CHATEAUBRIAND

COMPOSITION, IMAGINATION, AND POETRY

STANFORD FRENCH AND ITALIAN STUDIES

volume IX

ANMA LIBRI

CHATEAUBRIAND

COMPOSITION, IMAGINATION, AND POETRY

CHARLES A. PORTER

1978

ANMA LIBRI

Stanford French and Italian Studies is a collection of scholarly publications devoted to the study of French and Italian literature and language, culture and civilization. Occasionally it will allow itself excursions into related Romance areas.
Stanford French and Italian Studies will publish books, monographs, and collections of articles centering around a common theme, and is open also to scholars associated with academic institutions other than Stanford.
The collection is published for the Department of French and Italian, Stanford University by Anma Libri.

© 1978 by ANMA LIBRI & Co.
P.O. Box 876, Saratoga, Calif. 95070
ISBN 0-915838-37-0
Printed in the United States of America

Contents

To Jean Boorsch

Preliminary

In the last couple of decades Chateaubriand has practically been rediscovered. His life and career have been the subject of a new scrutiny. His works, reprinted in popular as well as learned series, appear in ever handsomer editions. Important new critical editions have been prepared. In 1968, bicentenary of his birth, special numbers of such journals as *La Table ronde*, *Etudes françaises*, *La Revue des Sciences humaines*, and *La Revue d'Histoire littéraire de la France* were devoted to him. The Société Chateaubriand has been publishing a fat annual volume of learned Proceedings and actively encouraging studies and workshops in and out of France.

Of particular interest to me in this reinvigorated bibliography have been the works devoted to Chateaubriand's literary style and themes. Up until recently the numerous and often good Chateaubriand studies had been largely limited to biographical questions and studies of influence (Chateaubriand and the Greeks, Chateaubriand Father of Romanticism, and so on), plus quite a few excellent critical editions. Responding to Chateaubriand's own view of himself, his biographers and bibliographers had thus laid a foundation for the more detailed analysis and new criticism that are now appearing. The studies of Jean Mourot, *Rythme et sonorité dans les Mémoires d'Outre-Tombe*, 1960, and Jean-Pierre Richard, *Paysage de Chateaubriand*, 1967, are two outstanding examples.

The field of stylistic investigation still most open and potentially rich is the study of Chateaubriand's prose. J.-M. Gautier's and Maija Lehtonen's books[1] are useful introductions and marvelous repertories of diverse

---

[1] J.-M. Gautier, *Le Style des Mémoires d'Outre-Tombe*, 1959; M. Lehtonen, *L'Expression imagée dans l'œuvre de Chateaubriand*, 1964. (For bibliographical details of these and all further

aspects of his style. Mourot's book concerning the prose of the *Mémoires d'Outre-Tombe* demonstrates a fruitful and exciting way of examining anew a long admired master; its method must some day be extended to the study of Chateaubriand's other major works.

My intention here is to examine certain structures—paragraphs, chapters, whole books—of Chateaubriand's composition larger than the sentences Mourot has definitively analyzed. One of the keys to Chateaubriand's appeal to a generation of readers whose poetic sensibilities were formed by the school of disorder, understatement, and unexplicitness of such masters as Rimbaud and T.S. Eliot, Mallarmé and Yeats, lies in Chateaubriand's particular manipulation of prose forms. Beginning with the paragraph, I would like to show how in his composition Chateaubriand often resembles these "difficult" poets of the post-Romantic schools, as he furnishes to his reader collections of eloquent, clear, noble, surely—but *disparate* pieces of prose from which only he, the reader, by an effort of imagination that approaches the writer's own creative imagination, can create the surprisingly "poetic" whole.

Chateaubriand's composition, that is, his way of putting together his paragraphs, chapters, and books, was not always appreciated by his contemporaries, whose admiration went rather to the lyricism and exoticism of his inspiration and subjects, the color and fervor of his prose, the torments of his soul, the flamboyancy of his convictions. Some of the Romantics found in him inspiration: Victor Hugo's "Etre Chateaubriand ou rien."[2] Some saw a reflection of their own souls: "[René] se pique . . . de n'avoir pas un *ami*; au fond, c'est qu'il se flatte de n'avoir pas un *semblable*. Erreur! il en a beaucoup (sauf le talent); et dès qu'il eut parlé, dès qu'il eut exprimé sa peine singulière, une multitude de Renés se reconnurent et se levèrent en s'écriant: *Moi aussi!*"[3] There was a wondrous new harmony of expression, and Madame de Beaumont only said more dramatically what many felt: "Le style de M. de Chateaubriand me fait éprouver une espèce de frémissement d'amour: il joue du clavecin sur toutes mes fibres."[4] But as far as composition was concerned—and not only in works like the *Essai sur les révolutions* and the *Vie de Rancé* (the beginning and the end and the most astounding in this respect)—there

references see the Bibliography beginning on p. 141.) See also Miss Lehtonen's study, "L'Evolution du langage imagé de Chateaubriand," in the *Bulletin* de la Société Chateaubriand, nouv. série (henceforth BSC), IX (1965-66), 20-24.

[2] A tradition dating back to Madame Hugo: see Clarac, "Quelques remarques sur les relations de Chateaubriand et de Victor Hugo," *Revue d'Histoire littéraire de la France* (henceforth RHLF), LXVIII, 6 (Nov.-Dec. 1968), 1006, reprinted in Clarac, *A la recherche de Chateaubriand*, p. 238.

[3] Sainte-Beuve, *Chateaubriand et son groupe littéraire*, ed. Allem, "Classiques Garnier," I, 306-7.

[4] *Ibid.*, I, 174.

was general dismay. Sainte-Beuve called the *Vie de Rancé* "un véritable bric-à-brac; l'auteur jette tout, brouille tout, et vide toutes ses armoires."[5]

In the twentieth century such apparent disorder is no longer censured. I should like to contrast two further disgruntled remarks of Sainte-Beuve with three parallel comments by more recent critics: although they do not touch on identical points, they do make clear that what once seemed a vice or at least a misfortune (and it may be assumed that in these passages Sainte-Beuve speaks for his contemporaries[6]) has come to be accepted as a virtue.

> Cette absence totale de plan et d'ordonnance qui se montre dans le premier ouvrage de M. de Chateaubriand [*l'Essai sur les révolutions*] se retrouve plus ou moins. . . . dans tous ceux qui suivront, si l'on excepte ses trois courts romans et *les Martyrs* . . . la seule grande composition . . . dans laquelle l'imagination de l'auteur se trouve dispensée sur une vaste étendue, avec une économie savante. . . . Le reste de ses écrits est composé toujours de pièces et de morceaux, de très beaux morceaux, mais qui ne réussissent à faire qu'un ensemble haché, saccadé. . . . Sa pensée est plutôt par accès, comme son style est tout en traits; il recommence à chaque instant; chaque paragraphe est une suite de *recommencements* successifs, brillants, saccadés.[7]

And this, in a note concerning the *Mémoires d'Outre-Tombe*: "Quant au fond, il se rappelle les faits, et a oublié les impressions: il les met après coup. Ce sont les gestes d'un jeune homme, et les réflexions d'un vieillard, de sorte que c'est vrai et c'est faux à la fois. Jamais on n'a mis l'intelligence d'autrui à une plus rude épreuve. Elle s'embrouille."[8]

I have quoted Sainte-Beuve at length for his acuity in analysis; his judgment and condemnation may be something else again. For a century later J.-M. Gautier looking at some of these disjointed pieces seems pleased to find them forming, by their very disjunction, metaphors.[9] Mourot signals as a kind of accomplishment "ces sortes de coq-à-l'âne que sont si souvent dans l'*Essai* [*sur les révolutions*] les passages du texte aux notes personnelles, ces raccords désinvoltes [qui] se retrouveront dans les paragraphes et les suites de paragraphes des *Mémoires d'Outre-Tombe* et de la *Vie de Rancé*; l'*Essai* offre la première et naïve manifestation de la démarche discontinue qui sera délibérée et calculée dans les deux derniers ouvrages de Chateaubriand."[10] For Miss Lehtonen, "La structure des *Mémoires d'Outre-Tombe* révèle un artiste qui sait calculer les effets

---

[5] *Ibid.*, II, 320.

[6] Cf. similar comments by Marcellus, *Chateaubriand et son temps*, pp. xii, xvii, and xix (quoted *infra*, Chap. 6, n. 2).

[7] Sainte-Beuve, *Chateaubriand et son groupe littéraire*, I, 127-28.

[8] *Ibid.*, II, 355.

[9] Gautier, *Le Style des Mémoires d'Outre-Tombe*, pp. 171-73.

[10] Mourot, *Etude sur les premières œuvres de Chateaubriand*, p. 188.

résultant de la superposition et de la juxtaposition de plusieurs époques."[11] In the metaphors that juxtaposition sometimes creates she sees the revelation of "une tendance elliptique. Cette technique pourrait être utilisée pour la création d'expressions hermétiques, comme dans la poésie moderne. Mais dans la plupart des cas, les comparaisons juxtaposées de Chateaubriand sont faciles à comprendre. Toutefois, le lecteur est obligé d'établir le lien logique qui manque; le procédé produit un effet de surprise, peut-être recherché par l'auteur."[12]

This essay will examine these juxtapositions and observe these missing links, in the parts of Chateaubriand's composition larger than his sentences. I will examine first the kinds of juxtapositions Chateaubriand creates in his paragraphs, showing their most characteristic forms and attempting to demonstrate—although Chateaubriand has made the task formidable—how the author has worked at bringing them into being. Then I shall consider the themes which are most characteristically associated with the discontinuous type of paragraph and try to define the correspondence between structure and message. In the following chapters I should like to consider the general structure of several of Chateaubriand's major works, which show to me a similarly surprising use of juxtaposition and discontinuity. Finally I should like to resume the previous considerations in a study of Chateaubriand's poetic method, attempting to demonstrate a new kind of unity in his work in general and to show how, essentially, he is a true poet in prose, through his particular appeal to the reader's imagination.

Though it will be apparent from the quotations in the preceding paragraphs that the discontinuity that is my subject has never gone unnoticed, I do not think it has ever been apparent to what extent Chateaubriand used it as the very basis of his particular poetic forms and structures.[13]

---

[11] Lehtonen, *L'Expression imagée dans l'œuvre de Chateaubriand*, p. 415. According to Poulet (*Etudes sur le temps humain*, pp. 35-36) such "superposition" and "juxtaposition" is characteristic of the Romantic search for a way to "posséder sa vie dans le moment."

[12] Lehtonen, *op. cit.*, p. 486. Dollinger, in *Les Etudes historiques de Chateaubriand*, had treated as well verbal juxtapositions—juxtapositions of words within the phrase or sentence—that are also quite characteristic of Chateaubriand.

[13] Much of Chapter 1 following was presented in an earlier version at the Chateaubriand Congress at the University of Wisconsin in 1968; my paper there was published in Switzer, ed., *Chateaubriand. Actes du Congrès de Wisconsin* (Genève: Droz, 1970), pp. 185-91, under the title, "The Poetics of Discontinuity in *La Vie de Rancé*."

I should like here to express my gratitude to the librarians and staff of the Yale University Library and the Bibliothèque Nationale in Paris, where much of the reading for this study was accomplished. Much of it was done during the academic year 1970-71 when I was in part supported by a fellowship from the American Council of Learned Societies, to which I here express my thanks. I also wish to thank particularly the President and Vice-President of the Société Chateaubriand, Messrs. Pierre Clarac and Maurice Chalvet, for counsel and encouragement they gave me during the writing of this essay.

> . . . il ne faut pas toujours tellement épuiser un sujet,
> qu'on ne laisse rien à faire au lecteur. Il ne s'agit pas de
> faire lire, mais de faire penser.
>
> Montesquieu, *De l'esprit des lois* XI, 20

1 A Poetry of Discontinuity

At the conclusion of Book Two in the *Vie de Rancé* one reads the following paragraph:

Dans ces premières années de la retraite de Rancé, on entendit peu parler du monastère, mais petit à petit sa renommée se répandit. On s'aperçut qu'il venait des parfums d'une terre inconnue; on se tournait, pour les respirer, vers les régions de cette Arabie heureuse. Attiré par les effluences célestes, on en remonta le cours: l'île de Cuba se décèle par l'odeur des vanilliers sur la côte des Florides. "Nous étions," dit Leguat, "en présence de l'île d'Eden: l'air était rempli d'une odeur charmante qui venait de l'île et s'exhalait des citronniers et des orangers."

les quatre *premières années* se passèrent sans que personne *entendît parler* de lui[1]
Le *Monastère* de la Trappe *répand* sa bonne odeur dans les Provinces les plus éloignées[2]
les vents du nord-est apportent, loin en mer, les *parfums* du Saba du rivage aromatique de l'*Arabie Heureuse*[3]
On n'est pas toujours à cette heure de la vie où l'on respire l'*odeur des vanilliers* dans *l'île de Cuba*[4]
Nous vîmes terre. `. . . `on voulut se flater de la douce pensée que ce pourroit être *l'Isle d'Eden . . .* l'air étoit parfumé *d'une odeur charmante qui venoit de l'Isle;* & qui apparem-

[1] Mademoiselle de Montpensier, *Mémoires*, XLII, 468-69 (Letessier's reference). Most of the sources of this paragraph are noted in Letessier's critical edition of the *Vie de Rancé*, pp. 213-14.

[2] Le Nain, *La Vie de* . . . *Rancé*, p. 198 (Letessier's reference). This sentence appears as a chapter heading in Le Nain.

[3] Milton's *Paradise Lost*, translated by Chateaubriand, in *Oeuvres*, ed. Pourrat, 1837, XXXV, 235. The passage is part of a simile for Eden.

[4] From MS 12.454 of the Bibliothèque Nationale, folio 64 (Letessier's note).

> ment *s'exhaloit* en partie *des Citron-*
> *niers & des Orangers* qui y sont en
> grande abondance[5]

A rapid comparison of Chateaubriand's text with the passages indicated in parallel to the right shows that its principal ideas and even its basic metaphors were either copied by Chateaubriand from his "sources" or originally composed by him in different contexts. At the same time it is apparent that in meaning as in poetic appeal this very lyrical paragraph is a self-contained unit. Its patchwork quilt of words and phrases may be called, in two different senses of the word, "composition": as an arrangement of previously discrete fragments and as a new and highly original poetic creation.

The subject of the paragraph appears to be the growing fame and expanding gracious influence of the Trappist monastery under Rancé's reform. The paragraph's principal structure is determined by the comparison between this widening fame and influence and a spreading perfume. After the initial sentence there is no mention of Rancé or the monastery; only the virtues of the sweet odor are developed, but the reader applies what is said about them to La Trappe. Although the statement of relationship between the two parts is brief and fragile—only the almost dead metaphor in "[sa renommée] se répandit"—it is perfectly clear and therefore sufficient; Chateaubriand is following common rhetorical practice and using a common metaphor. By the third sentence the reader has been brought easily and naturally from the monastery to the island of Cuba and understands that the winsome fragrance of the latter represents the former's merit.

Yet the structure of the paragraph is not all that simple. Its initial sentence, the topic sentence, is a direct enough statement of the subject: the gradual growth of the monastery's fame. Following that come a sentence and a half continuing and developing the idea to its normal conclusion: people turn their attention to La Trappe and soon are drawn by its virtues. The rhythms lead also to this natural conclusion. The three

---

[5] François Leguat, *Voyage et avantures*, I, 47-48. See Letessier's note. The "Isle d'Eden," Leguat informs us, was another name for the Island of Mascareigne, near Mauritius, since better known as the île Bourbon, then la Réunion. (He quotes DuQuesne who explains that the name of Eden, "c'est-à-dire, 'Pays de Délices,'" was given to the island by French travellers who "l'ont trouvée si excellente et si belle qu'ils l'ont regardée comme un petit Paradis Terrestre.") It is notable that Leguat and his group first saw and only then smelled the island from shipboard: "Si nôtre vûe étoit parfaitement satisfaite, nôtre odorat ne l'étoit pas moins. . . . Nous fûmes tous également frapez de cette suave odeur, à une certaine distance de l'Isle. Quelques-uns se plaignirent agréablement que ces parfums les avoient empêchez de dormir; & d'autres dirent qu'ils en avoient été si embaumez qu'ils se sentoient rafraichis, comme s'ils avoient été quinze jours à Terre."

approximately equal movements of the topic sentence, defining the state of affairs, give way to the more complex structure of the second sentence, of similar total length. Its first, unbroken half repeats the initial topic in imaged language; a three-part increasing rhythm[6] in the second half announces people's turning and then movement in spirit towards "cette Arabie heureuse" on which the sentence falls. The matter-of-fact two-part falling rhythm of the part of the third sentence that precedes the colon brings the conclusion that is expected: "Attiré par les effluences célestes, on en remonta le cours."

In terms of what we have so far presumed to be its meaning the paragraph is complete at the colon. But then it starts up again. After the pause marked by the colon we read what are essentially two new sentences about the far-reaching perfume of the island of Cuba and the "île d'Eden" that Leguat's crew was sailing toward. Introduced so abruptly these sentences take on a gratuitous and absolute quality, mysteriously portentous.

The two new sentences are parallel: a charming perfume reveals from afar the presence of an exotic isle.[7] On reflection—but that reflection is forced upon us by the abrupt change in both grammatical subject and the subject of discourse—we realize that these sentences too refer to the odor of sanctity permeating the atmosphere far from Rancé's monastery. Thematically they are the development of the Eden image suggested by the "Arabie heureuse"; the theme of exotic voyages has already been suggested by the idea of following after a heavenly effluence. Rhyth-

---

[6] I keep here Chateaubriand's original "oral" punctuation, the importance of which is stressed, for example, by Levaillant in the Introduction to Chateaubriand, *Mémoires de ma vie*, p. ix, and Mourot in *Rythme et sonorité dans les Mémoires d'Outre-Tombe*, pp. 266-69.

[7] Chateaubriand likes the spreading exotic perfume image; cf. other forms in the *Mémoires d'Outre-Tombe*, Pléiade ed. (henceforth MOT, with references in text), I, 205: "ce sage et brillant Orient . . . dont les parfums nous arrivaient à travers les champs de l'Arabie et les mers de la Grèce"; and the more descriptive passage from the *Voyage au Mont-Blanc* cited by Lebègue, "Réalités et résultats du voyage de Chateaubriand en Amérique," RHLF, LXVIII, 6 (Nov.-Dec. 1968), 928: "L'odeur du pin . . . a surtout pour moi un charme particulier, parce que je l'ai respiré[e] à plus de vingt lieues en mer sur les côtes de la Virginie: aussi réveille-t-elle toujours dans mon esprit l'idée de ce Nouveau-Monde qui me fut annoncé par un souffle embaumé, de ce beau ciel, de ces mers brillantes où le parfum des forêts m'étoit apporté par la brise du matin; et, comme tout s'enchaîne dans nos souvenirs, elle rappelle aussi dans ma mémoire les sentiments de regrets et d'espérance qui m'occupoient, lorsqu'appuyé sur le bord du vaisseau je rêvois à cette patrie que j'avois perdue, et à ces déserts que j'allois trouver." When Chateaubriand's ship nears the American coast, "nous ne voyions pas la terre, mais l'odeur des forêts de pins arrivait jusqu'à nous" (MOT I, 215). Cf. also Lehtonen, "Chateaubriand et le thème de la mer," *Cahiers de l'Association internationale des études françaises* (henceforth CAIEF), XXI (May 1969), 201-4, and its references: MOT I, 203 ("les vents parfumés de Ceylan"); II, 726 ("Vent des orangers de Palerme qui soufflez sur l'île de Circé"); II, 772 (personification of Venice: "le vent du soir soulève ses cheveux embaumés"). Cf. also *Vie de Rancé*, ed. Letessier, I, 79: "cette mer de la Grèce, d'où nous viennent tant de parfums."

mically they are introduced into the paragraph by a series of phrases gradually increasing in length. But all the same they still have no necessary connection with La Trappe. What they do is append to its already prosaically concluded description a new ending that is much more poetically evocative.

The "poetry" comes in part, of course, from rather traditionally exotic images: the names and trees of America, the bowers of Eden. Their effect is multiplied, I think, by the mounting rhythmic pattern of the final phrases, as a comparison with the original passage from Leguat reveals. The comparison with the sources shows as well how much Chateaubriand has accomplished by omitting precisions meaningless in his context and arranging his sentences so that they fall on the most sensuous words: "des citronniers et des orangers"—the now less scientific plural keeping perhaps the emphasis from being excessively visual in this context; "les Florides" certainly being more limitlessly evocative, as well as less abrupt in sound, than "Cuba."

Yet the principal poetic force of the paragraph comes, I think, from two factors that counter the reader's normal expectations from a prose paragraph. In the first place, the subject of the development following the colon is so much more general, so much more inviting than the matter-of-fact original presentation that it draws to itself the burden of meaning of the entire paragraph: during its very reading the paragraph ceases being a statement about the reputation of Rancé's monastery and becomes rather a declaration of the power of fragrance. But the change to this new development involves an abrupt juxtaposition of ideas and images not necessarily related; they are joined only by a moment of silence indicated in the punctuation, rather than by an explicit transition. In the second place, then, there is a break in continuity that constrains the reader to furnish for himself the transition for a widening analogy; forced to account in himself for the sudden change of direction he becomes for the moment, as it were, himself, the poet. Such a sudden change, from reading "for facts" or "for understanding" into a more active participation, is a largely pleasurable phenomenon, I think quite like what most of us enjoy in reading the poetry and particularly the "hermetic" poetry of the later nineteenth and twentieth centuries; it is in any case a kind of reading pleasure more common to the reading of "poetry" than of "prose."

The reader's mind is suddenly conscious of a space to be filled between rapidly diverging concepts; he is pleased to fill it with his own reverie.[8]

[8] Cf. Richard's analysis of a very different theme and subject (I have imitated his wording because I find it singularly apt): "La rêverie naît ici de l'écart que l'esprit se plaît à surprendre, puis à combler entre deux états extrêmes . . . d'une même existence." *Paysage de Chateaubriand*, p. 20.

"Très sommairement parlant, la technique du rapprochement, soit dans l'espace, soit dans le temps"—may I add, "soit dans l'espèce"?—"suppose l'existence d'un écart que l'imagination, de manière ou d'autre, se flatte de réduire ou de combler. Procédé poétique au sens plein du terme, dès l'instant que l'écart gît dans la nature des choses, et le rapprochement, dans une création *sui generis*. Ce qui compte en l'espèce, ce ne sont pas les données premières; c'est l'opération magique qui les intériorise et les restitue sous la forme d'un jumelage non pareil, intuitif, et rendu convaincant par la seule instrumentation du style."[9]

This sort of paragraph, the poetic structure that abruptly groups together otherwise unassociated ideas and generates through the friction of their juncture, in the mind of the reader, a set of similes, is found with some frequency at moments of emotional pitch in certain of Chateaubriand's works. I shall identify them later. It appears in several variations. The privileged form is the one we have seen in this paragraph from *Rancé*: the paragraph develops a certain subject according to the usual rules, and then, suddenly, at the end—"la place privilégiée," "l'endroit où il est le plus sensible, à la fin d'un paragraphe," "là où l'écrivain recherche toujours l'effet"[10]—it changes course; the distinctive marks of the change are the break, the broadening rhythms, and the increased scope of the subject of the final image.

The following example, also from the *Vie de Rancé*, shows a similar—though more astonishing—development with an even clearer transformation in the course of the paragraph from the apparent subject of the topic sentence to the "real" subject developed majestically at the end:

Mademoiselle de Scudéri était la grande romancière du temps, et jouissait d'une réputation fabuleuse. Elle avait gâté et soutenu à la fois le grand style, accoutumant les esprits à passer de *Clélie* à *Andromaque*. Nous n'avons rien à regretter de cette époque. Madame Sand l'emporte sur toutes les femmes qui commencèrent la gloire de la France. L'art vivra sous la plume de l'auteur de *Lélia*. L'insulte à la rectitude de la vie ne saurait aller plus loin, il est vrai, mais madame Sand fait descendre sur l'abîme son talent, comme j'ai vu la rosée tomber sur la mer Morte. Laissons-la faire provision de gloire pour le temps où il y aura disette de plaisirs. Les femmes sont séduites et enlevées par leurs jeunes années; plus tard elles ajoutent à leur lyre la corde grave et plaintive sur laquelle s'expriment la religion et le malheur. La vieillesse est une voyageuse de nuit: la terre lui est cachée; elle ne découvre plus que le ciel.[11]

[9] Bédé, "De Chateaubriand à André Malraux," CAIEF, XXI (May 1969), 220.
[10] Mourot, "Chateaubriand satirique; quelques aspects de son style," CAIEF, XXI (May 1969), 174, 171; "Réflexions sur quelques variantes de 'L'Itinéraire de Paris à Jérusalem,'" RHLF, LXVIII, 6 (Nov.-Dec. 1968), 959. Cf. Lehtonen, *L'Expression imagée dans l'œuvre de Chateaubriand*, p. 528.
[11] *Vie de Rancé*, ed. Letessier, pp. 34-35. (My references to the *Vie de Rancé* will always be to the first edition, edited by Letessier. The second, as Maurice Regard points out on p. 1365 of

Here there is little of the limpidity of form observed in the preceding
example. Several subjects precede the one plainly of greatest concern to
the author: the transformation of perspective occasioned by old age. In
determining the true subject of the paragraph the context is of little help,
for this passage occurs in an expository section devoted to various
habitués of the Hôtel de Rambouillet, showing "d'où Rancé était parti."
Here Mademoiselle de Scudéry is quickly abandoned, with no contextual
justification, for George Sand, George Sand for Chateaubriand himself,
and them all for the axiomatic and lyrical double conclusion, in the loose,
rambling manner characteristic of the *Vie de Rancé*.

The materials of the paragraph are this time compiled all from
Chateaubriand's own previous work. After the hasty generalizations of
the first two sentences and the curiously sudden transition, we come upon
a reworking of a paragraph of the *Mémoires d'Outre-Tombe*,[12] written
apparently in 1837 or 1838. From it I extract here only the parallel
elements:

> Madame Sand possède un talent de premier ordre. . . .*Lélia*. . .est. . .
> un chef-d'œuvre dans son genre. . . . la dépravation des maximes, l'insulte
> à la rectitude de la vie, ne sauraient aller plus loin; mais sur cet abîme l'auteur
> fait descendre son talent. Dans la vallée de Gomorrhe, la rosée tombe la nuit
> sur la mer Morte.[13] (MOT II, 892)
> [These elements are in the beginning and middle and end of one paragraph.
> After five paragraphs dealing rather severely with the moral aspect of
> George Sand's work, suggesting that as she grows older her judgment also
> might become more severe, follow two other consecutive paragraphs:]
>
> Madame Sand ne peut se convertir que par la prédication de ce mission-
> naire à front chauve et à barbe blanche, appelé le Temps. [Here I omit four
> sentences.] Laissons madame Sand enfanter de périlleuses merveilles jusqu'à
> l'approche de l'hiver; elle ne chantera plus *quand la bise sera venue*; en atten-
> dant souffrons que, moins imprévoyante que la cigale, elle fasse provision de
> gloire pour le temps où il y aura disette de plaisir. La mère de Musarion lui
> répétait: "Tu n'auras pas toujours seize ans. Chæréas se souviendra-t-il
> toujours de ses serments, de ses larmes et de ses baisers?"

the first volume of the Pléiade edition of the *Oeuvres romanesques et voyages* [henceforth ORV,
with references in text], is "moins belle littérairement"; it seems to me, for the reasons that
Letessier develops on pp. liii-liv of his edition, that one should prefer the "premier jet."
[12] Letessier suggests the comparison.
[13] Gautier, *Le Style des Mémoires d'Outre-Tombe*, p. 171, quotes this example as a "comparaison
par simple juxtaposition." He suggests that such juxtapositions, with their effect of surprise
making the image all the more striking, might have been suggested to Chateaubriand by the
Homeric or Biblical style typical of the *Martyrs* with simple suppression of the "tels sont,"
"ainsi," "de même." It seems to me that such an explanation underestimates the abruptness
of the break and the extent to which Chateaubriand moves away from the original subject of
the comparison.
   It should be noted that this final image may have originated in *Lélia*. Lélia says to Sténio at
one point, "Heureux ceux qui pleurent! Mes yeux sont plus secs que les déserts de sable où la
rosée ne tombe jamais. . . ." Sand, *Lélia*, ed. Pierre Reboul, Classiques Garnier, p. 98.

Au reste, maintes femmes ont été séduites et comme enlevées par leurs jeunes années; vers les jours d'automne, ramenées au foyer maternel, elles ont ajouté à leur cithare la corde grave ou plaintive sur laquelle s'exprime la religion ou le malheur.[14] La vieillesse est une voyageuse de nuit; la terre lui est cachée, elle ne découvre plus que le ciel brillant au-dessus de sa tête! (MOT II, 894-95)

It will be noted that the paragraph in the *Vie de Rancé* (written about 1843) is built thus of elements from three paragraphs of the *Mémoires*, all of which present the same composition: remarks relating to Madame Sand, expanded with an image, followed by a pause followed in its turn by a new development illustrating the initial one. The paragraphs about George Sand in the *Mémoires* are in no way associated with Rancé, although they are in a context sprinkled with references to aging Chateaubriand: ". . . l'admiration que je professe pour elle doit lui faire excuser des remarques qui ont leur origine dans l'infélicité de mon âge," "Le mérite et l'entraînement des passions de vingt ans ne se déprécieront-ils point dans son esprit, comme les ouvrages de mes premiers jours sont baissés dans le mien?" Now in the *Vie de Rancé* Chateaubriand has taken a number of sentences written about George Sand and used them to describe the effects of aging, from the aging of a culture to the aging of a writer. He has done it effectively, creating a paragraph full of the most jarring grouping of ideas and images which by their very abruptness jolt the reader into feeling the expanses and mutations of time. Here is a kaleidoscopic changing of image: the Dead Sea, provision of fame held in store against coming famine (cut off in the final version, however, from the specific reference to La Fontaine), youth seducing women, a lyre, a traveler. Several of the images are of so unusual a nature that they draw considerable attention to themselves, to the temporary disservice of the paragraph as a whole. But I think that there can be no doubt that the reader's perception of the relative importance of the paragraph's parts, like the theme, guides him straight to the final statement.

The movement of the paragraph from specific to general is similar to that noted in the first example, although it is organized more freely, by association of ideas rather than a logical development: Mademoiselle de Scudéry was a famous woman novelist, George Sand is our great woman writer; now it is true that there is evil in her life and immorality in her works, but age will bring to her nobler preoccupations. So far the thought is centered on George Sand, the subject of discourse if not always the

---

[14] From "ont été séduites" this sentence is almost identical to the concluding sentence of the final paragraph concerning French women writers and particularly (though she is not named) George Sand in the chapter "Nouveaux Romans" of Part V of the *Essai sur la littérature anglaise, Oeuvres*, ed. Pourrat, 1837, XXXIV, 291. Cf. Clarac, "L'exemplaire Pourrat de Chateaubriand," BSC, XIII (1970), 21, reprinted in Clarac, *A la recherche de Chateaubriand*, p. 277.

grammatical subject of all the sentences of the middle of the paragraph and, in a sense, almost the subject by anticipation in the early sentences. But now with the concluding sentence the movement suddenly becomes abstract: "la vieillesse" is the subject, old age that time will bring to George Sand, and to the reader, and to the author.

The secret and most important movement is not yet, however, in this movement towards the abstract: it is rather in the progression from a specific, Rancé-related topic—Mademoiselle de Scudéry—to Chateaubriand himself. And such a progressing, found throughout the book, is the key to the *Vie de Rancé* and all its digressiveness. Chateaubriand's finally dominating presence in the paragraph comes as a surprise, even though it is predicted by the "nous" of the third sentence and announced more insistently by the "comme j'ai vu" of the Dead Sea image—an insistence not present in the paragraph of the *Mémoires d'Outre-Tombe*. The abrupt changes of direction force the reader to feel the inconsistency of all human life and suggest a yearning for a calm and reflective conclusion to it. We begin to understand that the deeper meaning of the paragraph is something like this: one turns to religion in old age, from the flesh to the spirit, as Rancé turns from worldly pleasures to solitude and meditation, and as his profane memorialist turns from his own life to Rancé's. Chateaubriand is scenting the fragrance of the true Eden,

> And of pure now purer air
> Meets his approach, and to the heart inspires
> Vernal delight and joy, able to drive
> All sadness but despair: now gentle gales
> Fanning thir odoriferous wings dispense
> Native perfumes, and whisper whence they stole
> Those balmy spoils. As when to them who sail
> Beyond the *Cape of Hope*, and now are past
> *Mozambic*, off at Sea North-East winds blow
> *Sabean* Odors from the spicy shore
> Of *Araby* the blest, with such delay
> Well pleas'd they slack thir course, and many a League
> Cheer'd with the grateful smell old Ocean smiles.[15]

One should note with amusement that Milton refers in these words to Satan's voyage to destroy Eden. Milton's translator in 1836, Chateaubriand, one may assume, is concerned rather with the ultimate victory of Paradise.

Again, however, these movements—from specific to general, historical to abstract, Mademoiselle de Scudéry to us, Rancé to Chateaubriand—are only hinted at; the reader must himself furnish the links if he will have a

---

[15] Milton, *Paradise Lost*, IV, 153-65.

meaning. I think this paragraph may be one of the best examples of the staccato technique that annoyed Sainte-Beuve when he made his complaint[16] that the author of the *Vie de Rancé* "jette tout . . . et vide toutes ses armoires." We no longer require the kind of ordered, smooth continuity in composition that Sainte-Beuve did; perhaps we seek out rather the contrary.

So far I have cited examples in which Chateaubriand's paragraph suddenly opens out to a wider meaning by contrasting sentences and ideas and images that appear at first sight disparate. The contrast was emphasized and made all the more efficacious by a momentary pause in the paragraph, pause indicated in Chateaubriand's "oral punctuation" frequently by a colon, or less idiosyncratically by a change of sentence.[17] In these examples the contrast has been the result of a sudden change of apparent subject; elsewhere, as we shall see in examples below and in the following chapter, the change of subject can be emphasized or even replaced by tense changes, shifts in mood, the sudden shift from description to meditation or confession, an unintroduced quotation, notably different sentence construction. But the pause, momentary silence, or break is always caused and imposed by the opposition of dissimilar elements placed together, and the break in turn strengthens the effect of the opposition.[18]

Now in Chateaubriand's paragraph composition such a structure is but one manifestation of a more general form. The elliptical paragraph we have been looking at could be considered a particular version of a more common paragraph form in which a series of factual observations is resumed and concluded with a statement of general import.

A paragraph of the *Analyse raisonnée de l'Histoire de France* (1831) resumes quickly a series of principal events of the French Revolution, suddenly sweeps up to the barricades of 1830 that "faisaient disparaître en quelques heures trois générations de rois," and then, after the characteristic pause (here a full stop), concludes briskly, "L'histoire n'attend plus l'historien; il trace une ligne, elle emporte un monde."[19] In such a case, where the movement is towards a relatively abstract epigram rather than a pictural image, the effect is more declamatory and final than lyrically

---

[16] Cf. *supra*, p. 3 and n. 5.

[17] Cf. Lehtonen, *L'Expression imagée dans l'œuvre de Chateaubriand*, p. 483. Mourot uses the expression "ponctuation orale" in analyzing the "coupe suspensive, instant de silence entre l'appel et son écho inverse" in cases of opposition: "Chateaubriand satirique; quelques aspects de son style," CAIEF, XXI (May 1969), 182.

[18] Mourot, *loc. cit.* Cf. Gautier, *Le Style des Mémoires d'Outre-Tombe*, p. 212: "Chateaubriand réserve pour la 'clausule' la formule qui frappe; elle est d'ordinaire introduite par un silence marqué dans le texte par la ponctuation."

[19] Chateaubriand, *Oeuvres*, ed. Ladvocat, V³, 316.

suggestive. Another paragraph on the revolutionary theme that leads to an abstraction closes with a more picturesque image and seems closer to poetry. In this famous passage from the *Mémoires d'Outre-Tombe* (transcribed almost without variation from the *Congrès de Vérone* published in 1838) Chateaubriand is writing about his lack of will and easy disillusionment. Can anything make it worth one's while even to get out of bed? Change of sentence, then: "On s'endort au bruit des royaumes tombés pendant la nuit, et que l'on balaye chaque matin devant sa porte" (MOT II, 149). The abruptness of change in human affairs that is the subject of these final sentences is well served by the abruptness of their introduction. Their epigrammatic form breaks the rhythmical continuity of the paragraph preceding. The density of expression and the jar of rupture of continuity force the reader to participate actively in appreciating the sense. The political nature of the subject, the workaday world suggested by the very vocabulary ("trace," "balaye") give the feeling of prose,[20] but except that the ironical epigram is expressed with a falling rhythm, in shorter and shorter phrases,[21] the structural technique is very similar to the form used in the more poetic passages studied earlier.

Sometimes the reader comes upon a paragraph of abstract discussion concluded with a rapidly sketched tableau that transforms simultaneously rhythm, matter, and tone. In a long and richly detailed paragraph of Book XXXI of the *Mémoires* Chateaubriand relates, with considerable satisfaction, his accomplishments as ambassador to Rome. The final sentence falls, suddenly, "Eh bien! voyez-vous, je brochais cette besogne diplomatique comme le premier ambassadeur venu, sans qu'il m'en coûtât une idée, de même qu'un niais de paysan de Basse-Normandie fait des

---

[20] A prose surprisingly similar in this regard to what one finds in *L'Esprit des lois* of Montesquieu; the following paragraph and chapter endings in that work, among others, have for me a curiously Chateaubrianesque ring:

"Après la mort d'Attila, son empire fut dissous: tant de rois qui n'étaient plus contenus, ne pouvaient point reprendre des chaînes."

"Le prompt établissement du pouvoir sans bornes est le remède qui, dans ces cas, peut prévenir la dissolution: nouveau malheur après celui de l'agrandissement!"

"Les fleuves courent se mêler dans la mer: les monarchies vont se perdre dans le despotisme." (VIII, 17, "Propriétés distinctives de la monarchie," end chap.)

"Quand on jette les yeux sur les monuments de notre histoire et de nos lois, il semble que tout est mer, et que 'les rivages même manquent à la mer.' Tous ces écrits froids, secs, insipides et durs, il faut les lire, il faut les dévorer, comme la fable dit que Saturne dévorait les pierres." (Mid-XXX, 11)

Cf. *infra*, chap. 2, n. 20.

One should note here also what Chateaubriand says in the "Préface des ouvrages politiques" (*Oeuvres*, ed. Ladvocat, XXIII, ix): "mon esprit se refuse à mêler les genres, et . . . les mots de la poésie ne me viennent jamais quand je parle la langue des affaires."

[21]Mourot has much to say of this falling rhythm: *Rythme et sonorité dans les Mémoires d'Outre-Tombe*, part I, chap. IV.

chausses en gardant ses moutons: mes moutons à moi étaient mes songes" (MOT II, 356). The unexpected, explicit ("de même que") first comparison is pleasing here for its self-deprecating humor; the unannounced turn at the very last word to a new and higher theme, all the more by its contrast, is strangely appealing. A justly famous tableau with which less whimsically Chateaubriand transfigures and ennobles the description of moonlight in the *campagne romaine* is found further on in the *Mémoires*, in the dense and lyrical "Invocation à Cynthie": "Législatrice du monde, Rome, assise sur la pierre de son sépulcre, avec sa robe de siècles, projette le dessin irrégulier de sa grande figure dans la solitude lactée" (MOT II, 725).

Highly characteristic of the Chateaubriand style, these sudden illustrations or generalizations draw their effect from the magnificent generosity of their proportions and their discreet usage as well as the "sonorities" Mourot has analyzed. As we shall see in Chapter 3 Chateaubriand typically broadens and plumbs his thought when he touches on his most sensitive subjects, and he does it often at the ends of chapters and books. He also multiplies the effects of the special paragraphs by several variations in method.

One of the varieties is their own inverse form, in which the break precedes not a sudden opening but a sudden contraction of vision or narrowing of scope. On the way into Salzburg from Venice Chateaubriand makes a perilous descent from the Alps; immediately he thinks—thereby preparing for contrast a temporary expansion—of other descents, into Spain and Italy. But this slope "ne mène point à Grenade et à Naples. On ne trouve point au bas des lacs brillants et des orangers: il est inutile de se donner tant de peine pour arriver à des champs de pommes de terre" (MOT II, 843). All the parts here—short, choppy phrases, the expressions of decreasing affective import towards which they are directed (Grenade et Naples, lacs et orangers, champs de pommes de terre)—tend towards an ironic effect, an impression of disappointment and dashed hope, more characteristic of the author's political diatribes than his *Mémoires*. Yet even here, in the "on ne trouve point" clause, one has a sort of opening, also characteristic, towards the void, as in the example from the *Vie de Rancé* quoted at the end of this chapter.

A paragraph from the *Essai sur la littérature anglaise* (1836)[22] cited by Madame Durry for its Hugo-like cadence,[23] brings a personal reminiscence suddenly into the history of the misfortunes of King James II. Reflecting by analogy on the downfall of the Bourbon monarchy Chateaubriand asks with characteristic bitterness, "qu'importent toutes ces choses?" He remembers his own return from emigration in 1800, and

[22] Ed. Pourrat, 1837, XXXIV, 204.
[23] Durry, *La Vieillesse de Chateaubriand*, I, 575.

his coach running over a drunk peasant lying in the road: "Nous avions passé sur une vie et la roue s'était à peine élevée de terre quelques lignes." Without break he continues:

> Les Francs, nos pères, égorgèrent à Metz les Romains surpris au milieu d'une fête; nos soldats ont valsé, il n'y a pas encore vingt-cinq ans, au monastère d'Alcobaça avec la squelette d'Inès de Castro: malheurs et plaisirs, crimes et folies, quatorze siècles vous séparent, et vous êtes aussi complètement passés les uns que les autres! L'Eternité commencée tout à l'heure est aussi ancienne que l'Eternité datée de la première mort, du meurtre d'Abel. Néanmoins les hommes, durant leur apparition éphémère sur ce globe, se persuadent qu'ils laissent d'eux quelque trace: sans doute! Chaque mouche à son ombre.

In the following example, which I shall quote in full because of the vigor and passion and color of its political rhetoric, the paragraph comes to a sudden halt with an epigram that is at once, as a generalizing image, an opening, and, as devastating irony, a narrowing of scope. This paragraph begins the third chapter of Book XXXIII of the *Mémoires*, "Journée militaire du 28 juillet."

> Les groupes s'étaient reformés le 28 plus nombreux; au cri de: *Vive la Charte!* qui se faisait encore entendre, se mêlait déjà le cri de *Vive la liberté! à bas les Bourbons!* On criait aussi: *Vive l'Empereur! Vive le Prince Noir!* mystérieux prince des ténèbres qui apparaît à l'imagination populaire dans toutes les révolutions. Les souvenirs et les passions étaient descendus; on abattait et l'on brûlait les armes de France; on les attachait à la corde des lanternes cassées; on arrachait les plaques fleurdelisées des conducteurs de diligences et des facteurs de la poste; les notaires retiraient leurs panonceaux, les huissiers leurs rouelles, les voituriers leurs estampilles, les fournisseurs de la cour leurs écussons. Ceux qui jadis avaient recouvert les aigles napoléoniennes peintes à l'huile de lis bourboniens détrempés à la colle n'eurent besoin que d'une éponge pour nettoyer leur loyauté: avec un peu d'eau on efface aujourd'hui la reconnaissance et les empires. (MOT II, 403-4)

There are paragraphs in which the reader's imagination is suddenly invited to wander off to infinity because all the limits placed on it by precise description have been abruptly removed. The scope of reverie is widened as the scope of detail is reduced to nothing. Such is the case in this description of a moment in Bonaparte's Russian campaign: the date, the proper names, the precision of *"trois* ponts," the contrasting use of direct quotation, do not prepare us for the ending of the last sentence, which quickly falls away, in brief clauses each shorter than the last, to the "silence universel" it mentions.

> Le 23 juin 1812, Bonaparte reconnut de nuit le Niémen; il ordonna d'y jeter trois ponts. A la chute du jour suivant, quelques sapeurs passent le fleuve dans un bateau; ils ne trouvent personne sur l'autre rive. Un officier de Cosaques, commandant une patrouille, vient à eux et leur demande qui ils

sont. "Français.—Pourquoi venez-vous en Russie?—Pour vous faire la guerre." Le Cosaque disparaît dans les bois; trois sapeurs tirent sur la forêt; on ne leur répond point: silence universel. (MOT I, 788)

One also finds in Chateaubriand paragraphs that expand at the end without a break. The paragraph may come smoothly to its conclusion with a grandiose simile. There are many examples to choose from: here from Book I of the *Mémoires* is a remarkable description of the moon setting over the sea in Brittany.

> Etablie par Dieu gouvernante de l'abîme, la lune a ses nuages, ses vapeurs, ses rayons, ses ombres portées comme le soleil; mais comme lui, elle ne se retire pas solitaire; un cortège d'étoiles l'accompagne. A mesure que sur mon rivage natal elle descend au bout du ciel, elle accroît son silence qu'elle communique à la mer; bientôt elle tombe à l'horizon, l'intersecte, ne montre plus que la moitié de son front qui s'assoupit, s'incline et disparaît dans la molle intumescence des vagues. Les astres voisins de leur reine, avant de plonger à sa suite, semblent s'arrêter, suspendus à la cime des flots. La lune n'est pas plus tôt couchée, qu'un souffle venant du large brise l'image des constellations, comme on éteint les flambeaux après une solennité. (MOT I, 42)[24]

One can easily characterize the numerous poetic techniques used to create the magnificence and solemnity of this passage: personification; a controlling image of noble proportions; suggestive, unusual words like "intumescence."[25] For its subtle and intricate "imitative" rhythm the whole second sentence would bear close investigation. Indeed the combined effect of

[24] This paragraph, written probably in the early 1830's, occurs in the "Printemps en Bretagne" passage that is analyzed at length at the end of Chapter 3. In the *Lectures des Mémoires de M. de Chateaubriand*, 1834, the paragraph is substantially the same, particularly in regard to its ending.

One may properly see the origin of this passage in a paragraph that introduces a melancholy reflection on Greece, an evening contemplation of ruin and desolation from the temple of Sunium, in the *Itinéraire de Paris à Jérusalem* (ORV II, 901):

"Au plus beau coucher du soleil avait succédé la plus belle nuit. Le firmament répété dans les vagues avait l'air de reposer au fond de la mer. L'étoile du soir, ma compagne assidue pendant mon voyage, était prête à disparaître sous l'horizon; on ne l'apercevait plus que par de longs rayons qu'elle laissait de temps en temps descendre sur les flots, comme une lumière qui s'éteint. Par intervalles, des brises passagères troublaient dans la mer l'image du ciel, agitaient les constellations, et venaient expirer parmi les colonnes du temple avec un faible murmure."

The materials of the two paragraphs are almost identical, as is a certain portion of the vocabulary (vague, mer, disparaître, l'horizon, rayons, descendre, flots, s'éteint, brises [*brise*, vb., in the *Mémoires*] l'image, constellations) and most particularly the simile of the light being put out. But the paragraph of the *Itinéraire* is not built either to "open" or to "close"; it is simply part of an elaborate transition between architectural "reflections" and the political "contemplation."

[25] Gautier, *Le Style des Mémoires d'Outre-Tombe*, p. 91, lists "intumescence" among other "archaïsmes" like "effluence."

these elements might well serve to overpower the final simile: is not terrestrial activity a disappointment after the movement of the spheres? After the exit of the queen can one possibly be interested in the activities of the domestics? Yet there is a peculiar effectiveness in the concluding simile as it suggests the frequency of the majestic spectacle just viewed; it is carefully tied to the preceding passage—as an image of the breeze it remains with the celestial machinery; its carefully noble language (the precise but grandiose "flambeaux"; the vague grandeur of "solennité") maintains the solemnity of the main image.[26]

A more rapidly introduced comparison, one in completely different tone, is found further on in the *Mémoires*, in the description of 29 July 1830. A certain Berthier, son of the first victim "sacrificed" in 1789, appears at the court and assures the troubled ministers that all is going well for the royal cause: a "fatal" reminder of preceding doom. But—last sentence—"Ces malheurs n'étaient plus des nouveautés; depuis 1793, Paris était accoutumé à voir passer les événements et les rois" (MOT II, 412). Only the last three words cause the explosion of image, but how somber and, indeed, fatal an image retrospectively it is! The *comme* of the preceding paragraph, the *et* coupling two direct objects of *voir passer* here, make it difficult to speak of a "break" in grammatical continuity with what precedes the image. Yet the effect of the image results in large part from the break, though only a break in metaphor, or in manner. There is nothing "poetic" about the last paragraph until the image of the funeral cortege so suddenly evoked by zeugma at the very end.

The following example of a paragraph ending suddenly opened by an unexpected simile shows Chateaubriand once more typically adapting a text[27] and completely transforming the impression it makes. "Un homme

---

[26] It should be noted also that one recognizes here a quite characteristically "eighteenth-century" aspect of Chateaubriand's imagination: for him, I think, a "solennité" is of a higher order than a mere setting of the moon.

[27] See Letessier's comment, *Vie de Rancé*, p. 193, n. 4. Here, for purposes of comparison, is the equivalent passage in Le Nain, *Vie de . . . Rancé*, ed. 1719, p. 612: "Au reste, on ne peut dire combien cette exactitude à garder le silence a fait de conversions & produit de biens: En voici quelques exemples. Entre les Freres Convers, il y en avoit un nommé F. Mathurin, qui s'étoit converti à Dieu de cette maniere. Il étoit marchand, & s'étant égaré dans les bois de la Trappe, lorsqu'il alloit vendre sa marchandise aux environs; il entendit une cloche sur les huit heures du soir, qui lui fit juger qu'il y avoit quelque Monastère dans cette solitude; il poursuivit son chemin du côté qu'il l'avoit entenduë, & étant sorti du bois, il arriva à l'Abbaye, & comme il étoit nuit, il demanda l'hospitalité, on l'y reçut avec la charité ordinaire; mais sans lui dire un seul mot, parce que c'étoit le temps du grand silence. Ce silence le toucha si fort, que le lendemain à son réveil, il fit reflexion qu'il s'étoit heureusement perdu dans ce bois, parce que Dieu l'avoit voulu conduire au port du salut. Ainsi sans differer, si-tôt qu'il fut habillé, il s'en alla trouver le R. Pere qui commençoit encore à établir sa réforme, & lui fit de si grandes instances pour obtenir le saint Habit Religieux, qu'il lui fut accordé, & il a vêcu trente années dans la Maison, avec tant de perfection qu'il n'y avoit pas son semblable."

s'étant égaré entendit une cloche sur les huit heures du soir: il marche de ce côté et arrive à la Trappe. Il était nuit; on lui accorda l'hospitalité avec la charité ordinaire, mais on ne lui dit pas un mot: c'était l'heure du grand silence. Cet étranger, comme dans un château enchanté, était servi par des esprits muets dont on croyait seulement entendre les évolutions mystérieuses."[28] Because of the "comme" there is technically no break here either, but the "château enchanté" is more than a mere simile intended to enhance the passage: if it did only that it would be a poor simile indeed, carrying too many inappropriate connotations. As it stands it presents a new idea, that there is something magical to spiritual achievement; such a sentiment is not particularly Catholic and might not have appealed to Rancé, but it adds a marvellous touch to that intimate portrait of Chateaubriand that I think we now understand the *Vie de Rancé* principally to be.

Because they are so unexpectedly evocative or conclude with such surprisingly powerful metaphors these intermediate forms—paragraphs directed towards maxims, concluding tableaux, similes—may be considered to point towards the form first observed, the form with the more distinct "break"; they too may be considered part of a poetry of discontinuity.

Chateaubriand's discontinuity is too frequent not to be at least partially conscious, although the exact way in which he arrives at it is not easy to demonstrate: Chateaubriand scrupulously destroyed most of his manuscripts. Madame Durry has long since, however, brought to light one item of a manuscript notebook[29] that appears to reveal the author consciously suppressing a transition in order to arrive at a particularly bold form of the poetic leap we have been considering. The fragment, noted on a scrap of paper: "Andilly traduisit les pères du désert comme Rancé la vie du solitaire [Dorothée] d'autant plus curieuse pour moi que j'ai vu le désert d'[Ascalon] Gaza et les trois palmiers que me montrait mon guide." *La Vie de Rancé* rearranges this observation in a sequence almost as mysterious as a Rimbaud prose poem and as strangely beautiful.

> D'Andilly n'avait laissé à Rancé que l'histoire de Dorothée à traduire: c'était un mauvais grec du troisième siècle, difficile à entendre, et dont il n'existait qu'une paraphrase infidèle. J'ai vu entre Jaffa et Gaza le désert qu'avait habité Dorothée: il n'y avait point les soixante-dix palmiers et les douze fontaines.[30]

While remaining very close to the language of the original Chateaubriand has obviously written a completely different paragraph.

[28] *Vie de Rancé*, ed. Letessier, p. 193.

[29] Durry, *La Vieillesse de Chateaubriand*, I, 523.

[30] *Vie de Rancé*, ed. Letessier, p. 286. This very particular kind of description by absence, of evocation of a detailed nothing, appears several times already in the *Itinéraire*, though not in

Flung abruptly from one kind of reality—that subject to measurement, analysis, inspection, delimitation—into another—the past, the imagined, the ideal, the nonexistent, the archetypal—the reader of these paragraphs, like Marcel tasting the *madeleine*, experiences a liberation, a joyous freedom from contingency. Is this not one of the ways in which Chateaubriand has opened a new direction for poetic sensibility? I am struck by the parallel between this kind of composition and the lyric technique of André Chénier as Sainte-Beuve analyzed it in the fourteenth *pensée* of *Joseph Delorme*. In Chénier's style Sainte-Beuve noted the collusion of two elements that forms an effect much like that of the paragraphs we have observed. First, instead of the abstract or metaphysical and sentimental word favored by the typical eighteenth-century poet, Chénier used a picturesque *mot propre*: "lac bleu," not "lac mélancolique." But then, on occasion, he would add

> quelques-uns de ces mots indéfinis, inexpliqués, flottants, qui laissent deviner la pensée sous leur ampleur. . . . C'est comme une grande et verte forêt dans laquelle on se promène: à chaque pas, des fleurs, des fruits, des feuillages nouveaux; des herbes de toutes formes et de toutes couleurs; des oiseaux chanteurs aux mille plumages; et çà et là de soudaines échappées de vue, de larges clairières ouvrant des perspectives mystérieuses et montrant à nu le ciel.[31]

the same kind of paragraph structure as here in *Rancé*: "Le 8, nous avions à notre gauche Leucate, aujourd'hui Sainte-Maure, qui se confondait avec un haut promontoire de l'île d'Ithaque et les terres basses de Céfalonie. On ne voit plus dans la patrie d'Ulysse, ni la forêt du mont Nérée, ni les treize poiriers de Laërte: ceux-ci ont disparu, ainsi que ces deux poiriers, plus vénérables encore, que Henry IV donna pour ralliement à son armée, lorsqu'il combattit à Ivry." ". . . plus d'acclamations, plus de chants, plus de pompes sur le rivage; plus de cris guerriers, plus de choc de galères, plus de tumulte sur les flots. Mon imagination ne pouvait suffire, tantôt à se représenter la procession religieuse d'Eleusis, tantôt à couvrir le rivage de l'armée innombrable des Perses qui regardaient le combat de Salamine." And most curiously of all, as it is merely a seasonal absence: "En avançant vers Eleusis, je ne vis point les anémones de diverses couleurs que Wheler aperçut dans les champs; mais aussi la saison en était passée" (ORV II, 778, 852, 850). One should note also the paragraph of absences, "Quand on parle d'une vallée, on se représente. . . . Ici, rien de tout cela," that Chateaubriand adds to a description of the Jordan Valley in the *Itinéraire*, lengthening thus a parallel passage of the *Martyrs* (ORV II, 997; cf. II, 412). Of course in the *Itinéraire* Chateaubriand is even capable of equating nothing with nothing, one step better than these evocations of nothing present by something past: "Il faisait encore nuit quand nous quittâmes Modon; je croyais errer dans les déserts de l'Amérique: même solitude, même silence" (ORV II, 785).

[31] Sainte-Beuve, *Vie, poésie et pensées de Joseph Delorme*, ed. Antoine, p. 147.

Je m'esgare, mais plustot par licence que par mesgarde.
Mes fantaisies se suyvent, mais par fois c'est de loing, et se
regardent, mais d'une veuë oblique.

J'ay passé les yeux sur tel dialogue de Platon mi party
d'une fantastique bigarrure, le devant à l'amour, tout le
bas à la rhetorique. Ils ne creignent point ces muances, et
ont une merveilleuse grace à se laisser ainsi rouler au vent,
ou à le sembler . . . J'ayme l'alleure poetique, à sauts et à
gambades . . . Il est des ouvrages en Plutarque où il
oublie son theme, où le propos de son argument ne se
trouve que par incident, tout estouffé en matiere es-
trangere . . . O Dieu, que ces gaillardes escapades, que
cette variation a de beauté, et plus lors que plus elle retire
au nonchalant et fortuite.

Montaigne III, ix

2   *Achieving Discontinuity*

The preceding chapter suggested that Chateaubriand consciously intended to write, at times and in certain places, discontinuously. Discontinuity can also, however, be the result of incompletion—one thinks of the
Pensées that Chateaubriand admired so highly[1]—as it can be the sign of
carelessness. I suggested at the end of the last chapter that it was difficult
to demonstrate, in the general absence of manuscripts and drafts, that the
discontinuity observed in certain passages was consciously contrived. But
it is perhaps not impossible to do so. Here and there one can pick up
variants in passages Chateaubriand chooses to repeat; one finds, occasionally, manuscript fragments of versions later abandoned. These variants do point to a method, and a method is exactly what one would expect

---

[1] He wrote of the *Pensées*, "On croit voir les ruines de Palmyre, restes superbes du génie et du
temps, au pied desquelles l'Arabe du désert a bâti sa misérable hutte." "Pascal avoit entrepris
de donner au monde l'ouvrage dont nous publions aujourd'hui une si petite et si foible
partie. Quel chef-d'œuvre ne seroit point sorti des mains d'un tel maître!" (*Génie du christianisme*, III, ii, vi). On the other hand, at least in 1802, Chateaubriand does not seem to be
attracted consciously, otherwise, to a literature of fragments.

Raymond Lebègue has suggested another very plausible relation: with the style of Montaigne (and—after 1829—Saint-Simon of the *Mémoires*). "L'allure poétique par sauts et par
gambades convenait à Chateaubriand, quand il n'était pas emprisonné dans les règles de la
composition classique." "Quant à la forme, Montaigne a aidé à l'émancipation de Chateaubriand. A son exemple ce dernier cultive le développement discontinu, les digressions, et à
partir des *Mémoires* il renouvelle ses images, remplaçant les néo-classiques par des images
imprévues, voire triviales." Lebègue, "Essai sur Chateaubriand lecteur de Montaigne," BSC,
XVI (1973), 62, 63.

to find in the case of so careful and attentive[2] a writer as Chateaubriand.

One of the richer sources for such variants is the version of his Letters to Madame Récamier that Chateaubriand inserts in his *Mémoires*. Chateaubriand is very conscious of the difference between a private correspondence and public knowledge of it—even at a delay of many years—and comparison shows that in the case of this correspondence his main concern was to remove anything too "personal" from the letters (which already Madame Récamier had never seemed to find tender enough!). He also endeavored as he revised his letters for publication to ennoble their diction and unify their tone.[3] But we may also identify a third concern. The letters I am about to cite date from Chateaubriand's stay in Rome as ambassador in 1829; they are doubtless inserted into the *Mémoires* during the 30's:[4] this is the period in which Chateaubriand seems to be making considerable use of abruptly expanding paragraph endings. It is possible to identify very precisely a transformation that aims at such contrast and opening in his revision of the Letters.

A simple example is found in the letter of 17 March 1829. Chateaubriand is complaining of the lack of direction given him from Paris for the diplomatic maneuvering involved in the election of a new Pope. Continuing his complaint—and his paragraph—he writes in 1829:

> Je suis persuadé qu'on n'y pense seulement pas à Paris, et qu'entre les salons et les Chambres, les plaisirs et les lois, les joies du monde et les inquiétudes ministérielles, on se soucie de l'Europe comme de Colin Tampon. Il n'y a que moi qui, dans mon exil, ai le temps de songer creux du haut de mes ruines et de regarder autour de moi.[5]

In the *Mémoires d'Outre-Tombe* Chateaubriand keeps this passage almost whole, omitting only the trivial "Colin Tampon" (the phrase becomes, "on se soucie de l'Europe comme de rien du tout") and the dreadful—but oh!

---

[2] See for instance Marcellus' comments (*Chateaubriand et son temps*, pp. ix-xii) about the author's meticulous and repeated revisions, both silent and oral, of his manuscripts. As for a method leading to discontinuity, cf. Clarac, *A la recherche de Chateaubriand*, pp. 71-72: "Précisément parce qu'il a une pente naturelle à la facilité oratoire, Chateaubriand, dans sa vieillesse, s'appliquera, comme Flaubert, à rompre le rythme de ses phrases, à changer de ton sans crier gare, à surprendre le lecteur, qu'endormirait un ronron continu, par de brusques dissonances."

[3] In "Le Thème du 'Miserere' de la Sixtine," RHLF, LXXII, 2 (Mar.-Apr. 1972), 247-63, Raymond Lebègue compares various states of yet another letter to Madame Récamier: "Ici, comme pour les autres lettres à Juliette, le mémorialiste supprime les déclarations d'amour. Il biffe aussi une phrase sur les tracas de l'ambassadeur qui, dans cette méditation si élevée, apportait une note un peu vulgaire" (p. 250).

[4] Lebègue, *ibid.*, p. 249, basing himself in part on Marcellus, feels that the "Miserere" letter, dated 15 April 1829, may have been prepared for the *Mémoires* within the following month.

[5] Chateaubriand, *Lettres à Madame Récamier*, ed. Levaillant et Beau de Loménie, p. 297 (henceforth *Lettres*, with references in text).

so characteristic—"songer *creux* du *haut* de mes ruines" (for the flatter and wiser "le temps de songer creux et de regarder autour de moi").

The 1829 version continues in a new paragraph:

> Hier, je suis allé me promener par une espèce de tempête sur l'ancien chemin de Tivoli. Je suis arrivé à l'ancien pavé romain, si bien conservé qu'on croirait qu'il a été posé nouvellement. Horace avait pourtant passé par là et foulé les pierres que je foulais. Et où est Horace? Allons vite vous retrouver pour ne plus vous quitter. C'est le résultat de toutes mes réflexions. A jeudi.
> (*Lettres*, p. 297)

A new subject, then, in a new paragraph: leaving diplomacy behind him, he meditates on death, passage, and change, and Madame Récamier, the only solution. These themes are a commonplace in Chateaubriand and in these letters and so have no particular need of a raison-d'être; one could always consider them, however, to have been evoked by the "ruines" of the end of the preceding paragraph. The 1829 letter ends, thus, in a suitably intimate and elegiac fashion.

In the *Mémoires d'Outre-Tombe* (II, 327) all this has changed considerably. The letters to Madame Récamier are there presented alternately with political dispatches, with the double intention of showing the perpetual contrasts of the author's life, on the one hand, and the superiority of his diplomacy over his government's, on the other. In the new version the "Hier je suis allé me promener" movement becomes, with very few changes, part of the diatribe against Paris, instead of remaining an invitation to himself to return to his mistress. The passage of time comes to refer to the instability of the ineffectual government in power; the figure of the poet in Rome, however transitory his body, is all that remains. This major shift in sense is accomplished by two simple operations: the "Hier je suis allé" paragraph is simply run on to the preceding paragraph with no formal break, establishing thus a continuity between the political and the passage themes; and the new, longer paragraph ends with the sentence, "Horace avait pourtant foulé les pierres que je foulais; où est Horace?"[6] The resulting new paragraph ends then with an ironic twist, expansive in nature, by virtue of its increased chronological sweep and its open interrogative finish.

In another example, the letter of 25 February 1829, Chateaubriand adds sentences that make the death theme more grotesque, arranging the material again so that the new effect falls at a paragraph ending.

---

[6] The copy of the Bibliothèque Sainte-Geneviève adds back the two sentences "Allons vite vous retrouver . . . mes réflexions," but if I understand correctly Levaillant's description of the nature of that copy (MOT, ed. du Centenaire, I, lxxxiv-lxxxvi) this only substantiates the fact that Chateaubriand had cut them.

Lettres à Madame Récamier	*Mémoires d'Outre-Tombe*[7]
La mort est ici. Torlonia est mort hier au soir, après deux jours de maladie. C'est une grande perte pour Rome. C'était, comme vous le savez, la seule maison de *prince* ouverte aux étrangers. Au surplus, tout annonce la séparation de printemps [etc.]	La mort est ici: Torlonia est parti hier au soir après deux jours de maladie: je l'ai vu tout peinturé sur son lit funèbre, l'épée au côté. Il prêtait sur gages; mais quels gages! sur des antiques, sur des tableaux renfermés pêle-mêle dans un vieux palais poudreux. Ce n'est pas là le magasin où l'Avare serrait *un luth de Bologne garni de toutes ses cordes ou peu s'en faut, la peau d'un lézard de trois pieds, et le lit de quatre pieds à bandes de point de Hongrie.*
	On ne voit que des défunts que l'on promène habillés dans les rues; il en passe un régulièrement sous mes fenêtres quand nous nous mettons à table pour dîner. Au surplus, tout annonce la séparation du printemps [etc.]

A fairly nondescript notation then is played up in such a way as to underline a favored theme and simultaneously recall, sometime after 1829, one of the author's favorite French classical writers. The striking quotation, even one so grotesquely amusing, opens a literary vista: we shall see that this kind of use of quotation is a characteristic device.

The rest of the letter is altered so as to drop all intimate references to Madame Récamier. But it is also delicately changed so that once more instead of being a "closed" message, ever returning to Juliette, it becomes an open, expansive meditation: this time on the passage of all things in

---

[7] Without any further commentary Marcellus (*Chateaubriand et son temps*, p. 352) appends to this passage of the *Mémoires* the following letter, sent to him in Lucca, 3 March 1829:

"Rien de nouveau ici. Des scrutins nuls et variés. De la pluie, du vent, des rhumatismes, et Torlonia enterré l'épée au côté, en habit noir et chapeau bordé. Voilà tout. Ce soir, chez moi on chante à neuf heures, on soupe à dix, puis à minuit on jeûne pour les cendres de demain; avec un peu de pénétration vous devinerez que je vous écris le mardi gras. Tout cela, le mardi gras surtout, me fait dire, comme Potier [Charles Potier, 1775-1838: a famous comic actor of the Variétés à Porte-Saint-Martin theaters, according to *La Grande Encyclopédie*] dans le rôle de Werther: 'Mon ami, sais-tu ce que c'est que la vie? C'est un bois où on s'embarrasse les jambes.' Encore si les miennes allaient à la chasse comme les vôtres! Bonjour, voilà qui est bien peu sérieux pour un ambassadeur auprès d'un conclave. Je pleure si souvent, que, quand le rire me prend par hasard, je le laisse aller."

As well as casting an oblique light on Chateaubriand's state of mind at the time of the "original" letter to Madame Récamier, this text allows us to peruse a prose development of the same subject which is incoherent in a way quite different from the controlled incoherence typical of the paragraphs that are the subject of this chapter.

time. I italicize the differences of the two versions, whose overall effect, especially after the preceding expanded passage on death, is quite different. Instead of an anguished and embittered complaint turning inward we have a lyrical and elegiac meditation.

Lettres à Madame Récamier	*Mémoires d'Outre-Tombe*
L'année prochaine, ce seront d'autres voyageurs, d'autres visages, une autre société. *J'espère que je ne la verrai pas.* Il y a quelque chose de *trop* triste dans cette course sur des ruines. *Les* Romains sont comme les débris de leur *ville. Ils voient le monde passer* à leurs pieds. *Mais moi qui ne veux ni ne puis arrêter le monde, c'est auprès de vous que j'irai trouver quelque chose qui ne passe point et qui me restera.* Je me figure *toutes* ces personnes *que je viens de voir*, rentrant dans leurs familles, dans les diverses contrées de l'Europe, *toutes* ces jeunes *misses*,[8] *si fraîches, si blanches, si roses*, retournant au milieu de leurs brouillards. Si par hasard, dans trente ans d'ici, quelqu'une d'entre elles est ramenée en Italie, qui *la reconnaîtra? Qui* se souviendra de l'avoir vue dans *tels* palais dont les maîtres ne seront plus? Saint-Pierre et le Colisée, voilà tout ce qu'elle-même *reconnaîtra. Je griffonne plus mal que jamais, car je suis affreusement souffrant.*	L'année prochaine ce seront d'autres voyageurs, d'autres visages, une autre société. Il y a quelque chose de triste dans cette course sur des ruines: les Romains sont comme les débris de leur ville: le monde passe à leurs pieds. Je me figure ces personnes rentrant dans leurs familles, dans les diverses contrées de l'Europe, ces jeunes *Misses*[8] retournant au milieu de leurs brouillards. Si par hasard, dans trente ans d'ici, quelqu'une d'entre elles est ramenée en Italie, qui se souviendra de l'avoir vue dans *les* palais dont les maîtres ne seront plus? Saint-Pierre et le Colysée, voilà tout ce qu'elle-même *reconnaîtrait.*
[One brief paragraph follows, concerning a diplomatic dispatch.] (*Lettres*, p. 286)	[End of the paragraph, end of the letter in the quotation, end of a chapter.] (MOT II, 321-22)

In his adaptation of these two letters Chateaubriand has not yet fully developed the procedure of abrupt expansion of perspective whose birth I am trying to trace. Yet he does show a keen desire to amplify his subject rather than conclude it at the end of the paragraph, and he arrives thus at quite a different kind of paragraph, quite a different idea of paragraph closure. In a third and final example from the Récamier letters, 3 January 1829, we see him reworking a picture—again by the tiniest strokes—in order to create an expanding suggestion of passage, void, and death that

---

[8] *misses, Misses* emphasized by Chateaubriand in both texts.

was present but almost totally unaccented in the earlier, more intimate, "Chateaubriand en pantoufles," version.

Lettres à Madame Récamier	*Mémoires d'Outre-Tombe*
Voulez-vous savoir *comment je passe la journée et* exactement ce que je fais? Je me lève à *six* heures et demie; je déjeune à sept heures *et demie avec une tasse de chocolat dans la chambre de Mme de Chateaubriand.* A huit heures je reviens dans mon cabinet. Je vous écris ou je fais quelques affaires quand il y en a (les détails pour les établissements français et les pauvres *F*rançais sont assez grands). A midi je *m'habille, à une heure je prends une grande tasse de lait d'ânesse qui me fait un bien infini; ensuite je vais me promener deux heures avec Hyacinthe dans la campagne romaine.* Quelquefois, je fais une visite obligée avant ou après la promenade. A *quatre* heures, je rentre, je *me rhabille* pour la soirée. Je dîne à *cinq* heures, à sept heures et demie je vais à une soirée avec Mme de Chateaubriand ou je reçois quelques personnes chez moi. *Entre dix et* onze heures je me couche *et toujours je pense à vous.* Les Romains sont *déjà* si accoutumés à ma vie *méthodique*[11] que je leur sers *d'heures*[11] *pour marquer le temps comme j'en servais à vos voisins de l'Abbaye. Voilà n'est-il pas vrai un bien ennuyeux ambassadeur et bien différent de M. le duc de Laval? Jamais on n'a vu tant d'étrangers à Rome que cette année. Mardi dernier le monde entier était dans mon salon.*	Voulez-vous savoir exactement ce que je fais? Je me lève à *cinq* heures et demie, je déjeune à sept heures; à huit heures je reviens dans mon cabinet: je vous écris ou je fais quelques affaires quand il y en a (les détails pour les établissements français et *pour* les pauvres *f*rançais sont assez grands); à midi je *vais errer deux ou trois heures parmi des ruines, ou à Saint-Pierre, ou au Vatican.* Quelquefois je fais une visite obligée avant ou après la *promenade; à cinq* heures je rentre; je *m'habille* pour la soirée; je dîne à *six* heures; à sept heures et demie je vais à une soirée avec madame de Ch... ou je reçois quelques personnes chez moi. *Vers* onze heures je me couche, *ou bien je retourne encore dans la campagne malgré les voleurs et la malaria:*[9] *qu'y fais-je? Rien: j'écoute le silence, et je regarde passer mon ombre de portique en portique, le long des aqueducs éclairés par la lune.*[10]
[Follow here four more paragraphs, dealing for the most part with the ill-fated tragedy, *Moïse.*] (*Lettres*, pp. 242-43)	Les Romains sont si accoutumés à ma vie *méthodique,*[9] que je leur sers *à compter les* heures. *Qu'ils se dépêchent; j'aurai bientôt achevé le tour du cadran.* [End of the letter in the quoted version.] (MOᵀ II, 285)

---

[9] *malaria, méthodique* underscored by Chateaubriand.
[10] Richard gives a thematic analysis of this sentence in *Paysage de Chateaubriand*, pp. 90-91.
[11] *méthodique, d'heures* underscored by Chateaubriand.

Chateaubriand is here, then, not only concerned with correcting his image and purifying his style; as he takes the occasion to develop his favorite themes of resonant silence, repeated void, death he arranges a paragraph structure to lead up precisely to them. Although here there is still not the break in grammatical, rhythmical, or metaphorical continuity that we noted in examples quoted in the preceding chapter, the significant additions that close both the new paragraphs are suddenly more solemn than what precedes them, develop an image or a metaphor in a way quite different from the enumeration preceding, and are worked out in a much less prosaic rhythm—particularly the first which ends with an alexandrine close upon two phrases of six syllables.[12]

There are a few variants presently available for other parts of the *Mémoires d'Outre-Tombe* that show a similar development in the direction of discontinuous expansion. The most interesting from our point of view are the following, which I present from the simplest in variant to the most complex. First a paragraph (MOT I, 612-13) that shows the easiest possible move in the direction of discontinuity: the omission of an *et*. Chateaubriand is quoting, in alternation with his domestic Julien's itinerary, a passage of the *Itinéraire* describing his stormy voyage from Alexandria to Tunis: "Le 1ᵉʳ décembre, le vent, se fixant à l'ouest, nous barra le chemin." The middle of the paragraph, describing how he passes time by arranging his notes and chatting with a ship's officer, is essentially unvaried, though it picks up only two sentences from the middle of the second paragraph of the much longer passage in the *Itinéraire*. But the final sentence, a generalization based on the experience,

Itinéraire de Paris à Jérusalem

Les nuits passées au milieu des vagues, sur un vaisseau battu de la tempête, ne sont point stériles. . . . L'incertitude de *votre* avenir donne aux objets leur véritable prix: *et* la terre, contemplée du milieu d'une mer orageuse, ressemble à la vie considérée par un homme qui va mourir. (ORV II, 1157-58; my italics)

is transformed, more than by the abbreviation, more than by the generalizing change, *votre avenir* to *notre avenir*, by the dropping of the *et*. The continuing generalization of the *Itinéraire* gives way to a final, somber and didactic image, much more general yet in application.[13]

---

[12] For that matter the second ends with a "Romantic alexandrine."

[13] Occurring now after a break in continuity the final image seems even more striking for a peculiarity already present in one of Chateaubriand's first works: the comparison of the real to the abstract, the "fault" for which the author was criticized in *René*'s, "Quelquefois une haute colonne se montrait seule debout dans un désert, comme une grande pensée s'élève, par intervalles, dans une âme que le temps et le malheur ont dévastée": see *René*, ed. Weil, p. 25, n. 1 (quoting Sainte-Beuve).

A slightly more complex transformation occasioned by the dropping of an element in the conclusion with a resulting greater absoluteness and finality at the end of the paragraph occurs in the reworking (in 1837-38) of a passage from the *Voyage en Italie* (1803). Having recently[14] arrived in Rome for the first time, Chateaubriand is seeing the sights. During a nocturnal promenade he reflects on the simultaneous presence in one place of pagan Rome and Christianity's capital. "Qu'arriva-t-il, il y a dix-huit siècles, à pareille heure et aux mêmes lieux?" Without so indicating, Chateaubriand quotes almost exactly his earlier passage, with only minor additions and revisions before the last sentence. There (MOT I, 500) by eliminating the final clause (bracketed):

Voyage en Italie

Le Tibre sépare les deux gloires: assises dans la même poussière, Rome païenne s'enfonce de plus en plus dans ses tombeaux, et Rome chrétienne redescend peu à peu dans les catacombes [d'où elle est sortie]. (ORV II, 1458)

and eliminating the paragraph following, which terminates that section of the *Voyage*, Chateaubriand perfects his portrayal of disappearance and decay: no more a turn towards progress, if only in the past: now a chapter ending that echoes through the void.[15]

(The *Mémoires d'Outre-Tombe* include another, rather different example of evocativeness-by-elimination. It is the result of the apocopation of one of his own poems from which Chateaubriand quotes at length in XIV, 6 [MOT I, 496]. He is describing his first crossing of the Alps as he travels to Rome in 1803, and he quotes, exactly, from the poem dated 1822, "Les Alpes ou l'Italie," the third and fourth stanzas—plus the first line only of the fifth stanza. The complete poem had continued with a description of his further travels, to Rome and the Near East, but the penultimate paragraph of this chapter, into which the truncated poem is incorporated, leaves us at a vast perspective, viewed from the mountaintop:

L'Italie à mes pieds, et devant moi le monde!)

Thus elimination can be used to achieve an expanding paragraph. A less surprising and probably more characteristic evolution towards that

---

[14] (Much less recently in the *Voyage en Italie* [about six months] than is implied in the *Mémoires* [several days].)

[15] One notes, as Mourot would (cf. *Rythme et sonorité dans les Mémoires d'Outre-Tombe*, pp. 212-22), that the two parallel "Rome" clauses increase in length and now end on a nasal feminine syllable; according to Mourot, "Réflexions sur quelques variantes de 'L'Itinéraire de Paris à Jérusalem,'" RHLF, LXVIII, 6 (Nov.-Dec. 1968), 961, Chateaubriand "prodigue" "les finales consonantiques, surtout s'il s'agit de consonnes continues" "aux temps forts et à la fin des phrases; leur multiplicité et leur position à des places privilégiées coïncident avec le ton poétique et avec l'apparition de ses thèmes favoris."

form is by addition.[16] To a paragraph about Pius VII's return to Rome after his captivity at Fontainebleau, Chateaubriand dictates a metaphorical appendage at the last minute:[17] "Il semblait écouter la vie tombant dans l'Eternité" (MOT II, 207).

In another case he senses the opportunities present in a paragraph already expanding towards an impression of endless silence, reverberation, void—and adds to that impression.

"Manuscrit de 1847"[18]	*Mémoires d'Outre-Tombe*
	Après avoir traversé la Grèce, touché à Zéa et à Chio, je trouvai Julien à Smyrne. Je vois aujourd'hui, dans ma mémoire, la Grèce comme un de ces cercles éclatants qu'on aperçoit quelquefois en fermant les yeux. Sur cette phosphorescence mystérieuse se dessinent des ruines d'une architecture fine et admirable, le tout rendu plus resplendissant encore par je ne sais quelle autre clarté des muses. Quand retrouverai-je le thym de l'Hymète, les lauriers-roses des bords de l'Eurotas? Un des hommes que j'ai laissés avec le plus d'*envie* sur des rives étrangères, c'est le *douanier turc du Pirée*: il *vivait seul*, gardien de trois ports *déserts, promenant ses regards sur des îles bleuâtres, des promontoires brillants, des mers dorées.* Là, je *n'entendais que le bruit des vagues* dans le tombeau détruit de Thémistocle, *et le murmure des lointains souvenirs*: au silence des débris de Sparte, la gloire même était muette.[19] (MOT I, 603-4:
Quand je traversai le port du Pirée, j'enviai un douanier turc qui vivait seul dans les havres déserts, promenant des regards sur des îles bleuâtres, des promontoires brillants, des mers dorées, n'entendant que le bruit des vagues et le murmure des lointains souvenirs. (MOT I, 1104: brief paragraph introducing a most hasty sketch of his *Itinéraire*)	

[16] Cf. Marcellus, *Chateaubriand et son temps*, p. xi, concerning Chateaubriand's revision of his manuscripts: "il retranchait rarement de la pensée primitive, il y ajoutait plus souvent." But note also the characteristic "efforts de resserrement" that Pierre Clarac has pointed out in his studies of the "Manuscrit de Genève": Clarac, *A la recherche de Chateaubriand*, p. 374 *et passim*.

[17] Cf. Levaillant's comment in MOT II, 987: "addition dictée par CH. et transcrite par un secrétaire sur une des dernières copies."

[18] See Durry, "Un manuscrit retrouvé des *Mémoires d'Outre-Tombe*," *Revue des deux mondes*, 1 Dec. 1931, p. 668; on the preference to be accorded to the second version see Levaillant's comment, MOT I, xxvii.

[19] Cf. thematically the ending of Book XXIV (MOT I, 1033-34): "Je me décourage de durer. Ah! si du moins j'avais l'insouciance d'un de ces vieux Arabes de rivage, que j'ai rencontrés en Afrique! Assis les jambes croisées sur une petite natte de corde, la tête enveloppée dans leur burnous, ils perdent leurs dernières heures à suivre des yeux, parmi

a middle paragraph in the section
tracing the voyage to Jerusalem, al-
ternating his itinerary with Julien's.
I have italicized the elements from
the original version)

The newly resulting paragraph is as absolute as its final epigram and the
movement stops there, although the chapter continues.

In the chapter describing the author's arrival in Rome in 1803
Chateaubriand picks up his letter to Joubert of "28 juin, onze heures du
soir" (itself known only by the 1827 publication in the *Voyage en Italie*). The
"letter" is considerably changed, as it becomes part of the running narrative. Of particular concern here is the following paragraph; in transcrib-
ing it I have italicized the elements common to the two versions.

Voyage en Italie	*Mémoires d'Outre-Tombe*
J'ai couru tout ce *jour*, veille de la fête de Saint-Pierre. J'ai déjà vu *le Colisée, le Panthéon, la colonne Trajane, le château Saint-Ange, Saint-Pierre*; que sais-je? J'ai vu l'illumination et le *feu d'artifice* qui annoncent pour demain la grande cérémonie consacrée au prince des Apôtres: tandis qu'on prétendait me faire admirer un *feu* placé au haut du Vatican, je regardais l'effet de la lune sur le Tibre, sur ces maisons *romaines*, sur ces ruines qui pendent ici de toute part. (ORV II, 1437)	Le 28 juin, *je courus tout* le *jour*: je jetai un premier regard sur *le Colisée, le Panthéon, la colonne Trajane* et *le château Saint-Ange*. Le soir, M. Artaud me mena à un bal dans une maison aux environs de la place *Saint-Pierre*. On apercevait la girandole de *feu* de la coupole de Michel-Ange, entre les tourbillons des valses qui roulaient devant les fenêtres ouvertes; les fusées du *feu d'artifice* du môle d'Adrien s'épanouissaient à Saint-Onuphre sur le tombeau du Tasse: le silence, l'abandon et la nuit étaient dans la campagne *romaine*. (MOT I, 499)[20]

The "letter to Joubert" is composed of fragments, like many of the pages
of the *Voyage en Italie* and the *Voyage en Amérique*. The *Mémoires* are seldom
fragmentary in that sense, except in the rare case of unmanipulated

l'azur du ciel, le beau phénicoptère qui vole le long des ruines de Carthage; bercés du
murmure de la vague, ils entr'oublient leur existence et chantent à voix basse une chanson de
la mer: ils vont mourir."
[20] Cf. among the "Fragments de l'Esprit des lois non publiés," Montesquieu, *Oeuvres complètes*, Collection "l'Intégrale," p. 806, under the heading "Du jugement des crimes à Rome,"
another abruptly expanding paragraph curiously suggestive of this one of Chateaubriand's:
"On vit des sénateurs se cacher sous le toit d'un homme qu'ils voulaient accuser, pour
entendre ses discours. On vit Tibère porter au sénat tout ce que Drusus avait dit pendant les
. . . années de sa vie. La tristesse, le silence se répandirent dans Rome. Tout fut tendu de
noir dans la capitale de l'univers."

quotations. Chateaubriand in this passage orchestrates the "feu placé au haut du Vatican" with the sense of rhythm and feeling for exotic names he had used earlier in rewriting the "Sylphide" passage;[21] he eliminates the pallid, pre-Romantic "effet de la lune"; he takes care to present a less frivolous image of himself; but most importantly he replaces the undescriptive "ruines" with the expanding description of some of their connotations: tomb, silence, night; the perspective widens, and the declaration after the colon sets a completely new tone of high seriousness, stopping momentarily the busy details of the chapter.

In the "Life of Napoleon" section of the *Mémoires d'Outre-Tombe* we find a similar expansion, in the reworking of a paragraph from a *Conservateur* article concerning Napoleon's imprisonment. A carefully elaborated image in a third person description,

> . . . Bonaparte ne se peut remuer sur son rocher que nous n'en soyons avertis par une secousse; . . . sa seule présence sur le rivage américain de l'Atlantique forcerait l'Europe à camper sur le rivage opposé. (MOT I, 1026-27 [cf. also the original, 17 Nov. 1818, reproduced in the ed. Ladvocat, XXVI, 33])

is transformed and abruptly affixed to a double denunciation of Napoleon's solicitation of English asylum and England's eventual treatment of him:

> La haute fortune de Napoléon le servit mieux: les Anglais, se laissant emporter à une politique étroite et rancunière, manquèrent leur dernier triomphe; au lieu de perdre leur suppliant en l'admettant à leurs bastilles ou à leurs festins, ils lui rendirent plus brillante pour la postérité la couronne qu'ils croyaient lui avoir ravie. Il s'accrut dans sa captivité de l'énorme frayeur des puissances: en vain l'océan l'enchaînait, l'Europe armée campait au rivage, les yeux attachés sur la mer. (MOT I, 993)

The change from declaration to evocation is announced by the verb's passage from conditional to indicative; the evocation is drawn out by the supplementary final adverbial phrase; the final, geographically precise "rivage opposé" gives way to the limitless, unspecified "mer."

It will have been noted, in the examples preceding, that the discontinuous expanding paragraph is a mark of Chateaubriand's mature style, characterizing the writing of, roughly, his last twenty years. Its appearance cannot be dated with any great precision in the present state of our knowledge of Chateaubriand's composition, but there is no shortage of evidence indicating that its practice is born in the late 1820's.

Except for the almost always exceptional *Essai sur les révolutions* and a few rare examples that are generally unremarkable and that form in any

---

[21] Note Levaillant's comment, MOT I, 1133.

case no pattern—examples in such works as the *Itinéraire*—this structure is not found before 1826, either in the "literary" or the polemical works. There is, at least at present, no indication that this form was characteristic of the parts of the *Mémoires d'Outre-Tombe* written before the late 20's. But in the later revisions of the *Mémoires*, the later written parts of the *Mémoires*, the *Congrès de Vérone*, the *Vie de Rancé*—there it abounds.

The necessary predisposition for it does, however, appear early, as the following example from the *Itinéraire*, compared to its source, shows.[22]

Histoire de France de Velly[23]	*Itinéraire de Paris à Jérusalem*
Deux jours après l'armée se mit en marche, reprit la tour qui gardoit les citernes, et s'aprocha de Carthage, dont il étoit important de s'emparer, avant que d'assiéger Tunis [ville très fortifiée pour ce temps-là (p. 255)]. . . . Carthage fut prise en même temps que le château . . . le roi y établit des hôpitaux pour les malades; et les princesses, brus, fille, belle-sœur et niéce du monarque, y allerent demeurer, pour y être plus commodément. [End paragraph in Velly, whose paragraph is much longer than Chateaubriand's][24]	Saint Louis résolut de prendre Carthage avant d'assiéger Tunis qui était alors une ville riche, commerçante et fortifiée. Il chassa les Sarrasins d'une tour qui défendait les Citernes: le château fut emporté d'assaut, et la nouvelle cité suivit le sort de la forteresse. Les princesses qui accompagnaient leurs maris débarquèrent au port; et, par une de ces révolutions que les siècles amènent, les grandes dames de France s'établirent dans les ruines des palais de Didon. (ORV II, 1207)

Chateaubriand has rearranged the material so that, as so often in the paragraphs under consideration, the ending suddenly moves away from the particular situation into a vast historical and legendary perspective. There is no incoherence or abrupt juxtaposition here, however, as will be characteristic of similar, later transpositions.

For the study of the development of that later characteristic form the first three books of the *Mémoires d'Outre-Tombe* copied by Madame Récamier and Monsieur et Madame Lenormant in 1826 are particularly useful.

Of ten striking examples of the discontinuous expanding paragraph that I have noted in the final versions[25] of Books I-III three are para-

---

[22] Cf. Chateaubriand's later revision of Leguat in the *Vie de Rancé* passage quoted at the beginning of Chapter 1 (*supra*, p. 5).

[23] Quoted by Malakis in his edition of the *Itinéraire*, II, 296, n.

[24] Velly, *Histoire de France*, ed. 1770, III, 253-54 (Malakis' reference).

[25] I realize that the history of the manuscripts and the publication of the *Mémoires d'Outre-Tombe* makes it impossible to speak of a definitive version. By "final versions" I refer to those two syntheses of Chateaubriand's most determinable latest wishes published by Maurice Levaillant in the "Bibliothèque de la Pléiade" (with Georges Moulinier) and the "Edition du Centenaire."

graphs added that have no equivalent in 1826 (one, MOT I, 28, is a paragraph of historical summary ending in a metaphorical generalization; another, I, 46, a personal reflection ending in a little tableau; the third, I, 54, a description of a childhood scene ending with a historical quotation describing a similar scene). Only one exists already in near final form: it is the famous passage on the "gazouillement d'une grive" that recalls the author from Montboissier in 1817 to his childhood at Combourg.

The passage has two paragraphs in 1826; they are run together in the *Mémoires d'Outre-Tombe* without this causing any appreciable shift of meaning or notable change in style. The opposition between present and past is reinforced by the introduction of two transitional phrases in the second sentence after "paternel": "j'oubliai les catastrophes dont je venais d'être le témoin [i.e. the fall of the Empire], et, transporté subitement dans le passé, je revis ces campagnes [etc.]." The only other changes are a few small differences in wording ("le domaine paternel" for "les champs paternels," for instance) and the elimination of several short expressions not necessary to the sense. In

> Le chant de l'oiseau dans les bois de Combourg *ne* m'entretenait *que de l'avenir, et me promettait* une félicité que je croyais *bientôt* atteindre; le même chant dans le parc de Montboissier, *ne* me rappelait *que le passé, et* des jours perdus à la poursuite de cette félicité *fugitive. Naître, désirer, mourir, c'est donc tout? Désormais* je n'ai plus rien à apprendre, *rien à découvrir dans le voyage!* J'ai marché plus vite qu'un autre, et j'ai *déjà* fait *deux ou trois fois* le tour de la vie.[26]

the expressions I have italicized are omitted; the resulting two sentences are lighter and bring us sooner to the abruptly affixed image of the ending. That ending presents almost no variants at all:

> Mettons à profit le peu d'instants [1826: de jours] qui me restent; hâtons-nous de peindre ma jeunesse, tandis que j'y touche encore: le navigateur, abandonnant [1826: qui quitte] pour jamais un rivage enchanté, écrit son journal à la vue de la terre qui s'éloigne et qui va bientôt disparaître. (MOT I, 77)

Almost no variants—and yet a significant change, for the image of the sailor comes in the *Mémoires* at the end of a chapter, leaving our imagination to sail off with him during the blank space of a few inches of page, while in the undivided text of the *Mémoires de ma vie* the reader continues directly on towards new subjects.

In this case the situation of the image now at the end of a chapter is not all by itself significant, for that image, developed in an expanding rhythm, is part of a generalizing paragraph conclusion that slows down the reader

---

[26] Chateaubriand, *Mémoires de ma vie*, p. 101.

and causes him to dream a moment anyway. Such is not the case in another crucial paragraph, whose new importance assumed at the end of a chapter suggests a whole new set of meanings. The 1826 text read,

> Cependant le plaisir de la chasse ne me suffisait plus: à mesure que j'avançais dans la vie il se formait en moi un désir de bonheur que je ne pouvais ni régler ni comprendre; mon esprit et mon cœur s'achevait de former comme deux temples vides sans autels et sans sacrifices, où l'on ne savait encore quel Dieu serait adoré; je croissais auprès de ma sœur, et notre amitié était toute notre vie.
>
> Lucile comptait déjà dix-sept ans; elle était grande et d'une beauté remarquable mais sérieuse. . . .[27]

This first paragraph portrays indeed an uneasy adolescence that parallels the heartsickness of *René*; its structure supports its declaration that his malady is composed of both spiritual and sexual uncertainty and that his being is totally empty except for his comradeship with his sister, who is unnamed in the paragraph. Such no longer seems to me to be the case in the *Mémoires d'Outre-Tombe*, when the almost identical paragraph appears at the end of a chapter, "Passage de l'enfant à l'homme," when there is a period after "adoré," when the now other, shorter sentence, falling last in the chapter, comes to read as the answer to the two-fold malaise of the preceding sentence: "Je croissais auprès de ma sœur Lucile; notre amitié était toute notre vie" (MOT I, 86). While it is true that the incest theme of *René* is not elucidated by a parallel in the *Mémoires d'Outre-Tombe*, it seems to me that in this resulting chapter conclusion Chateaubriand is allowing himself the pleasure of ambiguity and encouraging his reader to dwell on it.

Another of the ten paragraphs is similarly endowed with a newly expanding and abrupt ending because of rearrangement. The ironical and humorous detached sentence, "Je n'ai pas rencontré à Athènes des personnages plus célèbres" that closes a paragraph describing various visitors received by Chateaubriand's father at Combourg (MOT I, 51-52) already exists in 1826[28] in almost the same words; there, however, it is much less visible, lost, as it is, in the middle of a paragraph later cut in two. ". . . voilà la société de Combourg: *on se souvient peut-être que* je n'ai pas rencontré à Athènes des personnages *beaucoup* plus célèbres." In dropping the transitional words italicized here Chateaubriand has also increased by abruptness the effect of his suddenly amusing observation.

The remaining four cases of prose development resulting in expanding discontinuous paragraphs are the most interesting because we can observe their gradual structural evolution. Two of them occur in the "Prin-

---

[27] *Ibid.*, p. 118.
[28] *Ibid.*, p. 63.

temps en Bretagne" section that closes Book I, chapter 6: they will be analyzed together with the rest of that passage in the following chapter. In the other two we can follow Chateaubriand's deliberate manipulation of all the material that forms the resulting paragraph in a manner to make its ending abruptly different from what precedes and take on by contrast an added force.

Jean Mourot has made a stylistic analysis[29] of the paragraph (MOT I, 29-30), "C'est sur la grève de la pleine mer . . . que j'ai été élevé. . . . Depuis cette époque, j'ai souvent cru bâtir pour l'éternité des châteaux plus vite écroulés que mes palais de sable," referring us to the earlier version of the passage in the *Mémoires de ma vie*. In its final form this concluding sentence ("fin lyrique," writes Mourot) stands out suddenly from the context: its reflective nature contrasts with the details and description of childhood adventures, its reference to the future is abrupt. In 1826 already the statement (almost identical) differs in these same respects from what surrounds it, but it is introduced by a much more eloquent development of the subject that precedes it and then returns at the very end: the "fours" or sand castles.

> Ils étaient plus ou moins vastes, plus ou moins beaux, selon la force ou le goût des architectes. Notre joie était extrême, lorsqu'à la mer montante, nous voyions s'approcher le premier flot pour envahir nos retranchements, comme Neptune lorsqu'il attaqua la muraille des Grecs. Souvent nous ménagions des ouvertures souterraines par où l'eau entrait dans l'intérieur de nos murs avant de les avoir renversés, le second flot sapait la base du monument qui disparaissait au troisième.[30]

All this disappears, including the rather overblown Greek simile; so does a somewhat demeaning phrase of the original second sentence: "C'est sur la grève *du côté* de la pleine mer entre ce château et *un fort appelé* le fort Royal que se rassemblaient les enfants *de la ville*. C'est là que *conduit par une bonne ou un domestique*, j'ai été élevé *comme le* compagnon des vents et des flots": everything I have italicized disappears. So does the "Combien de fois" that introduced the last sentence, one more transitional element thus removed. We are left after all the changes with a passage that is less descriptive, but, in its bareness, firmer, more thought-provoking and evocative.

In the final case, the paragraph that comes to begin Chapter 7 of Book I (right after the "Printemps en Bretagne"), Chateaubriand makes more subtle changes to effect an abrupt movement of reflection at the end. In 1826:

---

[29] In "Réflexions sur quelques variantes de 'L'Itinéraire ae Paris à Jérusalem,'" RHLF, LXVIII, 6 (Nov.-Dec. 1968), 963.
[30] Chateaubriand, *Mémoires de ma vie*, pp. 23-24.

Nous partîmes de Saint-Malo au lever du soleil, ma mère, mes quatre sœurs et moi. Nous étions dans une énorme berline dorée, traînée par huit chevaux parés comme les mulets en Espagne, avec des sonnettes et des houppes de laine de diverses couleurs. Tandis que ma mère soupirait en silence, mes sœurs parlaient à perdre haleine; il n'y avait pas jusqu'à ma pauvre Lucile qui n'eût perdu sa timidité. Pour moi, j'ouvrais de grands yeux; j'écoutais de toutes mes oreilles; je m'émerveillais à chaque tour de roue. En me rappelant ce premier voyage d'un homme qui devait voyager toute sa vie, j'ai fait souvent des réflexions sur les vicissitudes de la fortune et les changements plus déplorables qui arrivent dans le cœur de l'homme.[31]

The paragraph opens out into a generalization from its somewhat detailed description by means of a lengthy preamble, "en me rappelant . . ."; the form of the final sentence is similar to those preceding; the two parallel parts of the "reflections" are a cliché and a rather vague plaint. The corresponding paragraph of the *Mémoires d'Outre-Tombe* is quite different. The details of the first part of the paragraph are considerably expanded, in the direction of the picturesque, in two long sentences of similar construction. The middle section, the reactions of the travelers, is pared down to the essential. After "tour de roue" comes a colon to replace the preamble and the very different and far more striking conclusion: "premier pas d'un Juif errant qui ne se devait plus arrêter. Encore si l'homme ne faisait que changer de lieux! mais ses jours et son cœur changent" (MOT I, 42-43). The break is complete: movement from detailed description to terse generalization, change in sentence form. Thus is set off one of the major themes stressed from the very beginning of the *Mémoires*: Time injures, I am not what I was.

One further case of development from the 1826 version to the final text is of interest; although it involves no "break" because of the use of the "comme" of simile, it provides a sudden and very marked expansion of perspective. Chateaubriand writes (MOT I, 53-54) of the officers his father invited to dine at Combourg; they disturbed the solitude of the boy's life by introducing troubling vistas of other places, other ways of life. At the end of the long paragraph in the *Mémoires de ma vie* come the sentences parallel to the second paragraph of the equivalent passage in the *Mémoires d'Outre-Tombe*.

Quand j'entendais quelque officier parler de Paris et de la Cour je devenais triste. Je cherchais à deviner ce que c'était que la société. J'entrevoyais quelque chose de confus et de lointain, *je supposais des choses cachées, des mystères*. Mais bientôt je me troublais. Des tranquilles régions de l'innocence en jetant les yeux sur le monde j'avais des vertiges. Comme *la tête tourne* lorsqu'on regarde la terre du haut des tours qui se perdent dans le ciel, *je*

[31] *Ibid.*, pp. 47-48.

reculais effrayé et me retrouvais avec joie le petit François dans la retraite de mes bois, à l'abri de l'amitié de mes sœurs et sous l'aile de ma mère.[32]

The paragraph is a closed one; peace and solitude are interrupted and then return. The opening suggested by "vertiges" and the metaphor of the "tours" is carefully confined inside the body of the paragraph; its expression is not enhanced by the somewhat clumsy and confused handling of the two phrases: "vertiges" is not explained in its sentence and thus hardly forms an image, the "tours" image is lost in the explanatory part of the following sentence and unclearly attached to the other elements of the passage.

The final form of this passage is considerably more dramatic. The Paris paragraph has been separated from what precedes, taking on thus already special importance; coming at the beginning of a new paragraph the idea of "Paris" automatically evokes temptations and seductions certainly inherent in the myth of Paris by the 1830's. In the parts maintained there are few word changes, but all that I have italicized above is simply dropped. What remains of the first four sentences becomes one sentence, semi-colons after "triste" and "lointain," a colon after "société," a period after "troublais." The result is, I think, to suggest more clearly the adolescent's confusion and emotional uneasiness. What remains of the original paragraph becomes the second sentence. The image of the high towers leads the reader's imagination to wander off bemusedly at the end of the paragraph. Chateaubriand marks off by commas the four movements of the new sentence: "Des tranquilles régions de l'innocence, en jetant les yeux sur le monde, j'avais des vertiges, comme lorsqu'on regarde la terre du haut de ces tours qui se perdent dans le ciel."[33] Everything is explained in the one sentence, whose very bumpiness[34] now emphasizes the emotional upset that is the subject.

It is indeed a pity that we have no more than three books of the "Manuscrit de 1826," but from fragments of the "Mémoires de ma vie" that Chateaubriand disperses elsewhere in his published works one suspects that they would confirm the evidence just displayed: the abruptly expanding discontinuous paragraph as a regular feature comes after 1826. And so in this paragraph that finally appears at the very end of Book III of the *Mémoires d'Outre-Tombe*, after appearing in 1827 in the "Intro-

---

[32] *Ibid.*, pp. 66-67.

[33] The final form appears to have been substantially fixed by 1834. One reads the isolated sentence with a résumé of the surrounding general sense in the *Lectures des Mémoires de M. de Chateaubriand*, p. 289: "Des tranquilles régions de l'innocence, jetant les yeux sur le monde, j'éprouvais des vertiges comme lorsqu'on regarde la terre du haut de ces tours qui se perdent dans le ciel." "Une belle phrase," comments the editor.

[34] Reminiscent in this regard of Pascal's great sentence concerning "Le plus grand philosophe du monde, sur une planche plus large qu'il ne faut. . . ."

duction" to the *Voyage en Amérique* (ORV I, 669; quoted also in the notes, MOT I, 1054). Although in 1827 the paragraph ends already in an image almost identical to the image of the final versions, that image has been extended and broadened into a generalized portrayal of destiny that goes far beyond the evocativeness of the early version.

> Si mes ouvrages me survivent, si je dois laisser un nom, peut-être un jour, guidé par ces *Mémoires*, quelque voyageur viendra visiter les lieux que j'ai peints. Il pourra reconnaître le château; mais il cherchera vainement le grand bois [here 1827 adds, "il a été abattu," phrase that falls doubtless because its implication of a human agency is not in keeping with the theme of destiny now to be emphasized[35]]: le berceau de mes songes a disparu comme ces songes. Demeuré seul debout sur son rocher, l'antique donjon pleure les chênes, vieux compagnons qui l'environnaient et le protégeaient contre la tempête [1827: "les tempêtes," the abstract plural reinforcing the earlier suggestion that man in his violence as well as nature cut down the trees]. Isolé comme lui, j'ai vu comme lui tomber autour de moi la famille qui embellissait mes jours et me prêtait son abri: heureusement [replacing 1827: "grâce au ciel," that, while a cliché, adds an idea of height too soon in the image developing] ma vie n'est pas bâtie sur la terre aussi solidement que les tours où j'ai passé ma jeunesse [1827 ends with "jeunesse"], et l'homme résiste moins aux orages que les monuments élevés par ses mains. (MOT I, 106)

Although there is certainly no abrupt break to be noted here, the ending of the paragraph moves definitely further towards lyrical meditation in the final versions than in the earlier one.[36]

May one interpret the revelations of the "Manuscrit de 1826" to mean that this particular paragraph structure is, as a practice, unknown before 1826? Not quite. Though it disappears as a practice after the *Essai sur les révolutions*, it is a not uncommon feature of the *Essai*, which thus in still another respect is one with the works of Chateaubriand's later years. The

[35] I note here only the variants that are in keeping with my subject; there are a few others of minor stylistic significance.

[36] The dating of the forms of this important paragraph does, however, pose a conundrum, for the last paragraph of the *Mémoires de ma vie* (pp. 145-46) reads:

"Si mes ouvrages me survivent, si je dois laisser un nom après moi, peut-être un jour un voyageur guidé par ces mémoires, viendra visiter les lieux que j'ai peints; mais il cherchera vainement le grand bois. Le berceau de mes songes a disparu comme ces songes; demeuré seul debout sur son rocher, l'antique donjon semble pleurer les chênes, vieux compagnons qui l'environnaient et le protégeaient contre les tempêtes. Isolé comme lui, j'ai vu comme lui tomber la famille qui embellissait mes jours et me prêtait son abri; heureusement ma vie n'est pas bâtie sur la terre aussi solidement que les tours où j'ai passé ma jeunesse et l'homme résiste moins aux orages que les monuments élevés par ses mains."

Thus "1826," unlike "1827," is most like the "final version." I should suppose that Chateaubriand, at the time the "Manuscrit de 1826" was copied, revised this final paragraph as we here read it, and that the "1827" version referred to above is the one that corresponds to the original text of the "Manuscrit de 1826"—composed by and large, as we know, long before that date. But note that Levaillant, in MOT, ed. du Centenaire, I, 141, n. 17, considers "1827" to be "intermédiaire, pour le texte" between "1826" and the text of the *Mémoires*.

expanding paragraphs of the *Essai* are in general less spectacular than those found later, but they are structurally similar, as the following examples will show. As in the *Mémoires* we find paragraphs expanding at the end both with and without transitions: in effect, similes and metaphors. And the widening of attention is occasioned sometimes by an image or little tableau, sometimes by a maxim or epigram. As in the *Mémoires* these paragraphs come often at the ends of chapters.

Thus at the end of characteristic Chapter I, xiii, entitled "Sparte—Les Jacobins," after an introductory paragraph and two paragraphs of comparison, we find a paragraph of contrast: "Ici finit la ressemblance." Lycurgus transformed Sparta without overthrowing all tradition, without terror. The comparison of his times and reforms with those of the Jacobins is interesting and instructive.

> Sans cette comparaison, il seroit impossible de se former une idée juste des rapports & des différences des deux systèmes, considérés dans le génie, les tems, les lieux & les circonstances: ce sera alors au lecteur à prononcer sur les causes qui consolidèrent la révolution à Sparte; & sur celles qui pourront l'établir, ou la renverser en France. Celui qui lit l'histoire ressemble à un homme voyageant dans le désert, à travers ces bois fabuleux de l'antiquité, qui prédisoient l'avenir.[37]

After the break, then, an epigram, one that would be almost a little tableau were it not for the visual conundrum posed by *désert-bois fabuleux*; the epigram is a generalization perfectly in keeping with the subject but presented in a style of a different level.

A second example of a discontinuous expansion does not come at the end of a chapter but demonstrates a more complete break than the preceding one. In the seventh paragraph of II, ii, "Athènes. Les Quatre Cens," as in the preceding passages and the paragraphs following, we read a calmly detailed account of the rise of Alcibiades and the Four Hundred, with occasional, general, muted comparisons to the time of the *Conventionnels* in France. But the seventh paragraph is very abruptly concluded by a most bitter image, all the more apparent in the 1826 edition for the footnote Chateaubriand appends.

> Les Quatre Cens . . . entrèrent au Sénat dont ils chassèrent les membres. . . . firent massacrer ou exilèrent les ennemis de leur despotisme; mais ils ne rappellèrent aucun des anciens bannis, dont ils avoient d'abord embrassé la cause, soit dans la crainte d'Alcibiade, soit pour jouir des biens de ces infortunés. Je me figure le monde comme un grand bois, où les hommes s'entr'attendent pour se dévaliser.[38] (Ed. de 1797, p. 404)

---

[37] Chateaubriand, *Essai sur les Révolutions*, édition de Londres, 1797, p. 70; the quotations from this work below come from the same edition.

[38] "J'avais là une idée bien peu gracieuse du monde. Cette allure d'un esprit qui se permet tout, est assez amusante [*Note de 1826*]."

Here we have a much clearer break than in the preceding case: the subject of the epigram is more removed from the subject of the paragraph, and there is no "ressemble à" to ease the transition. There is, by the nature of the remark, on the other hand, little expansion of perspective, other than that implied by generalization; the effect is mildly picturesque but lyrical only—and yet truly lyrical, there—in the curious intrusion of that "je" which tempts the reader of the *Essai* often to read the work as autobiography.[39]

Chapter I, lxx (lxxi in 1797), "Sujets & Réflexions détachées," is a loosely woven tissue of remarks by the author contemplating his just completed first development, the "Révolution républicaine" of ancient Greece.[40] His tone is in general argumentative, harsh, embittered, reflectively personal. The paragraph beginning, "J'ai réflechi long-tems sur ce sujet: je ne hais point une constitution plus qu'une autre, considérée abstraitement" continues the contrast that had already been established between the mutability of governmental structures and the persistence of human vices and virtues, among both the revolutionary Greeks and the revolutionary French. "Prises en ce qui me regarde comme individu, [les constitutions] me sont toutes parfaitement indifférentes: mes mœurs sont de la solitude & non des hommes. Eh! malheureux, nous nous tourmentons pour un gouvernement parfait, & nous sommes vicieux! . . . Nous nous agitons aujourd'hui pour un vain système, & nous ne serons plus demain!" The paragraph is long, and its sinuous reflections continue the motifs of death and ennui announced in these opening phrases. The tone becomes more personal, already a foreshadowing of *René*:[41] "Est-ce un instinct indéterminé, un vuide intérieur que nous ne saurions remplir, qui nous tourmente? Je l'ai aussi sentie cette soif vague de quelque chose. Elle m'a trainé dans les solitudes muettes de l'Amérique, & dans les villes bruyantes de l'Europe. . . . Homme, si c'est ta destinée de porter partout un cœur miné d'un désir inconnu; si c'est là ta maladie, une ressource te reste." The author recommends scientific or metaphysical speculation under the starry heavens, or if that is too sublime,

> Au lieu de t'entretenir des haines sociales, observe les paisibles genérations,
> les douces sympathies, & les amours du Règne le plus charmant de la nature.
> Alors tu ne connoîtras que des plaisirs. Tu auras du moins cet avantage, que

[39] It is "autobiography" in the strange way that much of Malraux's *Antimémoires* is.

[40] It is parallel in many respects to the "Nuit chez les Sauvages de l'Amérique" that concludes the *Essai*.

[41] In 1826 Chateaubriand notes of this chapter, "étrange. . . extraordinaire. . . une sorte d'orgie noire d'un cœur blessé, d'un esprit malade, d'une imagination qui reproduit les fantômes dont elle est obsédée; c'est du Rousseau, c'est du René, c'est du dégoût de tout, de l'ennui de tout." He criticizes its ideas, development, language—and adds that he finds in it nevertheless "une inspiration, de quelque nature qu'elle soit, qu'on ne retrouve dans aucune autre partie de mes ouvrages."

chaque matin tu retrouveras tes plantes chéries: dans le monde que d'amis ont pressé le soir un ami sur leur cœur, & ne l'ont plus trouvé à leur réveil! Nous sommes Ici Bas comme au spectacle: si nous détournons un moment la tête, le coup de sifflet part, les palais enchantés s'évanouissent; & lorsque nous ramenons les yeux sur la scène, nous n'appercevons plus que des déserts & des acteurs inconnus. (Ed. de 1797, pp. 390-92)

A sentimentalized "Rêverie du Promeneur Solitaire" to an extent. A lyrical meditation quite in keeping with the rest of the paragraph. Still the final sentence takes one suddenly far from such clichés—and even such temporally definable concerns—into a generalized and yet much more visual image, carefully worked out rhythmically—the rapid cuts of the awakening, the sweep of the empty new vision—and powerful in its sudden bitterness.

The *Essai* also includes expanding paragraphs of a less abrupt construction, in which the final image is brought into play via a simile. The barbarous principles of the Carthaginians and their commercial genius are compendiously described and suddenly concluded with the epigrammatical last sentence of Chapter I, xxx: "Malgré l'état imparfait de la navigation, l'avarice, plus puissante que les inventions humaines, leur avoit servit [*sic*] de boussole sur les déserts de l'Océan" (Ed. de 1797, p. 171). One is not at all surprised to find appended to this chapter a note of 1826 in which Chateaubriand expresses his satisfaction with such passages: "à quelques anglicismes près, je les écrirois aujourd'hui tels qu'ils sont." A more melancholy and no doubt personal reflection is found in the image terminating Chapter I, xlvii, a comparison of Scythia and "la Suisse pauvre & vertueuse." The topic sentence of the last paragraph, "C'est ainsi que malgré soi, on s'arrête à contempler le tableau d'un peuple satisfait," leads to the final development: in times of trouble especially we grasp on to others' happiness: "Comme le matelot qui se noie, il [l'homme avide de bonheur] tâche de saisir son voisin heureux, pour se sauver avec lui. Si cette ressource lui manque, il s'accroche au souvenir même de ses plaisirs passés, & s'en sert comme d'un débri [*sic*] avec lequel il surnage sur une mer de chagrins" (Ed. de 1797, p. 257). At the end of the chapter once more the reader has been led far into a lyrical meditation concerning the émigré, and far from the topic in its narrower sense.

The same phenomenon occurs at the end of the development of the first part, in Chapter I, lxviii (lxix in 1797), "Différence générale entre notre Siècle & celui où s'opéra la Révolution Républicaine de la Grèce," though now the image is developed with greater grandeur. "Heureux si les Grecs en acquérant des lumières n'eûssent pas perdu la pureté des mœurs"—and from the theme of contrast thus announced Chateaubriand devotes his final paragraph to the warning that history, like life, alternates the picture of man's happiness and misery.

> La nature nous traite comme des enfans malades, dont on refuse de satisfaire les appétits, mais dont on appaise les pleurs par des illusions & des espèrances. Elle fait danser au-tour de nous une multitude de fantômes, vers lesquels nous tendons les mains, sans pouvoir les atteindre: & elle a poussé si loin l'art de la perspective, qu'elle a peint des Elysées jusques dans le fond de la tombe. (Ed. de 1797, pp. 375-76)

In 1826 once again Chateaubriand can't keep from noting his admiration for these sentences—despite, of course, his disapproval of "l'homme qui croit et qui veut douter" that in 1826 he is determined to show in the *Essai*.

Another expanding paragraph form that is common in the *Mémoires d'Outre-Tombe*, the paragraph opened out at the end with a quotation, is also seen in the *Essai*. In the eighteenth-century atmosphere of the work it is no surprise that the quotation is from Bernardin de Saint-Pierre, a paragraph ending from the *Chaumière indienne* that Chateaubriand simply makes his own. The fourth paragraph of the Introduction to Part I develops without much coherence the idea that the author can write disinterestedly and dispassionately about Revolution because, although he is an émigré, he is near death.

> La position où je me trouve est d'ailleurs favorable à la vérité. Attaqué d'une maladie qui me laisse peu d'espoir, je vois les objets d'un œil tranquille. L'air calme de la tombe se fait sentir au voyageur qui n'en est plus qu'à quelques journées. Sans désirs & sans crainte, je ne nourris plus les chimères du bonheur, & les hommes ne sauroient me faire plus de mal que je n'en éprouve. "Le malheur," dit l'auteur des *Etudes de la Nature*, "le malheur ressemble à la montagne noire de Bember, aux extrémités du royaume brûlant de Lahor; tant que vous la montez, vous ne voyez devant vous que de stériles rochers; mais quand vous êtes au sommet, vous appercevez le ciel sur votre tête & le royaume de Cachemire à vos pieds." (Ed. de 1797, p. 4)

It is easy to see why Chateaubriand noted down this passage, thematically and structurally so close to habits of composition that guide him, as we have seen, as early as 1797 and as late as the 1840's. Despite his footnote to the quotation, explaining how difficult it is for him in the conditions of his emigration to check his quotations, he quotes exactly—except, curiously, at the very end, where he reverses two elements that in the order of Bernardin's text (the most poetic word at the end; the voiced continuing consonant at the end; the increasing length of parts) were much closer to the order and habits one would consider Chateaubriand's: "et à vos pieds le royaume de Cachemire."

To summarize, then, it seems possible to claim that Chateaubriand has recognized the value of abrupt generalization and sudden opening of perspective. To force by such discontinuity the reader's poetic collaboration in the text appears to be an aim he seeks more and more frequently in his later years. He may do it consciously or not, but he does it with a certain consistency. He does not, so far as I know, ever speak directly of the practice, any more than he does of any of his literary practices other than the most elementary (such as when he points out proudly the careful documentation of the historical background of his fiction and gives suspiciously ex post facto rationales for various subjects, as in the preface of *Atala* or the *Génie*'s introduction of *René*). On the other hand, there is a kind of discontinuity of which he is quite conscious: of the many bold contrasts and inconsistencies in his life and experience he speaks with defiant frankness.

Thus it is that his references to literary juxtapositions appear only in passing and are not particularly enlightening, whether it concern others (he thinks of the *Astrée* while travelling along the banks of the Lignon in 1805, and on reflection finds "quelque chose d'ingénieusement fantastique dans cette résurrection des nymphes et des naïades qui se mêlent à des bergers, des dames et des chevaliers: ces mondes divers s'associent bien, et l'on s'accommode agréablement des fables de la mythologie, unies aux mensonges du roman"[42] [MOT I, 582]) or his own practice: "La postérité viendra; elle prononcera sur le *livre* et sur le *commentaire* [de l'*Essai sur les révolutions*]. . . . Le *livre* et les *notes* me mettent devant les hommes tel que j'ai été au début de ma carrière, tel que je suis au terme de cette carrière" (MOT I, 661). Or whether it concern imagistic (like nymphs mixed with shepherds) or temporal (mixture of two periods) juxtapositions. But conscious that his "souvenirs se font écho" (MOT I, 61, in reference to the woods of Brittany and the American forests) he does hint occasionally that the juxtapositions with which his life has been filled can be turned into a general method for parts of his *Mémoires*.

[Chapter on his arrival in Rome as ambassador]

Vous venez de parcourir mon journal de route, vous allez lire mes lettres à madame Récamier, entremêlées, comme je l'ai annoncé, de pages historiques.

Parallèlement vous trouverez mes dépêches. Ici paraîtront distinctement les deux hommes qui existent en moi. (MOT II, 235)

This consciousness of being simultaneously two or more different people is at times expressed with real anguish ("C'était comme la prière du soir au bord de la mer dans ma pauvre Bretagne, et j'étais au bord du lac de Lucerne! Une main renouait ainsi les deux bouts de ma vie, pour me faire mieux sentir tout ce qui s'était perdu dans la chaîne de mes années." [MOT II, 579]), sometimes with pomp and portentous pretentiousness,

---

[42] He is conscious of his own similar mixtures in the *Natchez* and the *Martyrs*: ORV I, 163-64; II, 29-30.

Je me suis rencontré entre deux siècles, comme au confluent de deux fleuves; j'ai plongé dans leurs eaux troublées, m'éloignant à regret du vieux rivage où je suis né, nageant avec espérance vers une rive inconnue. (MOT II, 936: a complete paragraph, finishing the penultimate chapter of the *Mémoires d'Outre-Tombe*)

and often with querulous complaints against "ma mémoire des lieux, étonnante et cruelle à la fois" (MOT II, 235), "la tyrannie de ma mémoire," which, however, perhaps, "en faisant entrer le passé dans le présent, ôte à celui-ci une partie de ce qu'il a de misérable" (MOT II, 452).

"Ma mémoire est un panorama; là, viennent se peindre sur la même toile les sites et les cieux les plus divers avec leur soleil brûlant ou leur horizon brumeux" (MOT II, 743). "Ma mémoire oppose sans cesse mes voyages à mes voyages, montagnes à montagnes, fleuves à fleuves, forêts à forêts, et ma vie détruit ma vie" (MOT II, 585). Of the two processes by which, through juxtaposition, memory can lead to a prose style—addition and an artistic offering, in the first of these quotations; subtraction and destruction, in the second—we have come to see the former as the operating principle in Chateaubriand's prose composition. It is a technique that, not unlike the successive scenes portrayed in early paintings of certain saints' lives, allows us to view within one frame a sequence of events whose relationship and emotional structure the viewer himself must furnish. It has taken until our generation for readers to appreciate how basic and profound the "oppositions" of "memory" are in Chateaubriand's life and work. I have tried to show in this chapter to what extent oppositions and juxtapositions of all kinds reach even into the form of Chateaubriand's paragraph.

Le suject, selon qu'il est, peut faire trouver un homme
sçavant et memorieux, mais pour juger en luy les parties
plus siennes et plus dignes, la force et beauté de son ame, il
faut sçavoir ce qui est sien et ce qui ne l'est point, et en ce
qui n'est pas sien combien on luy doibt en consideration
du chois, disposition, ornement et langage qu'il y a fourny.

Montaigne III, viii

3   The Feeling of the Unimaginable

In the preceding chapters I analyzed a certain type of discontinuous
paragraph which I claimed to be characteristic of an important part of
Chateaubriand's prose. This elliptical form, which suddenly opens its
perspective, causing the reader to join his imagination to the author's in a
leap forward to a greatly expanded vision, was seen to reappear in significant places. In Chapter 1 I pointed out that it is a development of
certain less specifically Chateaubrianesque forms, less elliptical, and ironical or antithetical in nature, and it was seen in Chapter 2 as an evolving
form in Chateaubriand's own work.

This kind of paragraph is not the most common sort to be found in
Chateaubriand's work: indeed it occurs only occasionally even in those
works which make the greatest use of it, drawing some of its effect (in this
respect rather like the "Romantic alexandrine") from its very difference.
A disjointed, surprising, evocative form, it tends to be a sign of emotional
tension, when the author's subject leads him to one of those themes—
death, the effects of age, passing time, silence, the shifting perspectives of
historical events, in general any manifestation of impermanence—that
regularly give rise to his most distinctive efforts. Nor indeed is this paragraph to be found in all of Chateaubriand's "manners." Except for the
ironical variation, it is absent from the political works, including the
pamphlets of the early 1830's. It is rare also in the literary works of what
was once considered Chateaubriand's great period—the 1800's, *Atala*
through the *Itinéraire*. We noted examples of this kind of paragraph most
often in the first and the last compositions: the *Essai sur les révolutions* of
1797, the *Mémoires* and the *Vie de Rancé* of the last years.

45

They are, of course, together with the *Itinéraire*, "Mémoires d'une année de ma vie" (ORV II, 701), Chateaubriand's most directly autobiographical works. It is perhaps natural for him to cluster all his poetic effects for emotional intensity there. For other kinds of discontinuity in composition are also noted in these works, works which either precede the period during which Fontanes, "sa muse . . . pleine d'un dévouement étonné," exerted such an influence on Chateaubriand, urging him to place "la langue classique dans la bouche de [ses] personnages romantiques" (MOT I, 451-52) or come at the end of the author's long and increasingly independent career. But, particularly if we divide his work into a "classical" and a non-"classical" manner and pay especial attention to the latter, I think we can see that discontinuous composition is one of Chateaubriand's most characteristic tendencies. The general structure of the *Essai* and the *Natchez* cycle rests on the immediate confrontation of contrasting subjects or styles necessary in the total plan. The *Mémoires d'Outre-Tombe* insert between Chateaubriand's story of beginning the writing of those *Mémoires* and his stormy career as a Restoration politician a whole history of Napoleon. *La Vie de Rancé* deals only occasionally with Rancé. Such composition by juxtaposition, peculiarly sympathetic to Chateaubriand, may no longer be explained as a result of only partly assimilated sources, slapdash writing, or contradictory and irreconcilable aims on the part of a pagan and sensual man who chose to become the author of the *Génie du christianisme*. I shall return to these larger confrontations after this chapter.

Having examined its form I should here like to examine the importance of our comparatively rare paragraph structure, to show how Chateaubriand uses this composition for maximum effect, show where and, as far as possible, when it tends to appear, and particularly examine the themes which most often bring it into play.

My first example in Chapter 1 was taken from the end of a book of the *Vie de Rancé*. It is very common for Chateaubriand to leave for the ending of a chapter or section this kind of effect. It would be foolish to claim statistical accuracy for the following indications,[1] but the trends are clear. I have noted for instance in the *Mémoires d'Outre-Tombe* 118 signal examples of the paragraph whose subject suddenly expands after a pause near the end. Of these examples, forty-four—more than a third of them—occur at the end of a chapter, and of them four occur in chapters terminat-

---

[1] Unnecessary also, for the phenomenon has been recognized by many sensitive critics. See for instance Durry, *La Vieillesse de Chateaubriand*, I, 245-46; Mourot, *Rythme et sonorité dans les Mémoires d'Outre-Tombe*, pp. 252-60. "Personne n'a poussé plus loin que M. de Chateaubriand l'art si justement apprécié de ramener au récit, après une digression, par une réflexion touchante, de terminer un chapitre par des pensées profondes ou mélancoliques, et de le clore toujours par une phrase mélodieuse, comme pour laisser dans l'oreille du lecteur un son qui l'attire et lui plaît": Marcellus, *Chateaubriand et son temps*, p. 156.

ing a book (in the Pléiade edition's arrangement of the *Mémoires* there are forty-four books). The pattern is reinforced if we add to these 118 examples forty-six more which also show a sudden expansion though without the "break": of the resulting 164 paragraphs, sixty-four occur at the end of a chapter, eight terminate books, and two of the four "Parties" reestablished by Levaillant in the "Edition du Centenaire" arrangement of the *Mémoires* are so terminated. Similarly in the *Vie de Rancé*, the other major source for paragraphs of this type, two of the four parts of the first edition, and one of the three in the second, are thus concluded.

One may state with confidence then that these paragraphs with the striking ending appear to be favored by the author as a striking ending for his chapter or book. One can maintain also that in still more cases, because of their very peculiarity, they occasion for the reader a pause similar to that of a chapter ending, in those cases where Chateaubriand continues his chapter after inserting one in the midst of a subject development.

It is not surprising that the majority of these favored paragraph endings have as their theme one of three of the great characteristic themes of Chateaubriand: passage or change in human affairs, death, the contrasting perspectives of history. I shall here examine some further examples in which the author treats the themes of impermanence and death, plus certain other, less frequent themes. Historical contrasts I shall save for the following chapter, because they occur with particular frequency in Chateaubriand's history of Napoleon.

As in all French Romantic poetry the theme of passage and change receives a place of honor among Chateaubriand's topics. It is a theme that lends itself naturally to the discontinuous paragraph.

> Quand l'abbé de Rancé introduisait la réforme dans son abbaye, les moines eux-mêmes n'étaient plus que des ruines de religieux. Réduits au nombre de sept, ce reste de cénobites était dénaturé par l'abondance ou par le malheur. Les moines, depuis long-temps avaient mérité des reproches. Dès le onzième siècle, Adalbéron déclare "qu'un moine est transformé en soldat." En Normandie, un supérieur ayant prétendu admonester ses moines fut flagellé par eux après sa mort. Abailard, qui tenta en Bretagne d'user de sévérité, se vit exposé au poison: "J'habite un pays barbare, disait-il, dont la langue m'est inconnue; mes promenades sont les bords d'une mer agitée, et mes moines ne sont connus que par leur débauche." Tout a changé en Bretagne, hors les vagues qui changent toujours.[2]

The reader who has noted with Richard Chateaubriand's regular pattern of voids that generate voids will spot a parallel design here in the final image: change within change. The reader of *Rancé* cannot fail to note also that this last sentence has but a tenuous and most unclear relationship to

---

[2] Chateaubriand, *Vie de Rancé*, ed. Letessier, pp. 136-37.

the apparent subject of the paragraph, although it has a lot to do with the author: once again its reader begins to suspect that any unity to be found in this strange book must be sought only in the book's depiction of the author's soul. Chateaubriand has once more lifted from the notes and books he is dutifully copying "pour obéir aux ordres du directeur de [sa] vie" the one image that sets in movement his imagination—here it is the "mer agitée"—and breaks wide open his running narrative of Rancé's initial reforms with a sentence of endless perspective and reiteration in harmony with his own inner music.

But there remains still a secret lesson to be drawn from this broken paragraph. What, precisely, has "changé en Bretagne," and when? Is it the religious order? Chateaubriand's Brittany is the home of loyalty to King and Church, the place of his childhood vows and his final salvation. Such a present religious order can only signify, coming as it does after a history of religious disorder, a sudden turning to order; conversion after debauch. Yet one notes that Chateaubriand does not cry in triumph about all this: in this paragraph conversion is an afterthought, while inconstancy is the stable element. Between this kind of ecclesiastical history and the fickle and worldly Chateaubriand whose early "je pleurai et je crus" hardly introduced a story of sainthood, who turns at the end of his life to a real saint's life—a saint whose sins he lovingly portrays—but only with "une répugnance naturelle," there is a strange parallel: rhetorical cohesion by virtue of incoherence, moral stability in change. Its abrupt ending makes the paragraph double, unstable, contradictory; Chateaubriand describes himself in both parts.

The kind of discontinuous paragraph that is most often devoted to a theme of passage presents the traveler, moving away from one place or time to another. Of all the leitmotifs of the *Mémoires d'Outre-Tombe* it is perhaps the one closest in spirit to the epigraph: "Sicut nubes ... quasi naves ... velut umbra." The best possible example occurs in the famous passage, already examined in the preceding chapter, referred to by Proust in *A la recherche du temps perdu*.[3] "Je fus tiré de mes réflexions par le gazouillement d'une grive" (MOT I, 76-77). Chateaubriand explains in the paragraph how the magical sound, heard at Montboissier in 1817, suddenly reopens for him whole vistas of his childhood at Combourg. A *tristesse* common to both moments, but one the *tristesse* of unknown, unrequited desire, the other that of a blasé quinquagenarian, is caught up in the sound. Will he ever be able to finish his *Mémoires*? "Mettons à profit le peu d'instants qui me restent; hâtons-nous de peindre ma jeunesse, tandis que j'y touche encore:"—and after the colon and the break—the break that stops the immobility—comes the rhythmically flowing maxim con-

---

[3] In *Le Temps retrouvé* (*A la recherche du temps perdu*, ed. Pléiade, III, 919).

cluding the initial chapter of Book III: "le navigateur, abandonnant pour jamais un rivage enchanté, écrit son journal à la vue de la terre qui s'éloigne et qui va bientôt disparaître."[4]

The image of the traveler is one of Chateaubriand's favorite images for himself, containing all together, as it were, a seafaring Breton ancestry, his own travels, and his profound concern with impermanence. Several times in the *Mémoires d'Outre-Tombe* we find him returning to this image after the break in an expanding paragraph. Thus, when he goes off for the first time to Combourg (again in a carefully revised paragraph whose development was traced in Chapter 2): ". . . je m'émerveillais à chaque tour de roue: [colon, and break after this logical finish of a paragraph in which each of three and a half sentences has given a detailed description of the boy's experience; after the break comes the double epigram, the second part more generalizing than the first] premier pas d'un Juif errant qui ne se devait plus arrêter. Encore si l'homme ne faisait que changer de lieux! mais ses jours et son cœur changent" (MOT I, 42-43).

It is the image of the sea voyage that comes back with greatest frequency in these paragraphs, an image that presents an almost archetypal picture of observable space between present and past, allowing but a tenuous link—a glance, a memory—between the two. Two ships draw near, hail each other, pass, move apart: "Le temps emporte et sépare les voyageurs sur la terre, plus promptement encore que le vent ne les emporte et ne les sépare sur l'océan; on se fait un signe de loin: *Adieu, va!* Le port commun est l'Eternité" (MOT I, 201-2).[5] Passengers on a ship meet briefly, in this "hôtellerie errante," react to each other, separate. "Quand vont et viennent ces jeunes femmes nées du sang anglais et du sang indien, qui

---

[4] Cf. the image terminating an early example of the expanding paragraph: "Il était six heures vingt-neuf minutes, lorsque je perdis de vue la Cité Sainte: le navigateur marque ainsi le moment où disparaît à ses yeux une terre lointaine qu'il ne reverra jamais" (*Itinéraire de Paris à Jérusalem*, ORV II, 1128). As to the mental structure called into play here, note Gautier's suggestive comment, in *Le Style des Mémoires d'Outre-Tombe*, p. 172: he considers "cette sorte de comparaison par rappel . . . un trait caractéristique du style des *Mémoires*; c'est à la fois une manière de penser et une manière d'écrire."

[5] Marcellus is one of the first connaisseurs of this discontinuous technique, as one can see from his objection to the next sentence which in the final versions forms a paragraph all by itself: "Il valait mieux finir là ['l'Eternité']. Les deux lignes qui suivent renferment une boutade survenue en relisant: 'Et si le vaisseau rencontré était celui de Cook ou de La Pérouse?'

"Cette pensée se rattache mal à l'autre, et nous fait descendre trop brusquement du ciel et de l'éternité dans le monde des navigateurs." *Chateaubriand et son temps*, pp. 49-50.

On the other hand, *ibid.*, pp. 11-12, in reference to the passage concerning the dogs of Saint-Malo, one may note that he was not automatically well-disposed to discontinuous paragraphs.

In the "Lectures" of 1834, the paragraph ends with "éternité"; the sentence about Cook and La Pérouse is already a one-sentence paragraph immediately following. *Lectures des Mémoires de M. de Chateaubriand*, pp. 209-10.

joignent à la beauté de Clarisse la délicatesse de Sacontala, alors se forment des chaînes que nouent et dénouent les vents parfumés de Ceylan, douces comme eux, comme eux légères" (MOT I, 203).[6] Chateaubriand leaves his English embassy and sets sail from Dover in 1822, as, in 1800, he had returned from emigration in England. And he writes this passage in 1839. "Lorsqu'on regarde ou qu'on écoute sa vie passée, on croit voir sur une mer déserte la trace d'un vaisseau qui a disparu; on croit entendre les glas d'une cloche dont on n'aperçoit point la vieille tour" (MOT II, 100-1: end of Book XXVII). In each of these cases the pause just before the final sentence marks the rupture between the former state—the measurable, objective, described—and the conclusion, subjective and lyrical, or, more properly, elegiac when as here the motif of movement away implies everlasting separation between the known and the inevitable unknown.

A similar technique, but developed with a metaphor of temporal rather than spatial passage, is a great commonplace of the *Mémoires*, bringing together moments widely separated by time—this is the method for that matter of the *Essai sur les révolutions*. I quote the most astonishing of these passages in full, because in it Chateaubriand manages to express temporal distance by spatial movement. During the summer of 1829, on leave from his post as ambassador to Rome, Chateaubriand goes to the Pyrenees to the spa at Cauterets. Memories are awakened of his first view of these mountains:

> Au lever des Pyrénées sur l'horizon, le cœur me battait: du fond de vingt-trois années sortirent des souvenirs embellis dans les lointains du temps: je revenais de la Palestine et de l'Espagne, lorsque, de l'autre côté de leur chaîne, je découvris le sommet de ces mêmes montagnes.[7] Je suis de l'avis de madame de Motteville; je pense que c'est dans un de ces châteaux des Pyrénées qu'habitait Urgande la Déconnue. Le passé ressemble à un musée d'antiques; on y visite les heures écoulées; chacun peut y reconnaître les siennes. Un jour, me promenant dans une église déserte, j'entendis des pas se traînant sur les dalles, comme ceux d'un vieillard qui cherchait sa tombe. Je regardai et n'aperçus personne; c'était moi qui m'étais révélé à moi. (MOT II, 374-75)

The walking up to one's own image, as in a mirror, is particularly effective here because of the double temporal perspective from the break between "les siennes" and "un jour." The anecdote of the man in the church which serves as an image for "visiting the past" (already itself an image) tells really of a brusk coming to face with the future. The only element

[6] Passage essentially the same in *Lectures des Mémoires de M. de Chateaubriand*, p. 212.
[7] Cf. the analysis of Grevlund, in *Paysage intérieur et paysage extérieur dans les Mémoires d'Outre-Tombe*, p. 200, in the case of "ces échos, ces correspondances [qui] se rejoignent dans une parfaite identité sensible. Perçue par l'esprit, cette identité paraît alors se dérober aux

common to both sides of the final metaphor, museum and tomb, is the absence of the present; the suddenness of the suppression of that present here coincides with the sudden interruption of the death theme in the theme of memory. It is notable furthermore that the approach of death is marked here at the break by an indication of time, "un jour," and in a context of religion and solitude, "église déserte."

The memory theme, a variant of the theme of passage, is a major theme in any autobiography. Chateaubriand reserves for it a very characteristic epigram, the generalizing conclusion of a paragraph that terminates the description of a visit he made to Oxford at the time of his emigration. It answers the question, can one give new life to the memories of youth? "Les plaisirs de la jeunesse reproduits par la mémoire sont des ruines vues au flambeau" (MOT I, 424). Yet however flickering memory's powers may be, even if it can come up with nothing but a ruin, it is all we have to give us an identity through time; we must treasure memory, however weak: "Notre existence est d'une telle fuite, que si nous n'écrivons pas le soir l'événement du matin, le travail nous encombre et nous n'avons plus le temps de le mettre à jour. Cela ne nous empêche pas de gaspiller nos années, de jeter au vent ces heures qui sont pour l'homme les semences de l'éternité" (MOT I, 143: end of a chapter and paragraph concerning Chateaubriand's friends in Paris in 1789 and mentioning Fontanes who, as he writes in 1821, has recently died).

The rapidity of change in time, another major related theme, is also seen in this passage, as in the one quoted in Chapter 1 about kingdoms fallen overnight and swept up in the morning. Yet, although memory is one protection against such change, it is not a final, complete protection: such is the lesson of a complex and elaborate tableau terminating a paragraph in the *Congrès de Vérone* concerning the gradual destruction of the aristocratic ideal by an encroaching spirit of democracy. The paragraph as a whole is a reflective and abruptly personal one, following the "appel des morts" at the end of the section "Colonies espagnoles"; it speaks eloquently of the necessity of historical change. But the concluding image opens doubly the perspective: historically, by reference to Roman history; lyrically, by the ambiguity suddenly developed in the idea of "souvenirs." Still the rhythm here is a narrowing, falling rhythm, mixing a suggestion thus of discouragement and acquiescence in the theme of inevitable change:

> On ne se défend point de l'invasion des années avec des souvenirs: Sabinus vainement entassa les statues des ancêtres sur le seuil des portes du Capitole pour empêcher l'ennemi d'y pénétrer la torche à la main; les Aigles mêmes

contingences de la durée traditionnelle. . . . Les catégories temporelles en sont comme annulées."

qui soutenaient les voûtes, s'embrasèrent et mirent le feu à l'édifice, leur nid paternel.[8]

A very special case of impermanence may be seen in the following examples, where the metaphor used is of such an amazingly bold and visual sort that one would like to call it a metamorphosis. One paragraph is short, and I quote it whole: it appears at the end of the chapter describing Napoleon's divorce and remarriage and criticizing him for "trompant lui-même son propre lit par son intimité avec Marie-Louise avant la célébration du mariage religieux":

> L'archiduchesse Marie-Louise, le 20 mars 1811, accouche d'un fils: sanction supposée des félicités précédentes. De ce fils, éclos, comme les oiseaux du pôle, au soleil de minuit, il ne restera qu'une valse triste, composée par lui-même à Schœnbrünn, et jouée sur des orgues dans les rues de Paris, autour du palais de son père. (MOT I, 776)

The other passage contains a comparison of a city to a woman, bringing to mind that stunning sentence in the *Vie de Rancé* where Chateaubriand speaks of the château de Chambord as "une femme dont le vent aurait soufflé en l'air la chevelure." Here Chateaubriand is writing elegiacally of Venice, the city of disappearances: the sun is setting, Dante, Petrarch, and Byron have passed through and beyond the city, and Venice is no longer the city it was in the days of its political dominance nor even what it was when Chateaubriand had visited it in 1806. Now, moreover, in 1833, Chateaubriand is serving his "embassy" from the Duchesse de Berry to the exiled royal family from which she is estranged, a lost cause, as Chateaubriand knows, within the larger lost cause, as he also knows, of the monarchy. The theme of death has already just been played on most specifically, for in the preceding chapter is repeated the somber "Appel des morts" of the Verona conference of 1822. The last paragraph of Book XL, chapter 4, describes the sunset in Venice, "cette ville en harmonie avec ma destinée." The light transforms everything; the chapter ends, "Venise est là, assise sur le rivage de la mer, comme une belle femme qui va s'éteindre avec le jour: le vent du soir soulève ses cheveux embaumés; elle meurt saluée par toutes les grâces et tous les sourires de la nature" (MOT II, 772).[9]

---

[8] *Congrès de Vérone*, "Négociations.—Colonies Espagnoles," chap. 28, in Chateaubriand, *Oeuvres complètes*, ed. Furne, 1862, X, 500.

[9] A passage of the *Mémoires* describing the Austrian oppression of Italy in 1803 ends in a similar manner and a similar vein, but with a less abruptly introduced personification: "Rome est rentrée dans ses ruines, Venise dans sa mer. Venise s'est affaissée en embellissant le ciel de son dernier sourire; elle s'est couchée charmante dans ses flots, comme un astre qui ne doit plus se lever" (MOT I, 498). Cf. four other concluding personifications of a city as a woman: "Rome, assise sur la pierre de son sépulcre" (MOT II, 725; quoted *supra*, p. 15), "Moscou, comme une princesse européenne aux confins de son empire, parée de toutes les richesses de l'Asie, semblait amenée là pour épouser Napoléon," "Moscou chancelait silen-

Death is the last, absolute impermanence, and this second great theme, as in the example just cited, frequently appears with the first. Death of all kinds is one of the most frequent subjects of the *Mémoires d'Outre-Tombe*, from the death of the ancien régime and its society to the death of the author's friends and his meditation on his own death. At the end of Book XXIX, the book devoted to Madame Récamier, in the third paragraph before the end, Chateaubriand speaks of all their friends who are no more. The paragraph ends with a fine generalizing image, tying together admirably an image of death and the idea of movement away. "Mon inséparable camarade de route, M. Ballanche, s'est trouvé seul au commencement et à la fin de ma carrière; il a été témoin de mes liaisons rompues par le temps, comme j'ai été témoin des siennes entraînées par le Rhône: les fleuves minent toujours leurs bords" (MOT II, 222). The abrupt pause before the epigram that is signaled by the colon is the sign of the breaking off of life.

Chateaubriand treats the theme of death in his expanding paragraphs with a virtuosity that is astonishing. His use of even such standard metaphors as a voyage or the night can be fresh and gracious. Speaking of the death of Moreau he brings back the image of the traveler: "Les hommes disparus jeunes sont de vigoureux voyageurs; ils font vite une route que des hommes plus débiles achèvent à pas lents" (MOT I, 780). Severely critical of the political situation around Charles X, Chateaubriand resigns his ambassadorship in Rome. With deepest regret he must give up the idea of an "exil éternel sur les ruines de Rome." "Le vieil oiseau tombe de la branche où il se réfugie; il quitte la vie pour la mort. Entraîné par le courant, il n'a fait que changer de fleuve" (MOT II, 383). Chateaubriand recounts the burial of the Duchesse de Lévis in Père-Lachaise near Fontanes and Fontanes' son. "C'est ainsi qu'en m'inclinant au monument de madame de Lévis, je suis venu me heurter à deux autres sépulcres; l'homme ne peut éveiller une douleur sans en réveiller une autre: pendant la nuit, les diverses fleurs qui ne s'ouvrent qu'à l'ombre s'épanouissent" (MOT I, 943). The technique of the break is particularly dramatic in such examples: it signifies the moment of death, after which comes the transfiguration of metaphor. A different variation on death, using more or less traditional means, comes in the following expansion by imaged maxim; the death theme occurs in a historical context, in a paragraph on Charles V: "Le lecteur de l'histoire est comme l'homme qui avance dans la vie, et qui voit tomber un à un ses contemporains et ses amis; à mesure

---

cieuse devant l'étranger: trois jours après elle avait disparu; la Circassienne du Nord, la belle fiancée, s'était couchée sur son bûcher funèbre" (MOT I, 804, 804-5) and the less visual image contrasting "Rome païenne" and "Rome chrétienne" (MOT I, 500) commented *supra*, p. 28.

qu'il tourne les pages, les personnages disparoissent; un feuillet sépare les siècles, comme une pelletée de terre les générations."[10]

The transfiguration can take the form of a reference to the eternal realm of literature rather than appear as an image. Many passages concerned with death are amplified with a quotation. When it is time to move with Napoleon to Saint Helena, Chateaubriand ends his chapter with all stops out, in his most magnificent full organ:

> Ores donc que, détaché de son temps, son histoire est finie et que son épopée commence, allons le voir mourir: quittons l'Europe; suivons-le sous le ciel de son apothéose! Le frémissement des mers, là où ses vaisseaux caleront la voile, nous indiquera le lieu de sa disparition: "A l'extrémité de notre hémisphère, on entend," dit Tacite, "le bruit que fait le soleil en s'immergeant, *sonum insuper immergentis audiri.*" (MOT I, 1010)

The movement into quotation, especially in a foreign tongue, is frequently used by Chateaubriand for an expansion into universal experience; here it is at once a movement from contemporaneity into history (Tacitus), from the idea of France to the concept of empire (Roman history), and, as we shall see again in the following chapter with Napoleon, from a great man to a natural force (the setting of the sun). The apostrophe to the reader, the rhetorical evocations of the sea, set the tone for a majestic metaphor; the break of pace, the movement into quotation, the passage from French to Latin, with stately finality mark the passing from life to eternity. A similar use of quotation may be noted in paragraphs referring to the death of a young Cossack in 1812 (the quotation is from a Scandinavian Edda: MOT I, 791-92), the death of Joubert (quotation from the Psalms: MOT I, 454), the death of the German poet Kœrner (quotation from Tyrtaeus: MOT I, 844). A quite curious case appears in a paragraph concerning the death from consumption of a sixteen-year-old Spanish girl at the Infirmerie Marie-Thérèse (MOT II, 623): Chateaubriand attributes his simple and poignant quotation to Lope de Vega and seems to refer to the play *La Niña de plata*: the quotation, however, would appear to have been invented by Chateaubriand.[11] If such is indeed the case Chateaubriand's dependence on the mechanism he is using seems all the clearer.

On still other occasions Chateaubriand expands his paragraph on death with so unusual and vivid an image that the person dead, like Napoleon's son in the example quoted above, seems to undergo an instantaneous metamorphosis. A paragraph referring to Pope Pius VII ends with this sentence: "Ma fidélité à la mémoire de mes anciens amis doit donner

---

[10] Chateaubriand, *Analyse raisonnée de l'Histoire de France*, in *Oeuvres*, ed. Ladvocat, V³, 186-87.
[11] According to Marcel Bataillon, referred to by Levaillant, MOT II, 1109, n. 8.

confiance aux amis qui me restent: rien ne descend pour moi dans la tombe; tout ce que j'ai connu vit autour de moi: selon la doctrine indienne, la mort, en nous touchant, ne nous détruit pas; elle nous rend seulement invisibles" (MOT II, 352-53). When he applies to himself a final transforming epigram an uncertain irony may emerge, as here after a reference to the deaths of Byron and Madame de Staël: "Ma trop longue vie ressemble à ces voies romaines bordées de monuments funèbres" (MOT II, 511).

But, as so often, the most remarkable instance of metamorphosis, if only that of an historical into a legendary woman, occurs in the *Vie de Rancé*:

> Marcelle [de Castellane] dansait avec grâce et chantait à ravir; mais élevée avec les flots [à Marseille], elle était indépendante. Elle s'aperçut que le duc de Guise commençait à se lasser d'elle; au lieu de se plaindre, elle se retira. L'effort était grand; elle tomba malade, et comme elle était pauvre, elle fut obligée de vendre ses bijoux. Elle renvoya avec dédain l'argent que lui faisait offrir le prince de Lorraine: "Je n'ai que quelques jours à vivre, dit-elle; le peu que j'ai me suffit. Je ne reçois rien de personne, encore moins de M. de Guise que d'un autre." Les jeunes filles de la Bretagne se laissent noyer sur les grèves après s'être attachées aux algues d'un rocher.[12]

This episode is most tenuously connected to the life of Rancé; the paragraph itself is tied together with very wispy thread. The paragraph is intended to illustrate "désintéressement" and "noblesse de sentiments," and it is plain that much of its interest for Chateaubriand lies in its theme of renunciation, a major theme of his *Rancé*—but all that has little to do with the structure of the paragraph, organized rather around the combined themes of the beautiful girl and the sea. The surprising effect at the end erupts with the word "noyer," the first direct announcement of death; that abrupt mention together with the abrupt change in grammatical subject give sudden importance to the idea of death, while simultaneously the strange and mysterious graciousness of the final image removes any excessive harshness in so sudden an intrusion.

A particularly complex case, in which the themes of death and historical change are brought together in the personified image of the Revolution, occurs in a paragraph terminating the chapter concerning the death of the author's parents. In this chapter Chateaubriand has contrasted the language and tone of the death certificate of his father, dated 1786, with that of his mother, "an VI de la République." In the first certificate there are all kinds of signs that the society of the ancien régime still exists: titles and names of notables, friends of the family. The second, which had been

---

[12] Chateaubriand, *Vie de Rancé*, ed. Letessier, I, 78. See the acute remarks on the final sentence by Raymond Lebègue in "Le Thème de la 'Bretonne noyée' chez Lamennais et Chateaubriand," *Mercure de France*, CCCXXII, 1093 (1 Sept. 1954), 180-81; and "Le succès d'une image mennaisienne: la Bretonne noyée," BSC, IV (1960), 32.

previously quoted, is resumed in the final paragraph, which moves vigorously from a sad objectivity, through mocking irony, to a sudden and powerful historical opening. It is one of the finest examples of the abruptly expanding paragraph in the *Mémoires*.

> Dans l'extrait mortuaire de ma mère, la terre roule sur d'autres pôles: nouveau monde, nouvelle ère; le comput des années et les noms mêmes des mois sont changés. Madame de Chateaubriand n'est plus qu'une pauvre femme qui obite au domicile de la *citoyenne* Gouyon; un jardinier, et un journalier qui ne sait pas signer, attestent seuls la mort de ma mère: de parents et d'amis, point; nulle pompe funèbre; pour tout assistant, la Révolution. (MOT I, 120)

The abrupt expansion is contained in but one word, "la Révolution," whose personification by apposition to "assistant" acquires enormous force.

The reader will have noted that in these paragraphs referring to death Chateaubriand is properly solemn, but not gloomy, perhaps self-pitying and at times nearly lachrymose, but never despairing. He tends to treat death with the sober detachment of the historian or with measured and reverential respect for its mystery; he is agreeably unsentimental and direct. Three rather different cases remain to be examined: two border on the grotesque and remind one that Chateaubriand is a "pre-Romantic" and the compiler of those astonishingly macabre notes in the *Génie du christianisme* on the opening of the royal tombs at Saint-Denis. The third contains a poignant note of discouragement.

A brief paragraph in the rapid and impressionistic "Journal de Paris à Venise" (MOT, Book XL, II, 765) refers to Madame de Custine, who had died in the place where now, some years later, Chateaubriand is changing horses.

> A Bex, tandis qu'on attelait à ma voiture les chevaux qui avaient peut-être traîné le cercueil de madame de Custine, j'étais appuyé contre le mur de la maison où était morte mon hôtesse de Fervaques. Elle avait été célèbre au tribunal révolutionnaire par sa longue chevelure. J'ai vu à Rome de beaux cheveux blonds retirés d'une tombe.

Now the paragraph is not composed with very clear logic. Rome has nothing to do with Chateaubriand's presence at Bex. The relationship established between death and long hair is fortuitous; the general effect is grotesque, when so weak a link is all there is to span the abrupt break. The thought resulting is curiously nuanced: beauty survives the tomb, but only cut off from that which gives beauty its final meaning.

The other grotesque note is in a more humorous vein. During the Hundred Days, emigrated with the King in Ghent, Chateaubriand had met a child who has since become a Duchess; he reflects now at the time of writing on later meetings with girls one has held on one's knees:

> Quand vous avez quitté une femme, mariée devant vous à seize ans, si vous revenez seize ans après, vous la retrouvez au même âge: "Ah! madame, vous n'avez pas pris un jour!" Sans doute: mais c'est à la fille que vous contez cela, à la fille que vous conduirez encore à l'autel. Mais vous, triste témoin des deux hymens, vous encoffrez les seize années que vous avez reçues à chaque union: présent de noces qui hâtera votre propre mariage avec une dame blanche, un peu maigre. (MOT I, 931-32)

The contrast here is the standard one of allegorical painting: the juxtaposition of the skeleton and the fleshed-out body. It might seem wrong to include this juxtaposition among those considered expansive: in the allegorical tradition the figure of death is the limiting presence that suddenly stops revelry, ambition, desire. Yet in the context of Chateaubriand death is almost always an opening towards the eternal.

Only once in these paragraphs do we come upon a note of discouragement, a sudden note of futility in the face of death, like that struck in the pages concerning the death of Armand Carrel. It is a sad generalization that follows after memories of Madame de Beaumont, in a paragraph relating Chateaubriand's summer at Savigny: "Par quel miracle l'homme consent-il à faire ce qu'il fait sur cette terre, lui qui doit mourir?" (MOT I, 455)

The other themes touched on in the expanding paragraphs appear with much less frequency than the themes of passage, historical contrasts, and death. Not surprisingly a catalogue of them would show them to be as much the great themes of French Romantic poetry as of Chateaubriand's work in general: the sea, night, time, age, dreams, memory, beauty, religion, the Poet. A few examples suffice.

The first is of particular interest, since it is not "Chateaubriand" at all but rather a quotation from Bourrienne's *Mémoires*.[13] It concerns the disastrous retreat of Napoleon's army from Syria in 1799. Chateaubriand has quoted extensively in the body of the chapter; now he uses this long quotation to terminate it. Bourrienne speaks of the terrible heat and thirst that demoralized the soldiers, causing them to abandon their sick and wounded. As they proceeded they burned villages and fields. Here are his last five sentences, revealing a vigor in descriptive résumé, a variety in method, an attention to contrast, and suddenly a sweeping and expanding overview after the details are finished that are all worthy of Chateaubriand and could, if he had written the passage, be called characteristic of

---

[13] Bourrienne, *Mémoires*, II, 251. Chateaubriand quotes, for once, almost without variation from the original. One major change for us, however: after "attendaient:" at the end of his paragraph Bourrienne added a clumsy "telle était notre position véritable"; Chateaubriand stops.

his historical pages at their best. That he has chosen to quote them so extensively indicates their appeal to his imagination.

> Nous n'étions entourés que de mourants, de pillards et d'incendiaires. Des mourants jetés sur les bords du chemin disaient d'une voix faible: *Je ne suis pas pestiféré, je ne suis que blessé*; et, pour convaincre les passants, on en voyait rouvrir leur blessure ou s'en faire une nouvelle. Personne n'y croyait; on disait: *Son affaire est faite*; on passait, on se tâtait, et tout était oublié. Le soleil, dans tout son éclat sous ce beau ciel, était obscurci par la fumée de nos continuels incendies. Nous avions la mer à notre droite; à notre gauche et derrière nous le désert que nous faisions; devant nous les privations et les souffrances qui nous attendaient. (MOT I, 731-32)

The "chois" and "disposition" (to use Montaigne's terms) are certainly Chateaubriand's in this study of devastation, even if the words are not. With "devant nous"—introducing in its sentence so parallel a construction, that is so well integrated into the rhythm of the whole paragraph as well—we suddenly leave history for prophecy, description for the idea of retribution, crime for punishment: in passing "devant" suddenly changes from an indication of place to one of time and retroactively becomes a kind of "break." The shift in the author's mood is all the more telling for the subtlety of its expression. According to Marcellus this quotation was originally followed by another, from Ariosto, but Chateaubriand crossed out the latter "pour ne pas affaiblir l'effet par trop de citations, et bien il fit."[14]

Two further passages, one concerning age, the other memory, are of particular interest because they come from texts of the author's "literary period."[15] One from *Atala*, the other from the *Itinéraire*, they are among the very rare examples of the expanding paragraph that precede the 1830's and the *Mémoires d'Outre-Tombe*.

> Déjà subjugués par notre propre cœur, nous fûmes accablés par ces images d'amour et de maternité, qui semblaient nous poursuivre dans ces solitudes enchantées. J'emportai Atala dans mes bras au fond de la forêt, et je lui dis des choses qu'aujourd'hui je chercherais en vain sur mes lèvres. Le vent du midi, mon cher fils, perd sa chaleur en passant sur des montagnes de glace. Les souvenirs de l'amour dans le cœur d'un vieillard sont les feux du jour réfléchis par l'orbe paisible de la lune, lorsque le soleil est couché et que le silence plane sur les huttes des Sauvages. (ORV I, 47-48)

---

[14] Marcellus, *Chateaubriand et son temps*, pp. 199-200. In connection with this Chateaubriand-like abruptly expanding paragraph found in another author's work, it is amusing to note, at least once, in Marcellus' own text a strikingly similar passage: the paragraph (p. 483) about his meeting with Abou-Gosch that ends—even with the colon!—"il ne reconnut même pas son nom quand je le lui prononçai: Dans le désert il n'y a pas d'écho" (passage quoted also by Malakis in the notes to his edition of the *Itinéraire*, II, 205 n.).
[15] "Ma carrière littéraire proprement dite": 1800-14, from the *Génie* through the *Itinéraire* (MOT I, 664).

One reason that the kind of paragraph we are examining is so rare in a work like *Atala* is that it temporarily stops the action: in *Atala*, as is proper for a novel, Chateaubriand typically makes each paragraph flow without pause into the succeeding one. Here the movement forward stops for a moment, so that Chactas, lyrically, can remind his listeners that he is recalling days long ago. Only because the reader has been caught up in the action as present is there a "break" after "lèvres." The sudden change from direct narration to reflection and image underlines the break, even though Chactas has already accustomed us to his vividly imaged "American" idiom, and here he extends its use only slightly beyond usual bounds.

As the *Itinéraire* is a much more retrospective and contemplative book than the little novel, one is surprised not to find more expanding paragraphs in it. But again there are almost none; Chateaubriand has not yet really developed this technique. Among the very few is a paragraph describing how Chateaubriand's departure from Megara is delayed by a meal his host insisted on serving him. The pièce de résistance is a kind of chicken that Chateaubriand believes comes from America.

> Je lui fis dire que j'avais voyagé dans la patrie de ces oiseaux, pays bien éloigné, situé au-delà de la mer, et qu'il y avait dans ce pays des Grecs, établis au milieu des bois, parmi des sauvages. En effet, quelques Grecs, fatigués du joug, ont passé dans la Floride, où les fruits de la liberté leur ont fait perdre le souvenir de la terre natale. "Ceux qui avaient goûté de ce doux fruit n'y pouvaient plus renoncer; mais ils voulaient demeurer parmi les Lotophages, et ils oubliaient leur patrie." (ORV II, 849)

The generalizing of the descriptive details of Chateaubriand's voyage by the use of quotations from ancient poets or authorities is of course a commonplace of the *Itinéraire*.[16] But here, where the link on which the final image is constructed—"fruits de la liberté"—is so far removed from the principal subject of the paragraph—the chicken—and the story of the Lotos-Eaters is so much more a part of universal legend than the detail of some modern Greek émigrés, we end up having an expansion from the particular and present into the realm of universal poetry, a transformation that leads us way beyond the more common historical or geographical matter of the *Itinéraire* in a manner much more characteristic of Chateaubriand's later works.

And so it is that the greatest examples of this structure do come from the *Mémoires d'Outre-Tombe* and the *Vie de Rancé*, as in this final example

---

[16] The author on quotations: "Le *Génie du Christianisme* est un tissu de citations avouées au grand jour. Dans les *Martyrs*, c'est un fleuve de citations déguisées et fondues. Dans l'*Itinéraire*, elles devaient régner par la nature même du sujet. Je les admets volontiers partout." Quoted by Marcellus, *Chateaubriand et son temps*, p. 289.

from Book I of the *Mémoires*, in a chapter dated 1812 but written certainly some twenty years later.[17] It is part of the description of springtime in Brittany.

> Entre la mer et la terre s'étendent des campagnes pélagiennes, frontières indécises des deux éléments: l'alouette de champ y vole avec l'alouette marine; la charrue et la barque à un jet de pierre l'une de l'autre, sillonnent la terre et l'eau.[18] Le navigateur et le berger s'empruntent mutuellement leur langue: le matelot dit *les vagues moutonnent*, le pâtre dit *des flottes de moutons*. Des sables de diverses couleurs, des bancs variés de coquillages, des varechs, des franges d'une écume argentée, dessinent la lisière blonde ou verte des blés. Je ne sais plus dans quelle île de la Méditerranée, j'ai vu un bas-relief représentant les Néréides attachant des festons au bas de la robe de Cérès. (MOT I, 41-42)

This is the fourth paragraph of six describing "Le printemps en Bretagne." All, except the fifth, which is a one-sentence transition, end with a particular flourish, three expanding suddenly after a break. The third ends with a quotation from Pliny and the last—quoted in Chapter 1 above—with the image comparing the setting of the moon with the extinguishing of torches after a banquet. Here we have a fine example of sudden expansion because the idea opens in so many ways simultaneously: contemporary landscape is compared with ancient times and an even more distant, mythological past; Breton Chateaubriand is presented as the Mediterranean traveler; agriculture is transformed into art. The break is underlined by the switch from third to first person, from present to past. And yet the whole is admirably held together by corresponding details ("pélagiennes"—"île"; "franges"—"festons"; "blés"—"Cérès") and the surrounding presence of the sea.

"Le printemps en Bretagne" is one of those lovingly and slowly elaborated passages, like the famous "Nuit chez les sauvages de l'Amérique," whose evolution can be observed in published texts. In the earliest fully elaborated text of this part of the *Mémoires*, the "Mémoires de ma vie" copied by Madame Récamier in 1826, the "printemps en Bretagne" is five sentences, not six paragraphs, in length. I quote the paragraph from which our text springs in its entirety:

> Le départ pour Combourg qui fut une grande peine pour ma mère fut une grande joie pour sa petite famille. Les enfants aiment la campagne. Je devais accompagner mes sœurs au château et être ensuite ramené au collège. Nous

---

[17] Levaillant, *Deux livres des Mémoires d'Outre-Tombe*, I, 46.

[18] The first part of this paragraph is notably close in spirit and method to Rimbaud's poem in free verse, "Marine." The comparison of sailor and plowman, wake and furrow, appears elsewhere in the *Mémoires d'Outre-Tombe*: "Le vieux matelot ressemble au vieux laboureur" (MOT I, 200); "le navire, avec sa quille, comme avec le soc d'une charrue, laboure à grand bruit le champ des mers" (MOT I, 201).

partîmes dans la première quinzaine du mois de mai. Le printemps en Bretagne est beaucoup plus beau qu'aux environs de Paris: il commence trois semaines plus tôt. La terre se couvre d'une multitude de primevères, de hyacinthes des champs et de fleurs sauvages. Le pays entrecoupé de haies plantées d'arbres offre l'aspect d'une continuelle forêt et rappelle singulièrement l'Angleterre. Des vallons profonds où coulent de petites rivières non navigables présentent des perspectives riantes et solitaires. Les bruyères, les roches, les sables qui séparent ces vallons entre eux en font mieux sentir la fraîcheur et l'agrément.[19]

When one compares this paragraph—charmingly picturesque, but in no way remarkable in composition—with the related passage in the *Mémoires d'Outre-Tombe* one discovers the sentence, "Le printemps en Bretagne . . .," almost word for word, with small stylistic improvements, at the head of the first paragraph. The rest of that paragraph is a considerably detailed expansion of the following sentence: the description of the birds and flowers, all named, occupies six sentences, and already the perspective of universal history is called into play. The sentence of 1826 becomes (I italicize the original elements): "*La terre se couvre* de marguerites, de pensées, de jonquilles, de narcisses, *d'hyacinthes*, de renoncules, d'anémones, comme les espaces abandonnés qui environnent Saint-Jean-de-Latran et Sainte-Croix-de-Jérusalem, à Rome"; at the end of the paragraph we learn that, "dans certains abris, le myrte et le laurier-rose croissent en pleine terre, comme en Grèce; la figue mûrit comme en Provence." The paragraph ends with the pretty, pre-Proustian comparison of the flowering apple tree to "un gros bouquet de fiancée de village."

The second paragraph of the final version has no correspondent in the 1826 text: it introduces another historical, and this time legendary, perspective, the presence in the region of "la forêt de Brécheliant," and is itself expanded at the end with a quotation from a fifteenth-century historical document.

The third paragraph, which in the final version presents an introductory reference to the "sylphide," is an expansion of the final three sentences of 1826: "Le pays entrecoupé de haies. . . ." It presents the first real expansion after break in the text: after the details of valleys, trees, ancient ruins (again adding historical depth), comes a colon and the phrase, "la mer borde le tout"; then a completely unexpected last sentence: "Pline dit de la Bretagne: *Péninsule spectatrice de l'Océan.*" Besides the expansion by reference to antiquity and by quotation, the play on "spectatrice,"[20] which in French abruptly personifies the whole preceding

---

[19] Chateaubriand, *Mémoires de ma vie*, p. 47. This portion of the "Manuscrit de 1826" is reproduced in the MOT, ed. du Centenaire, I, 549.

[20] "Contresens magnifique," writes Levaillant (MOT, ed. du Centenaire, I, 60, n. 14), who points out that Chateaubriand has misread Pliny's expression, "une péninsule *assez remarquable* (poeninsulam spectatiorem)."

description, serves as an admirable transition to the fourth paragraph, the one we are particularly concerned with, the one that paints, like Proust's Elstir, the blending of land and sea and then projects them suddenly into Greek myth.

This fourth paragraph has no correspondent in 1826, nor do the two following ones: the 1826 text moves directly to the sentence that becomes sentence two of the following chapter in the final version. But we may trace its development also, as we have traced its context, in previous incarnations. They are of two sorts. The first, chronologically, is the more distantly related: it concerns the impressions of Eudore in Armorique in the first versions of *Les Martyrs*; the parallel of these passages with the paragraph under our consideration was made in 1967 by Raymond Lebègue.[21] The text of 1805-6, referred to as "Termes":

> Je repris le chemin du château, accablé d'inquiétude. J'avois gravi une haute colline du sommet de laquelle on découvroit, d'un côté, le détroit britannique, et de l'autre les vallées que je venois de traverser. Rien n'étoit triste et grand comme cette double vue des bois et des mers de l'Armorique. La côte couverte de futaies et de rochers, se prolongeoit dans un lointain immense. L'Océan rouloit ses vagues sous l'ombrage des ormeaux et des chênes, dont les cimes répétoient dans l'air le bruit et le mouvement des flots. La mauve blanche, la noire barnacle que Dieu fit pour mesurer la solitude de l'abyme, embarrassoient leurs ailes dans les branches des bois, et des coquillages s'attachoient aux troncs des pins comme aux colonnes de ces temples de Neptune, que l'idolâtrie élève au bord de la mer.

The tone, as is fitting in this section of the *Martyrs*, is brooding and dark; the reference to pagan antiquity, as is fitting, is disapproving. The opening towards historical and legendary perspective is present, as it will be in the *Mémoires*, but it stands out much less: there is a simile, and not a break; reference to Greek religion is of course part of the givens of the *Martyrs*; and the comparison of terrestrial and marine activity remains unaccented, unrelated to the daily activity of man.

This passage has not been maintained in the published text of the *Martyrs*. But the comparison of landscape and seascape is introduced into the *Mémoires* some time after 1826, and by 1834 we can read a version of the paragraph that concerns us which is quite close to the final form.

> Entre la mer et la terre s'étendent des campagnes pélagiennes; frontière indécise des deux élémens: l'alouette des champs y vole avec l'alouette marine; la charrue et la barque à un jet de pierre l'une de l'autre, sillonnent la terre et les eaux. [   ] Des sables de diverses couleurs, des bancs variés de coquillages, *des fucus*, des vareqs, *des goémons*, des franges d'une écume argen-

---

[21] In the BSC, X (1967), 27, 44, 51. The text is also to be found in the notes to the *Martyrs*, ORV II, 1637.

tée, dessinent la lisière blonde ou verte des blés: [   ] j'ai vu *dans l'île de Céos* un bas-relief *antique qui* représent*ait* les Néréides attachant des festons au bas de la robe de Cérès.[22]

The "printemps en Bretagne" of 1834 is very close to the final version, and so provides an important indication of the date at which Chateaubriand began using the expanded paragraph with break. Like the definitive version the passage has six paragraphs, although only five of them are parallel to the last version: in 1834 the paragraph about the "forêt de Brécheliant" with its fifteenth-century quotation is not yet present. On the other hand immediately after "la robe de Cérès" there is a new paragraph that will be dropped in its turn, a paragraph that continues the comparison of land and sea and leads to a final, epigrammatic contrast:

> Dans les paysages intérieurs du continent, le plan terrestre et le plan céleste se regardent immobiles; dans les vues maritimes, le roulant azur des flots est renfermé sous l'azur fixe du firmament. De là un contraste frappant: l'hiver, du haut des falaises, le tableau est de deux couleurs tranchées; la neige, qui blanchit la terre, noircit la mer.

It is as if, under the impulse to develop all the juxtapositions of the Breton scene, Chateaubriand had forgotten he was describing spring in Brittany. This lapse of coherence and, more importantly, interruption into the gay spring scene of such relatively gloomy impressions are eventually suppressed.

Suppression is indeed characteristic of the changes from the version of 1834 to the final one. Although the definitive passage is about thirty words longer than its 1834 predecessor, two-thirds of the added length comes from the inserted paragraph, which itself is about twice as long as the one dropped (121 versus 58 words); forgetting for the moment the paragraph added and the one subtracted, in the five parallel paragraphs Chateaubriand removes 111 words, or half again as many as the 77 words he adds. And the additions are largely transitional in nature (an early reference to the Sylphide theme, a more appropriate topic sentence in the paragraph following the added one), except for one group of additions which I shall come to in a moment. The suppressions, on the other hand, are of substance; they serve to lighten the description, making its abrupt contrasts all the more obvious. Adjectives, detailed adverbial phrases of place, and particularly nouns—names of flowers, common nouns of people and places—disappear or are reduced to take the smallest possible space, as can be seen in the paragraph under consideration.

[22] *Lectures des Mémoires de M. de Chateaubriand*, p. 272 (reproduced in MOT, ed. du Centenaire, I, 551). I italicize the differences from the final version and mark by [   ] the places where new elements will be inserted.

But there is an important group of additions, and these are the ones that confer temporal space, the dimension of Time, on the picture. As is the case in the added paragraph with its medieval perspective and details, so for so small a detail as the "comme en Grèce" added to the expression "le myrte et le laurier-rose croissent en pleine terre, comme en Grèce; la figue mûrit comme en Provence"; the additions set the tone for the antiquity theme, which is to be more spectacularly exploited by the whole new sentence appended to the paragraph that immediately precedes the one under consideration: "Pline dit de la Bretagne: *Péninsule spectatrice de l'Océan.*"

In our paragraph the expansion and the break are both fully in force in 1834; indeed the break is made if anything less abrupt by the changes introduced after 1834. Still it is there, and this sudden expansion, from mere picturesque reality into a seascape of the mind, must rank as one of the best among Chateaubriand's attempts in the paragraph to impress on his reader a sublime feeling of literally indescribable distance. As Chateaubriand's imagination leaps, like lightning, from a positive pole of his experience ("Entre la *mer* et la *terre s'étendent* . . .": real places, a verb of being) to a negative pole ("*Je ne sais plus* dans quelle île . . . j'ai vu un bas-relief *représentant* les *Néréides* . . . *Cérès*") he illuminates for his reader one zone of the great dark hole of Time and Space; by successfully bridging particular and universal experience, he proves himself a poet.

> And of these one and all I weave the song of myself.
> I am an acme of things accomplished, and I an encloser of things to be.
> > Do I contradict myself?
> > Very well then I contradict myself
> > (I am large, I contain multitudes).
>
> Walt Whitman "Song of Myself" 15, 44, 51

4   The Life of Napoleon, or the Song of Myself

Sometime probably in the late 1830's,[1] not long after the time when Stendhal was penning his "Souvenirs d'Egotisme" and less than twenty years before Walt Whitman's famous explosion of egotism in the "Song of Myself," Chateaubriand started putting together from various collected notes and memoirs a history of Napoleon. He inserted it, curiously enough, into his own *Mémoires*. This Life of Napoleon in Chateaubriand's autobiography is a veritable Song of Myself, and by its simple presence there it is the greatest single example of surprising juxtaposition in Chateaubriand's work. The portion of the *Mémoires d'Outre-Tombe* that is devoted to Napoleon abounds moreover with its own kinds of juxtaposition: the elliptical expanding paragraphs that I have been considering and even abruptly expanding whole chapters.

Insistently in the *Mémoires d'Outre-Tombe*, and in a manner at times almost as incongruous as the famous comparisons of the *Essai sur les révolutions*, Chateaubriand abruptly brings himself and Napoleon together, glamorizing and adding perspective to each of their destinies, oddly, by the other. An example that seems to me particularly curious, because it is so offhand and totally unexpected (there is no other reference to Napoleon anywhere around), is a sentence in the middle of a paragraph explaining young Chateaubriand's plans for a voyage to the United States: "Personne ne s'occupait de moi; j'étais alors, ainsi que

---

[1] Likely after the recovery of the "coffre genevois" in 1836; see Gagnebin, "'J'ai fait la connaissance de M. Rigaud,'"RHLF, LXVIII, 6 (Nov.-Dec. 1968), 1046; see also Levaillant's introduction, MOT, I, xv.

Bonaparte, un mince sous-lieutenant tout à fait inconnu; nous partions, l'un et l'autre, de l'obscurité à la même époque, moi pour chercher ma renommée dans la solitude, lui sa gloire parmi les hommes" (MOT I, 188). It was surely the idea of this "même époque," at least as much as the political advantage of having "Buonaparte" born before Corsica became France, that convinced Chateaubriand that, like himself, Napoleon was born in 1768, not, as has since come to be accepted, 1769: "Vingt jours avant moi, le 15 août 1768, naissait dans une autre île, à l'autre extrémité de la France, l'homme qui a mis fin à l'ancienne société, Bonaparte" (MOT I, 17 n.)—a footnote fully as uncalled for, as much a "coq-à-l'âne," as any of those in the *Essai*.

Chateaubriand is everywhere at pains to keep before his reader the parallel unfolding of the two lives. Thus his literary career is begun, as later his *Mémoires* are written, under the sign of Napoleon: "il ne mit d'abord aucun obstacle à la publication d'un ouvrage utile à la popularité de ses desseins . . . heureux d'être défendu au dehors par l'opinion que le *Génie du Christianisme* appelait" (MOT I, 462); "Le livre précédent fut écrit sous la tyrannie expirante de Bonaparte et à la lueur des derniers éclairs de sa gloire" (MOT II, 75: second paragraph of Book III). Chateaubriand's first entry into a diplomatic career came about because "à la tête de l'Etat se trouvait une haute intelligence, qui ne voulait pas abandonner à des intrigues de bureaux une autre intelligence qu'elle sentait trop disposée à se séparer du pouvoir" (MOT I, 528). "Si Bonaparte n'eût pas tué le duc d'Enghien, s'il m'eût de plus en plus rapproché de lui (et son penchant l'y portait)," writes Chateaubriand, his life and his lot would have been quite other than they were: "mon sort a été . . . lié à cette catastrophe" (MOT I, 563).

Even when the connection is only the coincidence of chronology Chateaubriand marks it: "Je quittai l'Angleterre quelques mois après que Napoléon eut quitté l'Egypte;[2] nous revînmes en France presque en même temps, lui de Memphis, moi de Londres: il avait saisi des villes et des royaumes; ses mains étaient pleines de puissantes réalités; je n'avais encore pris que des chimères" (MOT I, 741: first paragraph of Book XX). But he takes pains to emphasize Napoleon's awareness of him. When Chateaubriand has fallen out of imperial favor Napoleon insists on seeing the portrait of him that a sycophant had put aside at the Salon of 1810 (MOT I, 633); indeed, the very Napoleon who wanted in 1807 to "le [faire]

---

[2] In *Chateaubriand et son temps*, pp. 200-1, Marcellus opposes to this passage a remark ironically pertinent: "Ce chapitre commence comme l'autre vient de finir, par le rapprochement favori, qui se glisse partout et comme il peut. Or ces deux noms, Bonaparte et Chateaubriand, je les ai lus gravés l'un à côté de l'autre sur la pierre qui couronne le sommet de la plus haute pyramide du désert, où aucun des deux passagers sur la terre égyptienne n'est monté."

sabrer sur les marches des Tuileries" (MOT I, 630), among his last remarks at Sainte-Hélène, states—and Chateaubriand dutifully transcribes his remark—that "Chateaubriand a reçu de la nature le feu sacré," that "tout ce qui est grand et national doit convenir à son génie" (MOT I, 1027).[3] Chateaubriand's life has been marked, he writes, by an encounter with each of the two military giants of his day: "J'ai rencontré une seule fois sur le rivage des deux mondes l'homme du dernier siècle et l'homme du nouveau, Washington et Napoléon. Je m'entretins un moment avec l'un et l'autre; tous deux me renvoyèrent à la solitude, le premier par un souhait bienveillant, le second par un crime" (MOT I, 491). His encounter with Napoleon is transcribed from the second page of the *Mémoires*—"cet homme, dont j'admire le génie et dont j'abhorre le despotisme, cet homme m'enveloppe de sa tyrannie comme d'une autre solitude" (MOT I, 6)—to the very last book, penultimate chapter, XLIV, 8, "Récapitulation de ma vie"—"Bonaparte m'arrête et se jette, avec le corps sanglant du duc d'Enghien, devant mes pas; je m'arrête à mon tour, et je conduis le grand homme de son berceau, en Corse, à sa tombe, à Sainte-Hélène" (MOT II, 934). Chateaubriand sees their destinies linked at the least by a perpetual parataxis.

Most of these remarks (all but three) precede Books XIX through XXIV of the *Mémoires*, the six-volume life and history of Napoleon. As is frequently the case in the *Mémoires d'Outre-Tombe* a great development has been announced and prepared by little but insistent repetitions of a motif. Now, as we get into the Life proper, we find a number of expanding paragraphs, placed with uncommon frequency at the end of a chapter, that suddenly throw Napoleon into relief against the background of history. Here is a characteristic example:

> Bonaparte négociait; il faisait des promesses: il laissait espérer au roi de Prusse la possession des provinces russes allemandes; le roi de Saxe et l'Autriche se flattaient d'obtenir des agrandissements dans ce qui restait encore de la Pologne; des princes de la Confédération du Rhin rêvaient des changements de territoire à leur convenance; il n'y avait pas jusqu'à la France que Napoléon ne méditât d'élargir, quoiqu'elle débordât déjà sur l'Europe; il prétendait l'augmenter nominativement de l'Espagne. Le général Sébastiani lui dit: "Et votre frère?" Napoléon répliqua: "Qu'importe mon frère! est-ce qu'on donne un royaume comme l'Espagne?" Le maître disposait par un mot du royaume qui avait coûté tant de malheurs et de sacrifices à Louis XIV; mais il ne l'a pas gardé si longtemps. Quant aux peuples, jamais homme n'en a moins tenu compte et ne les a plus méprisés que Bonaparte; il en jetait des

---

[3] Shortly before in the same chapter one reads, "La paix que Napoléon n'avait pas conclue avec les rois ses geôliers, il l'avait faite avec moi: j'étais fils de la mer comme lui, ma nativité était du rocher comme la sienne. Je me flatte d'avoir mieux connu Napoléon que ceux qui l'ont vu plus souvent et approché de plus près" (MOT I, 1026).

lambeaux à la meute de rois qu'il conduisait à la chasse, le fouet à la main: "Attila," dit Jornandès, "menait avec lui une foule de princes tributaires qui attendaient avec crainte et tremblement un signe du maître des monarques pour exécuter ce qui leur serait ordonné." (MOT I, 777)[4]

It is splendid historical writing, however ferociously partisan it may be; summing up in a rapid sweep of parallel but varied clauses months of complex projects, grouping a wide range of short and long phrases, quotations, epigrams, metaphors, it impels them with scathing irony and majestic scorn towards the final, insolent comparison. The break is marked this time not by a change in tense—though somehow the maintenance of the imperfect makes the contrast all the stronger—but by the direct quotation of Gothic historian Jornandès and the abrupt change in subject, announced right off by the shocking name, Attila.[5]

Many of the historical comparisons we shall see are hardly more flattering, especially those from mythological sources. How could the Allies have expected Napoleon to stay there on Elba, in plain sight of friends and accomplices and past triumphs? "Son ambition était déçue, non éteinte; l'infortune et la vengeance en ranimaient les flammes: quand le prince des ténèbres du bord de l'univers créé aperçut l'homme et le monde, il résolut de les perdre" (MOT I, 911). Indeed these comparisons seem to come from the realm of universal disaster: thus another one from Milton that precedes the Life of Napoleon, this time referring to the "changement dans la vie de Bonaparte" after the shooting of the Duc d'Enghien:

Ses grandes qualités restèrent les mêmes, mais ses bonnes inclinations s'altérèrent et ne soutinrent plus ses grandes qualités; par la corruption de cette tache originelle sa nature se détériora. Dieu commanda à ses anges de

---

[4] Cf. another concluding reference to Attila: "Napoléon foudroya les sections et dit: 'J'ai mis mon cachet sur la France.' Attila avait dit: 'Je suis le marteau de l'univers, *ego malleus orbis*'" (MOT I, 700).

[5] Such treatment is not reserved exclusively to Napoleon in Chateaubriand's historical writings: one may compare this passage to a structurally very similar one in the *Congrès de Vérone* (in Chateaubriand, *Oeuvres complètes*, ed. Furne, 1862, X, 18) written at the same period, in which the place of Napoleon is taken by the Spanish Captain Riego, the negative comparison to Louis XIV by a negative comparison to Don Quixote, and the abruptly expanding reference to history in the person of Attila by a reference to Columbus. The paragraph does not present quite as much rhetorical variety as the passage in the *Mémoires*, but it is just as vivid, detailed, full of movement, sweeping:

"Le trouble s'était répandu dans Madrid. Le général Freyre accourut, menant 13,000 hommes pour combattre les 10,000 insurgés: on pourparla. Riego, avec San-Miguel, sortit de l'île de Léon, accompagné d'une colonne de 15,000 hommes; il parcourut l'Andalousie, entra dans Algésiras, Malaga, Ronda, Cordoue; fut partout bien reçu, partout aussi vite oublié. Abandonné de ses troupes, il se cacha dans les montagnes célèbres par la pénitence du chevalier que la moquerie d'un beau génie fait vivre; héros plus grand et plus fou que Riego. Capitaine malheureux, Riego ne trouva point la société nouvelle qu'il cherchait au travers des tempêtes: Christophe Colomb, après avoir découvert un monde, dort en paix à Séville, dans la chapelle des rois."

déranger les harmonies de cet univers, d'en changer les lois, de l'incliner sur ses pôles: "Les anges," dit Milton, "poussèrent avec effort obliquement le centre du monde . . . le soleil reçut l'ordre de détourner ses rênes du chemin de l'équateur. . . . Les vents déchirèrent les bois et bouleversèrent les mers."

> They with labor push'd
> Oblique the centric globe........................the sun
> Was bid turn reins from th'equinoctial road
> ....(winds)
> ....rend the woods, and seas upturn.
> (MOT I, 571: end chap. XVI, 10)

At least the Fall of Man is grandiose high tragedy in Milton's poem; Napoleon does hold on to all the prestige of Milton's poetry here in Chateaubriand's *Mémoires*, in this thrice-repeated version of the catastrophic "changement" following the break at "détériora."

The poetry of tragedy and high crime is found also in Greek mythological references for the Emperor. On the occasion of the disastrous war in Russia, Napoleon accepts criticism because of his guilty conscience that is the result of the Duc d'Enghien affair: "Quand on a commis une chose reprochable, le ciel en punition vous en impose les témoins: en vain les anciens tyrans les faisaient disparaître; descendus aux enfers, ces témoins entraient dans le corps des Furies et revenaient" (MOT I, 817-18). Who will defend France if Napoleon goes off to battle in Russia? ask his advisors. "'Ma renommée,' répliqua l'empereur. Médée avait fourni cette réponse: Napoléon faisait descendre à lui la tragédie" (MOT I, 780). In cases such as these the sudden comparison to legendary heroes and criminals gives stature—an aura of power and greatness—to Napoleon, as it defines the author's subtle mixed attitude towards him. Attila, the avenging angels, Medea—history, religion, tragedy—form more than a backdrop for the figure of the Emperor when they are placed as here at the climax of the paragraph: they appear rather as the assumption of Napoleon into the company of the great and the horrendous. The break does not cut Napoleon off from the others, as was the case with the death theme noted in the last chapter, where the break marked dramatically the moment of passage; here the break reinforces the apposition in the manner of a slightly delayed musical attack, and the word immediately following the break presents an unexpected and immediate jolt: "Attila," "Dieu," "Médée."

Behind Chateaubriand's specific references to tragedy is massed an air of poetic foreboding, established already in the very early pages of Book XIX:

Ainsi donc il y a une avant-scène à la vie de l'empereur; un Bonaparte inconnu précède l'immense Napoléon; la pensée de Bonaparte était dans le monde avant qu'il y fût de sa personne: elle agitait secrètement la terre; on sentait en 1789, au moment où Bonaparte apparaissait, quelque chose de formidable, une inquiétude dont on ne pouvait se rendre compte. Quand le globe est menacé d'une catastrophe, on en est averti par des commotions latentes; on a peur; on écoute pendant la nuit; on reste les yeux attachés sur le ciel sans savoir ce que l'on a et ce qui va arriver. (MOT I, 684-85: end chap. XIX, 5)

The references to specific historical moments and great heroes are cheerier, though they do not always refer to Bonaparte at his happiest. Napoleon is of course compared to the greatest conquering hero of them all. Advised by Daru to spend the winter in Moscow, "'C'est un conseil de lion,' répond Napoléon: 'mais que dirait Paris? La France ne s'accoutumerait pas à mon absence.'—'Que dit-on de moi à Athènes?' disait Alexandre" (MOT I, 812). At Saint Helena Napoleon chose to rest and be buried in a little valley with a willow-planted spring. "Il disait en parlant de la source: 'Si Dieu voulait que je me rétablisse, j'élèverais un monument dans le lieu où elle jaillit.' Ce monument fut son tombeau. Du temps de Plutarque, dans un endroit consacré aux nymphes aux bords du Strymon, on voyait encore un siège de pierre sur lequel s'était assis Alexandre" (MOT I, 1023). It is notable that in these cases where, instead of declaiming doom for him, Chateaubriand is granting his protagonist a comparison of favor he builds towards the name of the hero in the clause after the break.

In other places the Emperor takes on almost the grandeur of a natural force. Napoléon Bonaparte is not the first Napoléon to carry the name. But the others, men of distinction, never yet had names imposing enough to stop a reader. No matter. "La gloire d'un homme ne remonte pas; elle descend. Le Nil à sa source n'est connu que de quelque Ethiopien; à son embouchure, de quel peuple est-il ignoré?" (MOT I, 674: end chap. XIX, 3). In a paragraph analyzed in the preceding chapter[6] Napoleon's death was compared to the setting of the sun as simultaneously a Latin quotation assimilated him into the permanent company of Tacitus' heroes (MOT I, 1010: end chap. XXIV, 8).[7] After such comparisons to nature and history it

---

[6] Cf. *supra*, p. 54.

[7] More traditionally Napoleon is also compared to the "noble" animals: a wounded lion (MOT I, 815, end of a paragraph), the eagle (MOT I, 995, end XXIV, 4). His "rocher" of Sainte-Hélène and the eagle are related to the myth of Prometheus, to whom he is specifically compared (MOT I, 1018).

The third paragraph of Book XXIII (MOT I, 915) compares him to a comet. The paragraph is of interest in the context of our discussion of the "expanding" paragraph, because its construction leads to a somewhat contradictory effect: after the exposition the comet metaphor expands the perspective, which is finally closed again by a maxim in falling rhythm concerning extraordinary individuals. The end result is much less flattering to Napoleon than if the maxim had preceded a concluding comet metaphor.

seems only natural to find an implicit comparison to Christ not far behind (MOT I, 1018-19).[8]

But Chateaubriand's epic of Napoleon is primarily a story of defeat, and disillusionment, and disintegration. It is well summarized in the following image which captures admirably the grandeur that was Napoleon's in his ambition and accomplishments, the disarray he caused more and more around him, and the death that comes to all things. It comes early in the *Mémoires*, where it terminates the last chapter of Book VI, the "Parallèle de Washington et de Bonaparte," one of the most important parts of the complex thematic prelude.

> Mais ce géant ne liait point ses destinées à celles de ses contemporains; son génie appartenait à l'âge moderne: son ambition était des vieux jours; il ne s'aperçut pas que les miracles de sa vie excédaient la valeur d'un diadème, et que cet ornement gothique lui siérait mal. Tantôt il se précipitait sur l'avenir, tantôt il reculait vers le passé; et, soit qu'il remontât ou suivît le cours du temps, par sa force prodigieuse, il entraînait ou repoussait les flots. Les hommes ne furent à ses yeux qu'un moyen de puissance; aucune sympathie ne s'établit entre leur bonheur et le sien: il avait promis de les délivrer, il les enchaîna; il s'isola d'eux, ils s'éloignèrent de lui. Les rois d'Egypte plaçaient leurs pyramides funèbres, non parmi des campagnes florissantes, mais au milieu des sables stériles;[9] ces grands tombeaux s'élèvent comme l'éternité dans la solitude: Bonaparte a bâti à leur image le monument de sa renommée. (MOT I, 224-25)

Although this is not a pure example of the expanding paragraph I have been considering—the last clause refers us back to the subject very precisely, and therefore makes the effect of the image much more that of an extended simile than an abruptly overwhelming metaphor-by-juxtaposition—the break is clear after "s'éloignèrent de lui." The apposition, "rois d'Egypte," is cleanly impressed, the flowing rhythm down to "solitude" presents to us, after all the details of "génie," "miracles," "force prodigieuse," the characteristic void-within-void, "tombeaux" in a "solitude." The slave-driving inhumanity of "les rois d'Egypte" is a condemnation of the Emperor compared to them, and the condemnation is all the

---

[8] Another comparison to Christ at the end of a paragraph ("Eût-on fait tant d'affaires pour sauver un homme qui eût apporté la liberté et la vertu au genre humain? Le Christ fut crucifié.") disappears from the final versions. Cf. the manuscript version parallel to MOT I, 1019-20 in Clarac, *"Mémoires d'Outre-Tombe: le manuscrit de Genève (suite),"* BSC, X (1967), 82.

[9]
> " 'My name is Ozymandias, king of kings:
> Look on my works, ye Mighty, and despair!'
> Nothing beside remains. Round the decay
> Of that colossal wreck, boundless and bare
> The lone and level sands stretch far away."

Chateaubriand's spirit and method are here very close to those of Shelley's fine sonnet of 1818. Is there perhaps a common source, or was this a *topos*?

more biting for its recall of Napoleon's disasters in his Egyptian campaign. The final clause, suddenly countering the expansion by a second, and contrary, apposition, effectively reduces Napoleon back down to normal human size after having built up his glory and power by the intimations of the comparison.

There is a comparable rhetorical movement in a paragraph in the Life of Napoleon that compares the emperor at the time of the Confederation of the Rhine to one of the greatest of artists; the expositional part of the paragraph terminates with a chiastic compound sentence that attempts to measure Napoleon's greatness and limitations: "Bonaparte, sa première visée de génie passée, n'apercevait plus que de l'argent et des soldats; l'exacteur et le recruteur prenait la place du grand homme." And then immediately in conclusion, the apposition of Michelangelo in a sentence that moves from praise to a certain judgment: "Michel-Ange de la politique et de la guerre, il a laissé des cartons remplis d'immenses ébauches" (MOT I, 752). It should be noted that all these paragraphs that lead us suddenly to a concluding historical or mythological contrast or example occur in a text strewn with comparisons of Napoleon to all sorts of great names. An outstanding example of this general feature of Books XIX-XXIV would be the single paragraph of XXII, 20, which contains references to "grands génies," "l'ange rebelle," an actor in the role of Flavius Attalus or Caesar, Briareus, Asmodée, and finally, again, the artist who could not finish his work: "il avait l'instinct de ce qui lui restait encore à peindre; il ne voulait pas que la toile lui manquât avant d'avoir achevé ses tableaux" (MOT I, 893).

The subject of Napoleon excites the rhetorical fervor of Chateaubriand to the point that he has composed whole chapters in the structure of the special paragraphs that have been examined. A couple of these chapters even appear before Book XIX. Chapter 4 of Book XIV (MOT I, 490-92) presents the dramatic and seriously comic meeting of Chateaubriand with Napoleon in 1802. It is the chapter in which, as we have seen above, Chateaubriand compares his single encounters with Washington and Bonaparte. Short—only seven paragraphs—and full of rhetorical figures throughout, the chapter begins by presenting Napoleon as someone greater than ordinary men: "l'Homme du temps" is envisaged in the context of "la marche gigantesque du monde." Napoleon's portrait is then sketched, his brief and rather intimidating conversation summed up, and with humorous relief Chateaubriand notes in the short fifth paragraph, "Bonaparte incontinent s'éloigna. Comme à Job, dans ma nuit, 'un esprit est passé devant moi; les poils de ma chair se sont hérissés. . . .'" When he then introduces the following comparison with Washington by the remark, "Mes jours n'ont été qu'une suite de visions . . . ," he—almost—

prepares us for the great and abrupt poetic conclusion of the last paragraph. There he has pictured himself watching Bonaparte watching him across the room:

> "*Chi è quel grande, che non par che curi*
> *L'incendio?*
> 'Quel est ce grand qui n'a cure de l'incendie?' (Dante.)"

Chapter 8 of Book XVI is also constructed like one of the abruptly expanding paragraphs, writ large. Here there is a résumé judgment of Napoleon after the Enghien affair. The chapter goes from a mock inquest, through a long quotation from the *Mémorial de Sainte-Hélène* and commentary on it, to a severe judgment of Bonaparte and a concluding maxim, separated from what precedes it by its calmer sarcasm and more impersonal expression: "Lorsqu'on ne peut effacer ses erreurs, on les divinise; on fait un dogme de ses torts, on change en religion des sacrilèges, et l'on se croirait apostat de renoncer au culte de ses iniquités" (MOT I, 567). It should be noted in addition that the whole of Book XVI is a carefully composed unit, in which the chapters are elements of a deliberate scheme. The whole book is devoted to an explanation of the place of the Enghien affair in Chateaubriand's life. It starts with his arrival in Paris from Rome and ends with a meditation on disappearance and death in the forest of Chantilly. This movement from historical event to the most intensely personal reflection is worked out through a succession of eleven short chapters which contain an expository account of Chateaubriand's resignation of the Valais ministry at the news of the Duc d'Enghien's execution (chap. 1); then, after the brief description of his November, 1838, visit to Chantilly, from which he dates the ten chapters he is now writing,[10] an account, point by point, of the arrest, court-martial, and execution of the Duc d'Enghien, with copious quotations from many of the persons involved and comments on their reports (chaps. 2-6), a brief résumé of the "Part de chacun" (chap. 7), the chapter 8 that has just been examined, a summary of the historical repercussions of the affair (chap. 9), a reference to Chateaubriand's famous 1807 *Mercure* article, "Lorsque, dans le silence de l'abjection," and the paragraph on Bonaparte's change that ends with the quotation from Milton about the avenging angels that was quoted earlier in this chapter (chap. 10); finally comes the reflective concluding chapter 11, "Abandon de Chantilly." It assimilates the Duc d'Enghien to the ruins of Chantilly where he was born and suddenly affiliates the destiny of the author of the *Mémoires d'Outre-Tombe* with the

---

[10] As so often this setting for the writing of the text appears to be the result more of a concern for narrative harmony ("[raconter] la mort de M. le duc d'Enghien, à la vue des ruines de Chantilly") than for the actual facts. See Levaillant, MOT, ed. du Centenaire, II, 136, n. 1.

destiny of this, the youngest Condé: "A diverses reprises la forêt entière est tombée sous la cognée. Des personnages des temps écoulés ont parcouru ces chasses aujourd'hui muettes, jadis retentissantes. Quel âge et quelles passions avaient-ils, lorsqu'ils s'arrêtaient au pied de ces chênes? quelle chimère les occupait? O mes inutiles *Mémoires*. . . . Hommes obscurs, que sommes-nous auprès de ces hommes fameux? Nous disparaîtrons sans retour . . ." (MOT I, 572-73). In the context and emotions of "Mémoires d'Outre-Tombe" such personal concern manages to be an expansive opening towards reverie even after facts that the author himself feels changed the world.

A striking "expanding" chapter in the Life of Napoleon occurs in Book XXII, the book that takes Napoleon from his return to Paris after the disastrous Russian campaign to his captivity on Elba. Chapter 19 recounts his abdication and the famous speech he made to his guard at Fontainebleau. At the end of the page-long quotation of his words there is a change of paragraph and this single sentence, which abruptly, by metaphor, metamorphoses Napoleon, up till then primarily pitiful, into an epic figure: "Cela dit, Napoléon lève sa tente qui couvrait le monde" (MOT I, 883).

Chapter 12 of Book XX, "L'empereur entreprend l'expédition de Russie," contains a whole series of abruptly expanding paragraphs. The very first paragraph ends with the reference to Medea, "Napoléon faisait descendre à lui la tragédie," that has already been mentioned. The second paragraph ends with a comparison to the Vandals and Alaric and a Latin quotation. Following paragraphs are concluded with epigrams or sudden generalizations. The chapter ends, after a rather long exposition concerning Napoleon's dealings with Poland, with a paragraph quoting Lamennais that raises suddenly the particular political issues to a general consideration of human values, sacrifice, suffering, and a very Chateaubrianesque figure of disquiet: the migrating bird.

> "Tant de sacrifices, tant de travaux", dit l'abbé de Lamennais, "doivent-ils être stériles? Les sacrés martyrs n'auraient-ils semé dans les champs de la patrie qu'un esclavage éternel? Qu'entendez-vous dans ces forêts? Le murmure triste des vents. Que voyez-vous passer sur ces plaines? L'oiseau voyageur qui cherche un lieu pour se reposer." (MOT I, 784)

Another chapter, XXII, 22, presents the inverse variant of the expanding unit, such as we saw also among the special paragraphs. After a very long paragraph describing in detail the odd contrasts and mixtures of old and new habits and characters of the "Première année de la Restauration," the chapter's other paragraph, much shorter, sarcastically opens a comparison to the Athenians. "Ces métamorphoses seraient odieuses, si elles ne tenaient en partie à la flexibilité du génie français." The Athenians were self-governed, listened to speechifiers, were "*regardeurs de discours et au-diteurs d'actions*, dit Thucydide. Mais quand, bon ou mauvais, le décret était rendu, qui, pour l'exécuter, sortait de cette masse incohérente et inex-perte? Socrate, Phocion, Périclès, Alcibiade" (MOT I, 900). Here we have exactly the reverse of the Lamennais chapter ending just examined: the suddenly much shorter paragraph, sentences rapidly diminishing in length, the four names suggesting an endless series of men, the glory of the human race, whose ironic contrast to their absent counterparts in the France of 1814 is so obvious that it is not mentioned.

Chateaubriand has ostensibly included the Life of Napoleon in his autobiography because the Emperor was so much a part of his times and had so much direct impact on his life that it would be impossible not to include him:

> Au reste, à qui ces contentions, ensevelies depuis quarante ans dans des liasses vermoulues, importent-elles? Des divers acteurs de cette époque un seul restera, Bonaparte. Nous tous qui prétendons vivre, nous sommes déjà morts: lit-on le nom de l'insecte, à la faible lueur qu'il traîne quelquefois après lui en rampant? (MOT I, 528-29)[11]

We have already noted the insistent and repeated way in which he makes their lives parallel. Then we examined paragraphs and chapters in which Chateaubriand expanded and deepened the presentation of Napoleon's life with comparisons and generalizations and sudden openings to images of vastness and heroism: treating Napoleon's life the way he treats his own—and will treat Rancé's. But there is yet a further and more essential relating of his life and the Emperor's.

> Nous entrons présentement dans [ma carrière politique]: avant d'y pénétrer, force m'est de revenir sur les faits généraux que j'ai sautés en ne m'occupant que de mes travaux et de mes propres aventures: ces faits sont de la façon de Napoléon. Passons donc à lui; parlons du vaste édifice qui se construisait en dehors de mes songes. Je deviens maintenant historien sans cesser d'être écrivain de mémoires; un intérêt public va soutenir mes confidences privées; mes petits récits se grouperont autour de ma narration. (MOT I, 668: first chapter of Book XIX)

The "vaste édifice[12] qui se construisait en dehors de mes songes": the

---

[11] We find an almost direct opposite to this evaluation of the importance of historical events in relation to his life when, speaking of his grief at the death of his sister Lucile in 1804, he writes, "Ce sont là les vrais, les seuls événements de ma vie réelle! Que m'importaient, au moment où je perdais ma sœur, les milliers de soldats qui tombaient sur les champs de bataille, l'écroulement des trônes et le changement de la face du monde?" (MOT I, 599)

[12] The image of the *édifice* picks up the metaphor Chateaubriand had used several pages earlier (MOT I, 665) in referring to his *Mémoires*: "Maintenant, le récit que j'achève rejoint les premiers livres de ma vie politique, précédemment écrits à des dates diverses. Je me sens un peu plus de courage en rentrant dans les parties faites de mon édifice."

phrase suggests that somehow Napoleon's life was the outcome, the fruition of his.

Thus we shall find in Chateaubriand's account Napoleon's life repeat-
ing his own (for though they are almost exact contemporaries, according
to Chateaubriand, Chateaubriand's life was told first). Since Napoleon's
greater fame makes him more real (if less approachable) than Chateaubriand, by means of him the author of the *Mémoires d'Outre-Tombe* will
become more real to their reader. Chateaubriand's *travaux* and *aventures*
are only *songes*: Napoleon has "fashioned" and "constructed" an "edifice"
of "facts."

Chateaubriand's story of Napoleon is obviously in part an effort to right
the balance in the growing Napoleonic myth. During his life Napoleon
had been both too much loved and too much hated; now in the 1830's he is
receiving a universal adulation that is also excessive, and unthinking;
Chateaubriand must set the record straight. Despite many reserves and
some severe criticisms Chateaubriand has an enormous admiration for
Napoleon, the one truly great individual in a generation of midgets, and
the last of his kind: establishing a just equilibrium is an adequate reason
for writing. But a further reason still, and the only one satisfactorily to
explain the large place Napoleon's Life takes in Chateaubriand's autobiography, is Chateaubriand's absolute personal fascination with Napoleon. Anything that really fascinates Chateaubriand—except his amorous
affairs, suppressed out of discretion—has found its way into the *Mémoires*,
be it French foreign policy or trees. If his own life of *songes* can seem even
to him at times lesser than Napoleon's "facts," still he can see, too, that
Napoleon is like himself a man of "imagination"—even, indeed, "imagination sans frein" (MOT I, 809; cf. I, 807, 813 n.). He is convinced of a
"mysterious kinship" between them.[13]

In Chateaubriand's account Napoleon's life strangely comes out to be a
function of Chateaubriand's. This is more than parataxis. It is not merely
egotism on the author's part, nor does it arise solely because the other's
story does appear, after all, in an autobiography. Though passages such as
the following are frequently ironic, they are not always so.

"Bonaparte, accouru à Paris, se logea rue du Mail, rue où je débarquai
en arrivant de Bretagne avec madame Rose"[14] (MOT I, 694). Chateau-

---

[13] Jean Boorsch, "Chateaubriand and Napoleon," *Yale French Studies*, XXVI (Fall-Winter
1960-61), 61. I am much indebted, and particularly in this chapter, to this impeccable
scholar.

[14] Chateaubriand was already using this type of comparison as early as the *Itinéraire de Paris
à Jérusalem*: "Puisqu'Homère avait eu pour hôte un armurier, à Néon-Tichos, je ne rougissais
plus d'avoir eu pour interprète un marchand d'étain, à Smyrne" (ORV II, 927: but note how
modest is the continuation of the comparison at the earlier date).

In addition to the parallels between Chateaubriand's and Napoleon's lives noted here see
also MOT I, 754, 991.

briand was there first, in the text of his *Mémoires* as also in life. "Il voit à la pointe du jour cette colonne de Pompée que j'apercevais du bord de mon vaisseau en m'éloignant de la Libye" (MOT I, 712). Napoleon saw it first, but Chateaubriand had already described his later sight of it. A year later "Napoléon prend la route que j'ai suivie: il longe l'Afrique par des vents contraires" (MOT I, 738).

"Remercions Bonaparte, aux Pyramides, de nous avoir si bien justifiés, nous autres petits hommes d'Etat entachés de poésie, qui maraudons de chétifs mensonges sur des ruines" (MOT I, 715). A justification that, ironically, preceded the political career accused. "Je comptais mes abattements et mes obscurités à Londres sur les élévations et l'éclat de Napoléon. . . . Napoléon était de mon âge: partis tous les deux du sein de l'armée, il avait gagné cent batailles que je languissais encore dans l'ombre de ces émigrations qui furent le piédestal de sa fortune. Resté si loin derrière lui, le pouvais-je jamais rejoindre?" (MOT I, 739-40). Here clearly Napoleon preceded him, but again the order of Chateaubriand's presentation gives Napoleon's lot after the description of his own. "Je n'eus pour moi dans le premier moment, parmi les souverains, que Bonaparte lui-même. Il parcourut ma brochure ["De Buonaparte et des Bourbons"[15]] à Fontainebleau" (MOT I, 868). Chateaubriand "wins": Napoleon follows. Definitively.

The most remarkable example comes in the famous and extraordinary description of the Battle of Waterloo. For in Book XXIII, Chapter 16, the recital of the climactic disaster of Napoleon's career is viewed uniquely through Chateaubriand's personal experience, as he stands silently at the edge of a field near Ghent: "auditeur silencieux et solitaire du formidable arrêt des destinées" (MOT I, 963). The procedure is similar to that subsequently used by Stendhal in the *Chartreuse de Parme*, and that is of course the point. Stendhal uses the scene for an ironic portrayal of history but also, and principally, to show something about the quality of his Fabrice's life; Chateaubriand is using the muffled and hard to interpret facts of Napoleon's career to emphasize by contrast the solidity of his own reflective thought. There has been more to the parallel than the simple simultaneity Chateaubriand refers to when he writes near the end of his Life of Napoleon, for instance, "Puisque c'est ma propre vie que j'écris en m'occupant de celles des autres, grandes ou petites, je suis forcé de mêler cette vie aux choses et aux hommes, quand par hasard elle est rappelée" (MOT I, 1026).

Je vous fais voir l'envers des événements que l'histoire ne montre pas; l'histoire n'étale que l'endroit. Les *Mémoires* ont l'avantage de présenter l'un

---

[15] In the much more sympathetic treatment of Napoleon in the *Mémoires* Chateaubriand transcribes the title of his pamphlet as "De Bonaparte . . . ."

et l'autre côté du tissu: sous ce rapport, ils peignent mieux l'humanité complète en exposant, comme les tragédies de Shakespeare, les scènes basses et hautes. Il y a partout une chaumière auprès d'un palais, un homme qui pleure auprès d'un homme qui rit, un chiffonnier qui porte sa hotte auprès d'un roi qui perd son trône: que faisait à l'esclave présent à la bataille d'Arbelles la chute de Darius? (MOT I, 952)

Chateaubriand is here referring to his rather grotesque portrayal of the circle surrounding Louis XVIII in Ghent during the Hundred Days, the circle of which he was an important part, contrasting its futile and silly ways with the vast and crucial events taking place around Napoleon. Yet he is also showing himself on the side being mocked, implying generally that the actions of his own life are part of the "envers," the reverse side of history, and not really a part of "history"—the history of the historians—at all. Surely such self-deprecating irony should not be taken at face value: it would be self-defeating, after all, on the part of an autobiographer. Chateaubriand remains clearly most interested in showing "l'autre côté du tissu"—his side. Despite the massiveness of the books devoted to Napoleon, he is writing them mostly to give depth and breadth to his portrayal of himself. Though not always as much as in the chapter on Waterloo, he is everywhere present; and though he and Napoleon start out simultaneously, it is he, not Napoleon, who finishes last. Napoleon, he makes it plain, never knew how to use Chateaubriand, but Chateaubriand finally, successfully, uses Napoleon.

The historian and the contemporary take on by association some of the glamour of the great hero. Chateaubriand, historian in the *Mémoires*, is conscious of this; in this respect he takes his place once more in the French "classical" tradition. What of the risk that the contrast between recorder and actor may suddenly be perceived, in reverse, to emphasize primarily the relative weakness of the former? Chateaubriand attempts to prevent this by his continuous parallels between himself and the Emperor, especially the ones drawn not too specifically. As in the paragraph expanding abruptly without transition, Chateaubriand gives it to the reader of his juxtapositions to draw the conclusions, seize the metaphor, make the point—carefully guided—for himself: for him, as he says in measuring his failure later to oppose Talleyrand forcefully enough, "j'aurais dû voir que la fortune de la France se trouvait liée dans ce moment à celle de mes petites destinées: ce sont de ces enchevêtrements historiques fort communs" (MOT I, 977).

Years later, in his last work, he is to do something rather similar with Rancé. It is well recognized that in the *Vie de Rancé* also Chateaubriand is writing a "Song of Myself." But when he talks about Rancé in that work it is nowhere near so shocking: after all the *Vie de Rancé* does not purport to be an autobiography of Chateaubriand, and so Rancé's role is secured. (For example, if Napoleon were to write a Life of Chateaubriand we would not be particularly surprised if he talked about himself in it and not at all if he talked about Chateaubriand.) Despite the difference of genre or title under which they appear the method is, however, the same in the Life of Napoleon and the *Vie de Rancé*, even though Rancé and René will be contemporaries not in time but in spirit: "Tout a changé en Bretagne, hors les vagues qui changent toujours" (ORV I, 1046). Again the text is filled with abruptly expanding paragraphs, but this time they form a backdrop of legend, romance, allegory, not the pageant of epic and history. Yet once more the thought, the "point," is in the empty space, the pause, the break. Chateaubriand, the real Chateaubriand, so runs the implication, lies between what he dares to say of himself and what he writes of Rancé or what he writes of Napoleon Bonaparte. Chateaubriand's self-portrait is thus in more than two dimensions; his reader reads between, on the one hand, the recorded and recognized, the admitted and claimed (that is, what Chateaubriand says about himself), and on the other (in what he says about Napoleon or Rancé) the potential and wished for. Chateaubriand paints his experience and his dreams, "Wahrheit und Dichtung," and asks his reader to find just where, between the two, the real he really is. It is a very dynamic way to write autobiography.

> Why do we conceive the desire to give expression to things
> that cannot be said—and sometimes succeed? Such suc-
> cess is a phenomenon that occurs when a subtle arrange-
> ment of words excites the reader's imagination to an ex-
> treme degree; at that moment, author and reader become
> accomplices in a crime of the imagination.
>
> Yukio Mishima *Sun and Steel*

5 At Cross-Purposes: The Christianization of René

Not only for its portrayal of a new kind of soul agony is *René* such a
watershed in French literature. It represents as well a new style and a new
form. "Je pris, par l'imagination, tous les maux de l'âme décrits dans ce
poème désolé," wrote George Sand, describing in her Memoirs many
years later the initial impact on her of reading *René*.[1] And *René* was indeed
a poem, even more than that *Atala* which younger Chateaubriand the
classicist was rather embarrassed to call "une sorte de poème":[2] it is
certainly much more like a poem than a novel in its brevity, its relative
plotlessness, its lyrical cry of anguish (for, essentially, it is much more a
"cry" than a "story"), its unity of tone, its lofty and sustained emotion. Yet
the most intriguing feature for me of both form and message of *René*
comes from their curious and troubled relationship to the *Génie du christianisme*.

The definitive story of the genesis of Chateaubriand's works up
through the *Génie* cannot yet be written. There is simply not enough
evidence to enable us to understand how the cynical, not so young author
of the chapter in the *Essai sur les révolutions*, "Quelle sera la religion qui
remplacera le Christianisme" (when he published it he was over twenty-
eight years old), came in four years or less to write the *Génie du christianisme*. The claims of crassest opportunism made by his detractors are
not wholly credible; neither is the instant conversion implied by the "j'ai

[1] Sand, *Histoire de ma vie*, IV, 6, in *Oeuvres autobiographiques*, Pléiade, I, 1092.
[2] See Préface to the first edition of *Atala*, ORV I, 18. Cf. Lucien Bonaparte's expression, "son
poème d'*Atala*," quoted in Riberette, "La lettre de Chateaubriand à Lucien Bonaparte,"
BSC, XIV (1971), 65.

pleuré et j'ai cru" of the first preface to the *Génie* and the *Mémoires d'Outre-Tombe*. God works in mysterious ways, but so does Chateaubriand.

Be that as it may, one may note striking resemblances in form between the *Essai* and the *Génie* and thereby find the two works less divergent than at first their subjects would suggest. Both are the result of considerable "research," both assimilate the results of those readings with method but no real domination of the material, both throw together topics of the most astonishing diversity (one may think of the parallel of the Athenians and Parisians, or the chapter on the rattlesnake that proves divine bounty), and both include passages inspired by the American and English travels of the 1790's that really have very little to do with the books' subjects: the occasional footnotes in the *Essai* relating the trials of the emigration and the astonishingly inappropriate last chapter, "Nuit chez les Sauvages de l'Amérique," that is placed at the end of the uncompleted study, on the one hand; on the other, there are *Atala* and *René*.

There seems no reason to doubt Chateaubriand's claim that *Atala* and *René* arise in some manner from a manuscript, the famous and unknowable *Natchez*, that in its turn antedates the *Génie du christianisme* (MOT I, 430, 399)—a supposition fairly well supported by Chateaubriand's own declaration (MOT I, 197) about the simultaneity of composition of *Atala*, the would-be "philosophique" *Essai sur les révolutions*, and the curiously "roman philosophique" *Natchez*.[3] Though the reasons for the 1801 publica-

[3] Cf. Butor, "Chateaubriand et l'ancienne Amérique," *Répertoire II*, pp. 160, 162, 165, 188. Much has been written on the striking parallels between *Atala* and the "roman philosophique": cf. particularly M.-J. Chénier cited by Lebègue, "Versions inédites des Livres IX et X des *Martyrs*," BSC, X (1967), 21; Monod-Cassidy, "Amours sauvages, Amours chrétiennes: Quelques prédécesseurs peu connus d'*Atala*," *Chateaubriand, Actes du Congrès de Wisconsin*, pp. 243-44, 248-49. Another curious parallel would be Voltaire's *Alzire*: see Ages, "Chateaubriand and the Philosophes," *Chateaubriand, Actes du Congrès de Wisconsin*, pp. 237-39; Chateaubriand has written in the *Génie du christianisme* (II, ii, vii) of the Christian ethic that directs Voltaire's tragedy.

On the other hand, mitigating possibly the "contradiction" that it is tempting to find in the work, is the fact, suggestively developed by Shackleton, "Chateaubriand and the Eighteenth Century," *Chateaubriand, Actes du Congrès de Wisconsin*, p. 23, that in French eighteenth-century thought there is already a psychological attitude towards religion which suggests "that religion and sexual passion meet the same psychological need on the part of the individual, and that religious ceremonial has a sensuous and even a sensual appeal."

As Butor points out, pp. 156-57, there is good reason to think that *Atala* was by and large written before the author's emigration in 1793; cf. Regard's introduction, ORV I, 3. Lebègue, on the other hand, is "convaincu que, pour la plus grande partie, l'*Atala* primitive, l'*Atala* peu ou point chrétienne a été écrite en Angleterre"—thus, after mid-1793: Lebègue, "Réalités et résultats du voyage de Chateaubriand en Amérique," RHLF, LXVIII, 6 (Nov.-Dec. 1968), 920.

More recently the dating and revisions of *Atala* and *René* have been discussed by Barbéris in *Chateaubriand, une réaction au monde moderne*, pp. 53-54 *et passim*; he discusses the rôle of *René* in the *Génie* particularly in chap. 6, "Fonction d'un roman," of *"René" de Chateaubriand, un nouveau roman*. He points out (*Chateaubriand, une réaction*, p. 126) that, like the *Essai sur les révolutions*, the *Génie* is an "espèce de somme historique et philosophique."

tion of *Atala* are not perfectly clear, it seems reasonable to think that Chateaubriand "detached" it from the *Natchez* and attached it and *René* to the *Génie* mostly because they were ready at the time he needed to make himself known, because he held them dear and considered them good, because he didn't quite know what to do with them as individual works. But what we can only guess at is what changes the author must have wrought in them to make them fit their new place. The *Natchez* does not seem originally to have been a very Christian work.[4]

Now from a standpoint of the Christian subject and preponderance of narrative form one may consider Chateaubriand's "literary" period to extend from *Atala* through the *Martyrs*, with the *Génie du christianisme* and the *Itinéraire* standing like bookends providing a philosophical and geographical frame for the works inside. Similarly, and conversely, one may consider, from a standpoint of *philosophique* subject and prose composition, the preceding *Essai sur les révolutions* and the *Natchez* to be Chateaubriand's "eighteenth-century" works. By "philosophique" I refer to the documented, historically oriented didacticism of the former work and the "roman philosophique" nature of the second, at once a tale of adventure and a parable.

What leads to a series of conundrums, however, is the fact that it is impossible to establish any firm kind of separation—even chronological—between the *Essai* and the *Natchez*, on the one hand, and the "Christian" "literary" later works. Major materials from the *Natchez*, *Atala* and *René*, are first published in the context of the *Génie*; the *Génie* is argumentatively structured like the *Essai*; the *Natchez*, *Essai*, and *Génie* were all composed by and large during the time and in the frame of mind of the author's emigration.[5] *Atala* and *René* are simultaneously "philosophique" and Christian, didactic and lyrical.

Now, like the *Essai* and the *Génie*, the *Natchez* is composed, from the point of view of the present study, with the most astonishing juxtapositions of both subject and method. It is difficult to know much of anything precise about the "eighteenth-century" *Natchez*, but it does seem certain

---

[4] Cf. the excellent introduction to the *Natchez* by Maurice Regard (ORV I) and to *Atala* (esp. ORV I, 3-5); see also the section, "Genèse de René," in the Introduction to *René*, critical ed. by J.-M. Gautier (Droz, 1970), pp. 7-9, and Barbéris, *Chateaubriand, une réaction au monde moderne*, p. 54.

[5] Chateaubriand makes this very clear in the *Mémoires*. When upon the news of his mother's death he resolved "à changer subitement de voie," he set right to work with ardor. "Mes matériaux étaient dégrossis et rassemblés de longue main par mes précédentes études. Je connaissais les ouvrages des Pères. . . . Quant à l'histoire proprement dite, je m'en étais spécialement occupé en composant l'*Essai sur les Révolutions*. . . Enfin mon terrible manuscrit des *Natchez*, de deux mille trois cent quatre-vingt-treize pages in-folio, contenait tout ce dont le *Génie du Christianisme* avait besoin en descriptions de la nature; je pouvais prendre largement dans cette source, comme j'y avais déjà pris pour l'*Essai*" (MOT I, 399).

that the fundamental juxtaposition of pagan "Nature" and Christian civilization was at the root of the subject: "Toutes les tribus indiennes conspirant, après deux siècles d'oppression, pour rendre la liberté au Nouveau-Monde, me parurent offrir un sujet . . . heureux" ("Préface" of the *Natchez*, ORV I, 160). The very formulation of this statement indicates that the author supports the "pagan" side. We may also suppose that the remarkable contrasts—"Christian," Miltonian contrasts—of hellish, heavenly, and earthly scenes were established from the origin, for Chateaubriand refers also (ORV I, 163) to the mixture of all kinds of "merveilleux," Christian, mythological, and Indian, as part of the "travail de ma jeunesse." The book thus balances, particularly in its more elaborate early part, divided, epic-fashion, into "books," scenes in Louisiana with episodes in the France of Louis XIV, flights of angels in the sky, prayers at the foot of the throne of Mary, plots in the "conseil des Démons." As it may seem normal for the *Essai* and the *Génie* to be disorderly in the way that *L'Esprit des lois*, one of their models, is,[6] it is also to be expected that a self-conscious epic will present a plenty of epic contrasts. These contrasts tend towards more troublesome confusion only when they are concentrated into the form of what at first sight appears a tightly unified short narrative.

The various problems of composition that have frequently been noted in *René*—lack of clarity in direction, curious juxtapositions—are comparable to the particularities of Chateaubriand's paragraph structure, as described in preceding chapters. These same problems are reflected if anything even more clearly in the structure of *Atala*. The composition of each of the little stories sheds a useful light on the other.

It seems to me plain that Chateaubriand originally set out to write *Atala* as a demonstration of the havoc wreaked on the state of nature by the encroachments of civilization, in particular by ill-understood or poorly-proclaimed Christianity. Then, having decided to use *Atala* as an example of the "harmonies de la religion, avec les scènes de la nature et les passions du cœur humain," he found himself constrained to take what he had already—written? planned out in some detail?—and transform its message. From this shift remains a most uneasy diffusion of interest in the story.[7]

---

[6] "Et certainement (si l'on peut comparer un chef-d'œuvre à une œuvre très-imparfaite) l'admirable *Esprit des Lois* est une composition qui n'a peut-être pas plus de régularité que l'ouvrage dont on essaie de justifier le plan dans cette défense. Toutefois la méthode étoit encore plus nécessaire au sujet traité par Montesquieu . . .": "Défense du Génie du christianisme," in Chateaubriand, *Oeuvres*, ed. Ladvocat, 1827, XIV, 273.

[7] Note the remarks on this subject that Weil makes in his critical edition of *Atala*, pp. lxv-lxviii, and the passages of Lemaître, *Chateaubriand*, to which he refers: pp. 92-94.

In the profusion of a luxuriant nature a European who has fled to America listens to an American Indian who has traveled in Europe at its height of civilized splendor. "C'est une singulière destinée, mon cher fils, que celle qui nous réunit. Je vois en toi l'homme civilisé qui s'est fait sauvage; tu vois en moi l'homme sauvage, que le Grand Esprit (j'ignore pour quel dessein) a voulu civiliser" (ORV I, 38). The glowing colors of the description of "les deux rives du Meschacebé" in the Prologue are thus contrasted immediately with the rather simplistic implications of a *roman philosophique* demonstration; the procedure is reminiscent of Bernardin de Saint-Pierre, in the line of the *Nouvelle Héloïse* or the "Vicaire Savoyard."

Chactas' story runs for a while true to the eighteenth-century pattern. The man of nature cannot stand the constraints of society. He chafes under the benevolent tutelage of Lopez and his sister. When he announces that he must return to the life of an Indian or die, Lopez' answer emphasizes the fact that Chactas possesses an inalienable independence; Chactas himself implies that Christianity would be an abrogation of this liberty: "'Va, s'ecria-t-il, enfant de la nature! reprends cette indépendance de l'homme, que Lopez ne te veut point ravir. . . .' Lopez finit par une prière au Dieu des chrétiens, dont j'avais refusé d'embrasser le culte, et nous nous quittâmes avec des sanglots" (ORV I, 39-40).

Captured by an enemy tribe, condemned to death, Chactas reacts with noble bravery and admires the joyous simplicity of his captors' life. One night he is rescued by a beautiful Indian girl whom he takes to be the "Vierge des dernières amours." The scene of her approach is erotic and graceful,[8] but when she speaks her words are dry and doctrinally severe. "A demi voilée," she is both virtuous and passionate in appearance; "une extrême sensibilité, unie à une mélancolie profonde, respirait dans ses regards"; on her breast glitters a crucifix. She speaks in a manner that juxtaposes abruptly the resonant Indian-Homeric style that Chateaubriand developed for the epic *Natchez* and a soberer, rather curt and harsh style that seems meant to be Christian. "La jeune fille me dit alors: 'Je ne suis point la *Vierge des dernières amours*. Es-tu chrétien?' Je répondis que je n'avais point trahi les Génies de ma cabane. A ces mots, l'Indienne fit un mouvement involontaire. Elle me dit: 'Je te plains de n'être qu'un méchant idolâtre. Ma mère m'a fait chrétienne; je me nomme Atala, fille de Simaghan aux bracelets d'or, et chef des guerriers de cette troupe. Nous nous rendons à Apalachucla où tu seras brûlé'" (ORV I, 42).

---

[8] The scene calls for and received an illustration: the fine Saint-Aubin engraving of the 1805 edition is reproduced in *Atala*, ed. Weil, and also, with four others from 1805, in the Classiques Garnier ed. of 1962. The picture of Atala is reminiscent in its apposition of sensuality and decency of such eighteenth-century delights as the prints for the *Nouvelle Héloïse*.

References to Christianity that follow bear out this stylistic suggestion that Christianity is somehow contrary to nature and that it is nature rather which deserves our sympathy in their confrontation. We of course see the story through unbeliever Chactas' eyes, but even in the reported words of Atala there is an implied criticism of something unnatural in the religion she has accepted: "'Ma religion me sépare de toi pour toujours . . . O ma mère! qu'as-tu fait? . . .'" (ORV I, 44). The lovers pursue their way through the landscape whose beauty is if anything enhanced by the morally harmonious—and pagan—tales of the young brave visiting his beloved, resembling the "Génie du printemps, parcourant les forêts pour ranimer la nature," and the pagan brides trying to gather the soul of a dead infant. Touched by such quite un-Christian harmonies, the lovers are about to submit to their passion.

Here again the difficulty arises. "Qui pouvait sauver Atala? Qui pouvait l'empêcher de succomber à la nature? [And one must note here that "nature"—even if in this case it is almost lost in the cliché—has heretofore been used in a very different way: "la grâce est toujours unie à la magnificence dans les scènes de la nature" (ORV I, 34).] Rien qu'un miracle, sans doute; et ce miracle fut fait! La fille de Simaghan eut recours au Dieu des chrétiens; elle se précipita sur la terre, et prononça une fervente oraison, adressée à sa mère et à la reine des vierges" (ORV I, 48). Such a miracle gives to Chactas a "merveilleuse idée" of the moral force of Christianity, "de cette religion qui, dans les forêts, au milieu de toutes les privations de la vie, [the idea of privation, one must note in passing, has certainly not been prepared by the splendors of the preceding description] peut remplir de mille dons les infortunés; de cette religion qui, opposant sa puissance au torrent des passions, suffit seule pour les vaincre, lorsque tout les favorise. . . ." At least Atala's real salvation comes less from the miracle than the sudden appearance of four braves who capture Chactas and return him to captivity.

A curious parenthesis is opened here: Christian missionaries have taught some tribes to substitute slavery ("un esclavage assez doux," it is true) for the cruel tortures that had formerly been inflicted on their captives. Not in the tribe of which it is here question, however! and this matter is under debate only to be rejected in favor of the "usage antique," the preparations for which are then long and carefully described. Atala again saves the "jeune idolâtre" and flees with him. But she is full of melancholy, proof of the "perpétuelles contradictions de l'amour et de la religion" (ORV I, 57) which make her incomprehensible to Chactas. During a storm, when she is once more about to succumb to their love, they are rescued by the missionary, Père Aubry, whose charity appears incomprehensibly great to Chactas.

Now, in the episode subtitled "Les Laboureurs," Chactas describes the benefits of civilization brought to the New World by the missionary. The Indian is filled with admiration. "Quiconque a vu, comme moi, le père Aubry cheminant seul avec son bâton et son bréviaire dans le désert, a une véritable idée du voyageur chrétien sur la terre" (ORV I, 65). Indeed, even in the precisely religious domain of the mass his emotion reaches a peak; he sees Nature herself join in harmony with the divine mystery.

> L'aurore paraissant derrière les montagnes, enflammait l'orient. Tout était d'or ou de rose dans la solitude. L'astre annoncé par tant de splendeur sortit enfin d'un abîme de lumière, et son premier rayon rencontra l'hostie consa- crée, que le prêtre, en ce moment même, élevait dans les airs. O charme de la religion! O magnificence du culte chrétien! Pour sacrificateur un vieil ermite, pour autel un rocher, pour église le désert, pour assistance d'innocents Sauvages! Non, je ne doute point qu'au moment où nous nous prosternâmes, le grand mystère ne s'accomplît, et que Dieu ne descendît sur la terre, car je le sentis descendre dans mon cœur. (ORV I, 71)

Chactas, resensitized, wanders delightedly amidst these "tableaux" in which he sees "le mélange le plus touchant de la vie sociale et de la vie de la nature"; he admires "le triomphe du Christianisme sur la vie sauvage." "Je sentis la supériorité de cette vie stable et occupée, sur la vie errante et oisive du Sauvage" (ORV I, 71-73). And yet nothing makes us feel that feeling of superiority, any more than earlier when the missionary claimed to have saved the Indians from a life "dont les mœurs étaient féroces et la vie fort misérable" (ORV I, 67) we saw too clear a relationship between that claim and the life of the unchristianized savages previously described. If only Chactas could have set up wigwam-keeping with Atala in the Mission village! The story seems to be on the point of claiming the victory of Christianity. But on his return to the hermit's grotto Chactas finds Atala near death. She has poisoned herself. Considering herself bound by a vow of perpetual virginity that her mother had made to the Virgin, she had preferred death to infidelity.

And now Chactas curses "cette religion que vous m'avez tant vantée," "le serment qui m'enlève Atala," "le Dieu qui contrarie la nature. Homme, prêtre, qu'es-tu venu faire dans ces forêts?" (ORV I, 76). The priest can only review the situation and try to satisfy both parties to the debate in a rather lame way:[9]

---

[9] See Mrs. Lowrie's analysis, "Motifs of Kingdom and Exile in *Atala*," *French Review*, XLIII, 5 (April 1970), 761-62. She feels that the claims of religion in *Atala* are "surreptitiously undercut" on two counts: the ultimate annihilation of Aubry's Mission and the regret over Christian virtue expressed by both Chactas and Atala and unconvincingly contradicted by Aubry. Cf. the subtle analysis of Butor, "Chateaubriand et l'ancienne Amérique," *Répertoire II*, pp. 163-64, indicating his belief that Père Aubry's speech, like Père Souël's in *René*, is

> . . . ma fille, tous vos malheurs viennent de votre ignorance; c'est votre éducation sauvage et le manque d'instruction nécessaire qui vous ont perdue; vous ne saviez pas qu'une chrétienne ne peut disposer de sa vie. Consolez-vous donc, ma chère brebis; Dieu vous pardonnera, à cause de la simplicité de votre cœur. Votre mère et l'imprudent missionnaire qui la dirigeait, ont été plus coupables que vous; ils ont passé leurs pouvoirs, en vous arrachant un vœu indiscret; mais que la paix du Seigneur soit avec eux! Vous offrez tous trois un terrible exemple des dangers de l'enthousiasme,[10] et du défaut de lumières en matière de religion. Rassurez-vous, mon enfant; celui qui sonde les reins et les cœurs vous jugera sur vos intentions, qui étaient pures, et non sur votre action qui est condamnable. (ORV I, 80-81)

The hermit comforts Atala in her last moments by pointing out the superiority of divine love to transitory earthly passion, but dying Atala tells Chactas that if she had life to live over again she would still prefer "le bonheur de vous avoir aimé quelques instants dans un exil infortuné, à toute une vie de repos dans ma patrie" (ORV I, 85). Chactas promises Atala to become a Christian one day.

The narrator of the story that Chactas recited to René tells us his reaction to it in a way which does not underestimate the conflicts it illustrates. "Je vis dans ce récit le tableau du peuple chasseur et du peuple laboureur, la religion, première législatrice des hommes, les dangers de l'ignorance et de l'enthousiasme religieux, opposés aux lumières, à la charité et au véritable esprit de l'Evangile, les combats des passions et des vertus dans un cœur simple, enfin le triomphe du christianisme sur le sentiment le plus fougueux et la crainte la plus terrible, l'amour et la mort" (ORV I, 93). He learns from a group of Indian exiles he encounters while visiting Niagara Falls that Chactas and René were both killed in the great Natchez massacre, that Chactas had been baptized, and that Père Aubry had been tortured to death by the Cherokees, several of whom were converted by the spectacle of his strength in suffering.

The presence in *Atala* of an eighteenth-century type parable of the "dangers de l'enthousiasme" conflicting with the new Chateaubriand-style picture of the beauties of religion may of course be "explained" by certain examples, such as *Les Incas* of Marmontel, likely present in the author's mind as he wrote; a similar struggle is also present in Voltaire's

almost certainly a late addition. Cf. also the curious article by Levitine, "Some unexplored aspects of the illustrations of *Atala*," *Chateaubriand, Actes du Congrès de Wisconsin*, pp. 143-44, in which he speaks of the "blatant contradiction" between certain words of Père Aubry and Atala that "could perhaps be explained in reference to the progressive stages of the composition of the novel" and then comments on interpretations of the novel's themes as revealed through contemporary illustrations.

[10] "Dangers de l'enthousiasme" recalls the Voltaire Chateaubriand greatly admired. Even in the *Génie du christianisme* he speaks of him having "tant de goût et un esprit si juste" (III, iii, vi). Cf. Robert J. Buyck, "Chateaubriand Juge de Voltaire" (in *Studies on Voltaire and the XVIIIth Century*, CXIV), reviewed by Raymond Lebègue, BSC, XVII (1974), 72.

tragedy *Zaïre*, which the author of the *Génie du christianisme* found worthy of comparison to the *Iliad*,[11] and in Chateaubriand's own later novelette, so reminiscent of *Zaïre*, "Le Dernier Abencérage." One may perhaps find in the conflict a reflection of movements of the author's soul at the time of the tale's elaboration, provided that one accepts Chateaubriand's own interpretation of his progress from the "doute et douleur" he knew as the writer of the *Essai* to the confidence and joy of a newly rediscovered faith. Yet all explanations that underscore the uneasy divergence of aims in the book and the resulting juxtapositions may be ultimately unfair: for it is true that to generations of readers by now the book has given an impression more of unity than disunity.

The truth and the essence of the character of Atala is that she contains irreconcilables:[12] " '. . . tantôt, sentant une divinité qui m'arrêtait dans mes horribles transports, j'aurais désiré que cette divinité se fût anéantie, pourvu que serrée dans tes bras, j'eusse roulé d'abîme en abîme avec les débris de Dieu et du monde![13] A présent même . . . le dirai-je? à présent que l'éternité va m'engloutir, que je vais paraître devant le Juge inexorable, au moment où, pour obéir à ma mère, je vois avec joie ma virginité dévorer ma vie; eh bien! par une affreuse contradiction, j'emporte le regret de n'avoir pas été à toi!' " (ORV I, 77) Chactas also contains irreconcilables: "Comment Chactas n'est-il point encore chrétien?" he asks himself years later (ORV I, 87). Now there is much "literature" here, too, of both the century of Racine and that of the Marquis de Sade. But there is, mostly, much Chateaubriand here.[14] The simultaneity of the irreconcilable forces in their character gives the major force and originality to Atala and Chactas. We should remember that they are the creatures of the very author who was at that period discovering the "chrétienne réprouvée" in

[11] "Une religion qui fournit de pareilles beautés à son ennemi mériteroit pourtant d'être entendue avant d'être condamnée. . . . Le polythéisme, ne s'opposant point aux passions, ne pouvoit amener ces combats intérieurs de l'âme, si communs sous la loi évangélique, et d'où naissent les situations les plus touchantes. Le caractère pathétique du christianisme accroît encore puissamment le charme de la tragédie de *Zaïre*." *Génie du christianisme*, II, ii, v.

[12] It could be maintained that in Atala, where I should prefer to see a reflection of Chateaubriand's soul and inner torments, Chateaubriand was giving a fictional form to the degradation and confusion of Indian ways as white colonists began to dominate North America. This would be in keeping with the "roman philosophique" tradition I sense behind *Atala*. Cf. MOT I, 249: "Les traditions religieuses sont devenues confuses; l'instruction répandue par les jésuites du Canada a mêlé des idées étrangères aux idées natives des indigènes: on aperçoit, au travers des fables grossières, les croyances chrétiennes défigurées; la plupart des sauvages portent des croix en guise d'ornements . . . ."

[13] Cf. young Chateaubriand with the "sylphide": "Plongeant dans l'espace, descendant du trône de Dieu aux portes de l'abîme, les mondes étaient livrés à la puissance de mes amours" (MOT I, 97 *et passim*).

[14] ". . . dans toutes les fictions romanesques de Chateaubriand, la croyance religieuse intervi[ent] comme une contre-force destinée à neutraliser de l'intérieur, puis à vaincre le double magnétisme d'un désir": Richard, *Paysage de Chateaubriand*, p. 40.

Phèdre. As *René* will in certain ways dramatize adolescent conflicts of Chateaubriand in a character supposedly older,[15] so Atala and Chactas, in Indian disguise, play out the drama of the child who came simultaneously upon "un *Horace* non châtié et une histoire des *Confessions mal faites*." Does not Chateaubriand himself attribute to this happy chance his success in painting "avec quelque vérité les entraînements du cœur mêlés aux syndérèses chrétiennes" (MOT I, 56, 57)?[16]

Is one perhaps justified in finding that the presence of simultaneously developing, opposing traits of character, which are the characteristic of Atala and her novel, is the thematic equivalent of the juxtapositions of materials of "philosophical" and "Christian" origins in the book? Carried to the level of plot structure these tensions come to resemble the "thème de l'hétéroclite" that Richard analyses: "Chateaubriand . . . n'accepte [ce type de partage] qu'à la condition d'adhérer personnellement aux deux côtés de l'être partagé."[17] As was true for a certain kind of paragraph typical of the *Mémoires d'Outre-Tombe* and the *Vie de Rancé* in the incoherence of this plot lie its coherence and its organizing principle.

René presents similar problems. If the disorganization in theme is more muted, more subtly handled in *René* than in *Atala*, the disorganization in form is more shocking. I refer to the "moralité plaquée" that Sainte-Beuve and later critics concerned with the author's "sincerity" have had to deal with. It is hard not to find a profound contradiction between the stern morality of Père Souël, to whom is given the novel's last word, and René's complaisance in melancholy, which is decidedly what entrances the reader for all the rest of the work. Still it must be seen that the "moralité" is "plaquée" in only the most superficial sense; indeed René is most deeply interesting because his story includes an attached contradictory moral.

As in *Atala* the contradictions are not only on the surface; their roots run deep into the matter of the tale. The "tendance visible à faire aimer la Religion et à en démontrer l'utilité" (ORV I, 114) is almost as essential an aspect of the novel as the basic portrayal of "amertume . . . inquiétude . . . aigreur" (ORV I, 112) that, as Maurice Regard points out (ORV I, 103), has nothing specifically Christian about it, nothing not quite in keeping with young Chateaubriand's "philosophique" period. Père Souël does not suddenly appear *ex machina* at the end: he is present, and in character,

---

[15] Cf. *infra*, p. 91, n. 21.

[16] Note also the confession concerning his voyage to America and its famous sunset: "Quand je peignis ce tableau dont vous pouvez revoir l'ensemble dans *le Génie du Christianisme*, mes sentiments religieux s'harmonisaient avec la scène; mais, hélas! quand j'y assistai en personne, le vieil homme était vivant en moi: ce n'était pas Dieu seul que je contemplais sur les flots dans la magnificence de ses œuvres. Je voyais une femme inconnue et les miracles de son sourire . . ." (MOT I, 215).

[17] Richard, *Paysage de Chateaubriand*, p. 141.

from the third sentence. "Hors Chactas, son père adoptif, et le père Souël, missionnaire au fort Rosalie, [René] avait renoncé au commerce des hommes. Ces deux vieillards avaient pris beaucoup d'empire sur son cœur: le premier, par une indulgence aimable; l'autre, au contraire, par une extrême sévérité" (ORV I, 117). The author could hardly announce more clearly that he is leading us toward a "moral" with two opposing faces.

The uncertain center of sympathy in *René* is paralleled moreover in the *Génie du christianisme* itself, for the melancholy the story is to exemplify— the melancholy so severely judged by Père Souël—is there explained as a new, a Christian emotion, little known to the *anciens* (ORV I, 112). It is unknown, we read in *René*, to the state of nature also:

> "Heureux Sauvages! Oh! que ne puis-je jouir de la paix qui vous accom- pagne toujours! Tandis qu'avec si peu de fruit je parcourais tant de contrées, vous, assis tranquillement sous vos chênes, vous laissiez couler les jours sans les compter. Votre raison n'était que vos besoins, et vous arriviez, mieux que moi, au résultat de la sagesse, comme l'enfant, entre les jeux et le sommeil. Si cette mélancolie qui s'engendre de l'excès du bonheur atteignait quelquefois votre âme, bientôt vous sortiez de cette tristesse passagère, et votre regard levé vers le ciel cherchait avec attendrissement ce je ne sais quoi inconnu, qui prend pitié du pauvre Sauvage." (ORV I, 125)

Real melancholy is thus one of the benefits of Christianity, and it is plain that it is not considered an unmixed blessing.[18]

René does not as simplistically as *Atala*, however, portray Christian civilization moving in and troubling an otherwise idyllic state of nature. For from the beginning René addresses himself to the sympathetic in- dulgence of Chactas who is an Indian and profoundly troubled himself already—though of course that had all begun with Atala's vow. *René* also is a study of *harmonies*, and René's melancholy is harmoniously reflected in all parts of the American backdrop, from Chactas' merciful sympathy to the uneven summits of the Appalachians against the morning sun and the

[18] In the fragment of the chapter "Du vague des passions" of the *Génie* quoted in the 1805 Préface of *René* this melancholy is affiliated with advancing civilization and certain "disposi- tions que nous acquérons dans la société intime des femmes." Chateaubriand omits there two paragraphs cited in ORV I, 1198-99, that contain significant sentences omitted in turn from later editions of the *Génie du christianisme*: "C'est dans le génie du christianisme, qu'il faut surtout chercher la raison de ce *vague* des sentiments répandu chez les hommes modernes" and "Une prodigieuse mélancolie fut le fruit de cette vie monastique; et ce sentiment, qui est d'une nature un peu confuse, en se mêlant à tous les autres, leur imprima son caractère d'incertitude: mais en même temps, par un effet bien remarquable, le vague même où la mélancolie plonge les sentiments, est ce qui la fait renaître; car elle s'engendre au milieu des passions, lorsque ces passions, sans objet, se consument d'elles-mêmes dans un cœur so- litaire." The Ladvocat edition and those following are different indeed. See the excellent discussion of "the ambivalent view of melancholy in relation to Christianity" in D.G. Charlton, "The Ambiguity of Chateaubriand's *René*," *French Studies*, XXIII, 3 (July 1969), 229-43.

magnificent silence of the rolling Meschacebé that "formait la bordure du tableau avec une inconcevable[19] grandeur." *René* is carefully staged, like most everything in Chateaubriand, and that "grandeur" of the scene is in any case the recompense of a Bernardin de Saint-Pierre-like Providence for the suffering that must take place in it.

But from the beginning of his story René takes almost all our sympathy. If we have a little left for blind Chactas whom we already know,[20] there is little or none for Père Souël, who can only listen and look on "avec étonnement" (ORV I, 125). It is not that René is unworthy of blame according to ordinary standards of morality. He is extraordinarily self-indulgent and generally uncritical of himself, though he does admit lucidly enough at the beginning that he is "sans force et sans vertu," that he "ne peut guère se plaindre que des maux qu'il se fait à lui-même" (ORV I, 119). He is indecisive and directionless. He is inconstant. He is childish.[21] We can understand Amélie's advice to him to "cherche[r] quelque occupation" (ORV I, 134). But, as Gerald H. Storzer points out,[22] when Père Souël's criticism contradicts René's point of view the reader finds it hard to agree with the missionary past a certain point: "his point of view has already been undermined by the narration. René has already shown a sensitivity that impresses us, and many of his general conclusions about the human condition seem valid enough. Then, too, René is an artist of sorts. . . . The process by which his imagination, memory and emotions internalize the exterior world, distort it to create new realities, corresponds closely to the romantic concept of creativity." And as Storzer concludes, "We never really know, then, what to think of René."[23]

Instead of a parable contrasting the "dangers de l'enthousiasme" in beautiful savage nature with the beauties of Christianity in nascent society, we have in *René* a conflict of interest between the duties of civilized man and the urge to "drop out." "Je vois un jeune homme entêté de chimères . . . qui s'est soustrait aux charges de la société pour se livrer à d'inutiles rêveries" (ORV I, 144), says Père Souël. (One might appropriately think here of young Chateaubriand, traveling like René in America,

---

[19] (The "inconcevable" is geographically exact . . . .)

[20] If we consider ourselves to have read *Atala* in 1801, *René* in 1802, though in the editions of the *Génie René* appeared first. The beginning of *René* assumes, by its brief reference to René's presence in America, that the reader is already acquainted with him from *Atala*. See Barbéris, *"René" de Chateaubriand*, pp. 95-104.

[21] Kathleen O'Flaherty has uncovered with great finesse the reasons for this impression of childishness, in "Adolescence in the Work of Chateaubriand," *Chateaubriand, Actes du Congrès de Wisconsin*, pp. 273-81: in *René* Chateaubriand has given to a 16- to 21-year-old hero his own emotions between the ages of 11 and 17.

[22] Storzer, "Chateaubriand and the Fictional Confession," *Chateaubriand, Actes du Congrès de Wisconsin*, pp. 128-29.

[23] He compares him for ambiguity to Michel of the *Immoraliste* and Camus's Jean-Baptiste Clamence.

before he is snapped back to duty in Europe at the news of the arrest of Louis XVI.[24]) "Que faites-vous seul au fond des forêts où vous consumez vos jours, négligeant tous vos devoirs?" There is a parallel here to the pattern of stasis and movement, sitting still and running, that Jean Boorsch has noted as a clear design in *René*.[25] From the opening lines of his tale René has shown how he prefers withdrawal into lyric and elegy to any dramatic advance, and we also have his own bad conscience condemning him for it. "Je ne puis, en commençant mon récit, me défendre d'un mouvement de honte. La paix de vos cœurs, respectables vieillards, et *le calme de la nature autour de moi* [my emphasis], me font rougir du trouble et de l'agitation de mon âme" (ORV I, 118). Whereas in *Atala* nature was on one side and Christianity seemingly on the other, here both nature— which includes a peacefully domesticized Indian village (it is characterized by the signs of establishment and society, "son bocage de mûriers, et ses cabanes qui ressemblent à des ruches d'abeilles") together with the French colony under the sunrise—and Christianity, like two other "respectables vieillards," condemn the one alone.

René tries to establish a way of life in which solitude in outdoor nature will dependably be a solace to him, for man's various relationships in society are always for him a source of grief or intolerable: "J'ai coûté la vie à ma mère en venant au monde. . . . J'avais un frère que mon père bénit. . . . je rassemblais autour de moi mes jeunes compagnons; puis, les abandonnant tout à coup, j'allais m'asseoir à l'écart . . ." (ORV I, 119).

Only with his sister Amélie can he enjoy the open, murmur poems inspired by "le spectacle de la nature." But his "matin de la vie . . . comme le matin du jour, plein de pureté, d'images et d'harmonies," (ORV I, 119) is of short duration. His father dies; a brief stay in a monastery and a period of voyages show him too few virtues and too many misfortunes among vanished as well as living peoples. He observes the poets whose life, resembling his with Amélie when they were children, seems to show man capable of uniting a civilized art, at least, with nature: "Leur vie est à la fois naïve et sublime; ils célèbrent les dieux avec une bouche d'or, et sont les

---

[24] Near the end of his brilliantly illuminating study of *"René" de Chateaubriand, un nouveau roman*, p. 229. Pierre Barbéris brings together the novel's ending and its place in Chateaubriand's life in the following manner: "René, un certain René, est mort en Amérique, jamais récupéré, malgré les exhortations concordataires du P. Souël, toujours et jusqu'à la fin fidèle à ses songes qui n'étaient pas seulement fantasmes et chimères, mais exigences et signe d'un besoin de totalité, sans perspectives de réalisation historique. René, . . . un autre René est rentré en France et a pris du service dans l'ordre nouveau, ayant liquidé ses 'chimères' au nom d'un 'réalisme.' . . . Il se trouve qu'en Chateaubriand coexistaient contradictoirement les deux René . . . celui qui était resté, figure de l'absolu, mais de fuite et d'absence; celui qui était rentré, figure de la pratique quand même, mais aussi de l'inévitable compromission."
[25] Boorsch, "Motion and Rest in *René*," *Yale French Studies*, XIII (Spring-Summer 1954), 76-82.

plus simples des hommes" (ORV I, 123). Ossian sings for him in the same natural setting that is now just as harmoniously the home of Christian art: "Sur les monts de la Calédonie, le dernier barde qu'on ait ouï dans ces déserts me chanta les poèmes dont un héros consolait jadis sa vieillesse. Nous étions assis sur quatre pierres rongées de mousse; un torrent coulait à nos pieds; le chevreuil paissait à quelque distance parmi les débris d'une tour, et le vent des mers sifflait sur la bruyère de Cona. Maintenant la religion chrétienne, fille aussi des hautes montagnes, a placé des croix sur les monuments des héros de Morven, et touché la harpe de David, au bord du même torrent où Ossian fit gémir la sienne" (*Ibid.*). The artistic monuments of Italy are described in terms of nature ("Qu'ils sont beaux ces bruits qu'on entend autour des dômes, semblables aux rumeurs des flots dans l'Océan, aux murmures des vents dans les forêts, ou à la voix de Dieu dans son temple!" [ORV I, 124]); while seated atop the natural monument, Etna, he sees a confusion of dehumanized civilization and anthropomorphized nature: "les fleuves ne me semblaient plus que des *lignes géographiques* tracées sur une carte," "mon œil. . . plongeait dans le cratère de l'Etna, dont je découvrais les *entrailles* brûlantes" (*Ibid.*, my emphasis).

Still at this point in the story the pattern seems to hold good: nature is basically good (here is where René interrupts himself, seeing "un groupe d'Indiens qui passaient gaiement dans la plaine," with the cry, "Heureux Sauvages!" quoted above), whereas society, as René shows in his next words in answer to a prompting of Chactas, indeed the ultimate civilization, the France of Louis XIV, has let him down: "Hélas! mon père, je ne pourrai t'entretenir de ce grand siècle dont je n'ai vu que la fin dans mon enfance, et qui n'était plus lorsque je rentrai dans ma patrie. Jamais un changement plus étonnant et plus soudain ne s'est opéré chez un peuple. De la hauteur du génie, du respect pour la religion, de la gravité des mœurs, tout était subitement descendu à la souplesse de l'esprit, à l'impiété, à la corruption" (ORV I, 126). (And once again one is tempted to transpose the episode into the future, and think of Chateaubriand returning from America and England[26] to find the *ancien régime* swept away.) When even his sister, inexplicably, seems to want to leave him even as society isolates him ("Je voulus me jeter pendant quelque temps dans un monde qui ne me disait rien et qui ne m'entendait pas" [ORV I, 126]) he attempts to abandon, though living "dans un faubourg," all contact with

---

[26] England was recalled just above (ORV I, 123) with the episode of the unnamed statue of Whitehall. See Barbéris, *"René" de Chateaubriand*, pp. 157 ff.: "la vraie coupure historique n'est pas celle de 1789-1793 mais celle de 1715-1725. . . . Comme, pour de complexes raisons, il n'est pas question de faire de René un émigré de 89-92 (comment dès lors se faire rayer?), Chateaubriand transpose et fait endosser à René le thème 'France classique/France philosophique,' au mépris même de sa propre biographie romanesque."

society. The natural penetrates into the City and he is simultaneously conscious of it and of his solitude, describing both in a passage that in many ways prefigures Baudelaire's Parisian "recueillement": "Quand le soir était venu, reprenant le chemin de ma retraite, je m'arrêtais sur les ponts pour voir se coucher le soleil. L'astre, enflammant les vapeurs de la cité, semblait osciller lentement dans un fluide d'or, comme le pendule de l'horloge des siècles. Je me retirais ensuite avec la nuit, à travers un labyrinthe de rues solitaires. En regardant les lumières qui brillaient dans la demeure des hommes, je me transportais par la pensée au milieu des scènes de douleur et de joie qu'elles éclairaient; et je songeais que sous tant de toits habités je n'avais pas un ami" (ORV I, 127). This is no solution either; René tires of the constant repetition of scenes and ideas: "Je me mis à sonder mon cœur, à me demander ce que je désirais. Je ne le savais pas; mais je crus tout à coup que les bois me seraient délicieux" (ORV I, 128).

At first he fills the shell of nature surrounding him from the riches of his inner self. But soon his heart can no longer suffice: "Bientôt mon cœur ne fournit plus d'aliment à ma pensée, et je ne m'apercevais de mon existence que par un profond sentiment d'ennui" (ORV I, 130). He decides to commit suicide. The pathetic fallacy has turned out to be no more than just that: a sad misconception; like society, nature has been tried and found wanting; there is nothing in harmony with René's soul. "Tout m'échappait à la fois, l'amitié, le monde, la retraite. J'avais essayé de tout, et tout m'avait été fatal. Repoussé par la société, abandonné d'Amélie, quand la solitude vint à me manquer, que me restait-il?" (ORV I, 131)

It is at this point that the "drame" takes place. Amélie, who has talked René into remaining alive, comes to stay with him. Overcome by her incestuous passion for her brother she flees to a convent and soon takes the veil. "On peut trouver des forces dans son âme contre un malheur personnel; mais devenir la cause involontaire du malheur d'un autre, cela est tout à fait insupportable" (ORV I, 140). The only hope for René on the side of society is not only gone, it has more fearfully turned against him than anything else. René is now "réellement malheureux" (ORV I, 141).

He decides suddenly to go off to America. While awaiting a ship and suitable weather he still takes some comfort in nature, a nature still at least in harmony with the greatness of his suffering: "Mes larmes avaient moins d'amertume lorsque je les répandais sur les rochers et parmi les vents. Mon chagrin même, par sa nature extraordinaire, portait avec lui quelque remède: on jouit de ce qui n'est pas commun, même quand cette chose est un malheur" (ORV I, 142). A letter he has recently received recounting Amélie's death is the occasion which has brought him to open his soul to Chactas and Père Souël. Chactas tries to find solace for René, but he must admit that the human comfort he once knew is no more, and he speaks of a nature now only metaphorical. "Mon enfant, dit-il à son fils, je voudrais que le père Aubry fût ici; il tirait du fond de son cœur je ne sais quelle paix qui, en les calmant, ne semblait cependant point étrangère aux tempêtes; c'était la lune dans une nuit orageuse; les nuages errants ne peuvent l'emporter dans leur course; pure et inaltérable, elle s'avance tranquille au-dessus d'eux" (ORV I, 144).

Père Souël is no père Aubry, in any case not as Chactas remembers père Aubry. He condemns René, as we have seen: in that judgment he represents the society which has always condemned René. Chactas, who also feels rebuked for his sympathy, tells a charming parable about the Meschacebé illustrating the moral, "il n'y a de bonheur que dans les voies communes." René tries to follow the advice of the two ancients, and "renonc[er] à cette vie extraordinaire qui n'est pleine que de soucis" (ORV I, 145).

It doesn't work. The novel ends with René's fruitless demise in social conflict after he had tried to leave meditation in nature in favor of activity: ". . . il retourna chez son épouse, mais sans y trouver le bonheur. Il périt peu de temps après avec Chactas et le père Souël, dans le massacre des Français et des Natchez à la Louisiane. On montre encore un rocher où il allait s'asseoir au soleil couchant" (ORV I, 146). The story is the story of a failure. Nature was never quite enough, society led to disaster for a René; Père Souël was right, and his advice was unsuitable. The *moralité* is *plaquée*, but in the way the end couplet sometimes found in La Fontaine's *Fables* is; it only points up something we knew all along. René's way is not society's, and René will no more find a solution for his anguish in a "natural" setting than he did in Christian Europe. His is a soul without a country.

Now it must be admitted that a reading of *René* as "René the ambiguous" is resolutely modern;[27] a reaction like Sainte-Beuve's that finds the ending contradictory rather than perversely illuminating is historically easier to justify. But precisely such "contradiction" is what one finds on all sides in Chateaubriand's work, to the extent that one may rightly ask if the attractiveness and meaning the mid-twentieth century finds in such incoherence are not more than a figment of critical imagination. In her analysis of the spatial and temporal structure of the *Mémoires d'Outre-Tombe* Miss Grevlund notes[28] the continual interference of past and present in that work: "nous sommes, à chaque page des *Mémoires*, en présence

[27] Cf. Barbéris' comment in *"René" de Chateaubriand*, p. 208: ". . . René est un héros moderne, et tout le piège idéologique est d'affirmer schématiquement l'équivalence: christianisme = modernité. . . . En fait, si *René* est moderne, c'est parce que c'est un texte critique de la société civile dans ses rapports avec l'individu, et par là un roman."
[28] In *Paysage intérieur et paysage extérieur dans les Mémoires d'Outre-Tombe*; see pp. 177-78 ff.

de la totalité de l'expérience . . . ; le présent pendant lequel l'auteur raconte son passé fait continuellement intrusion dans le récit suivi de ce passé et vice versa. Ces entrecroisements, d'abord peut-être reflets incon-scients des vicissitudes de la rédaction, deviennent le trait le plus carac-téristique de la dernière manière descriptive de René." Similarly the interference and interlacing of Christian morality and Romantic melan-choly, whether they be the immediate result of the Christianization of a "philosophical" tale or more profoundly the reflection of a complicated and troubled soul, are a characteristic and ever-present trait, like it or not, of Chateaubriand's early novelistic manner.

. . . ce Temps qui me fait pirouetter dans les espaces
avec lui (MOT I, 878)

Ma mémoire est un panorama (MOT II, 743)

6 *The Composition of the* Mémoires d'Outre-Tombe

For the Romantics Chateaubriand was first and foremost the author of
René. For most of us today, I suspect, he is primarily the author of the
Mémoires d'Outre-Tombe. Many are the parallels between the two works; the
protagonists particularly—unsatisfied, egocentric idealists, wandering,
soul-searching, intelligent and cultivated, conscious victims of the identity
crisis—present a striking resemblance. But *René* and the *Mémoires
d'Outre-Tombe* are also very different books; it says something about us and
our expectations—to what extent influenced by a book like the *Mémoires
d'Outre-Tombe* itself in this respect?—that we are much more patient with
the much longer and diffuse *Mémoires* than ever were its first readers.

This is in part precisely because they were the first readers, obliged to
read the *Mémoires*, as Sainte-Beuve put it, "découpés en feuilletons au
milieu des tempêtes civiles . . . jetés par lambeaux dans les carrefours
. . . lus, comme du Rétif, au coin de la borne."[1] Those who had earlier
known and sung the praises of the *Mémoires*—Sainte-Beuve among
them—had known only fragments, and moreover had known these fragments in the electrifying presence of the master himself and Madame
Récamier; the fragments were read aloud to the admiring chosen few, or
read in manuscript—again as by Sainte-Beuve—by the necessarily admiring chosen fewer. The *Mémoires d'Outre-Tombe* are still capable, by fragments, of appealing to all kinds of readers: one might easily cull from
them one of the most stimulating and attractive anthologies of political,
moral, or lyrical fragments of the nineteenth century. But they appeal

[1] Sainte-Beuve, *Chateaubriand et son groupe littéraire*, I, 80, n.

97

also, and I think particularly, to the twentieth-century reader as a composed whole, and it is to this whole that I now turn.

The *Mémoires*, we now know, *were* a composed whole, to an extent never properly appreciated by Chateaubriand's contemporaries.[2] Evidence abounds on all sides that the composition, the structure, the balancing and weighting of the materials composing the *Mémoires* were one of the author's major concerns. The division into parts, books, chapters, hidden by the early editions, much as the true architecture of another posthumous masterpiece, Pascal's *Pensées*, was hidden in the edition of Port-Royal, has now again become a part of the experience of the reader, who is guided by Maurice Levaillant's two editions, the "Pléiade" and the "Edition du Centenaire." Chateaubriand's own concern for the parts and the whole of his book is quite clearly illustrated by the wealth of architectural images he uses in speaking of his autobiography: *temple, cathédrale gothique, édifice, basilique* (MOT I, 7, 197, 435, 665; II, 222).[3]

OU EN SONT MES *MEMOIRES*

Il m'est arrivé ce qui arrive à tout entrepreneur qui travaille sur une grande échelle: j'ai, en premier lieu, élevé les pavillons des extrémités, puis déplaçant et replaçant çà et là mes échafauds, j'ai monté la pierre et le ciment des constructions intermédiaires; on employait plusieurs siècles à l'achèvement des cathédrales gothiques. Si le ciel m'accorde de vivre, le monument sera fini par mes diverses années; l'architecte, toujours le même, aura seulement changé d'âge. . . . (Book XIII, 2, MOT I, 435)

We know moreover that he was interested in the general effect of his

---

[2] Note, for instance, Marcellus' complaint about the *Mémoires*: "Ce dernier de ses ouvrages n'a point subi les combinaisons d'une composition uniforme. Revu sans cesse et soumis à des divisions multiples, il n'a jamais été, pour ainsi dire, coordonné. C'est une série de fragments sans plan, presque sans symétrie, tracés de verve, suivant le caprice du jour; l'imagination s'y confond avec la mémoire; la plume qui a passé à d'autres travaux revient à ceux-ci, retrempée dans toute son énergie, pour mêler à un présent assombri de mille vicissitudes un passé émaillé de mille souvenirs.

"Je ne sais si je me trompe, mais ce décousu, loin de nuire à la vivacité des impressions, y vient en aide" (Marcellus, *Chateaubriand et son temps*, p. xix). By and large a remarkably perspicacious comment on our subject, in which Marcellus lets his instinctive and generous good taste triumph finally over his "classical" prejudices.

Sainte-Beuve does refer to the *Mémoires* in one place (*Chateaubriand et son groupe littéraire*, II, 358), it is true, as "le livre peut-être le plus composé de Chateaubriand," but he seems there to be referring primarily to Chateaubriand's calculated efforts "pour produire l'effet et se mettre lui-même en lumière."

[3] A derivative and equally coherent series of images occurs at the end of the First Part (Book XII, 6, MOT I, 431) where Chateaubriand portrays himself in partly descriptive language, partly metaphor, as leaving the "asile . . . de la solitude" and "foyer de la famille" for the "carrefour . . . du monde": "Je jette un regard attendri sur ces livres qui renferment mes heures immémorées; il me semble dire un dernier adieu à la maison paternelle. . . ."

work, the effect that would be harmed—and indeed it was harmed—by a partial, cut up, or installment-style publication.[4]

He was aware of his diversity of materials and, particularly, of the contrast of tones and complexities of chronology that resulted from the way in which over the years he wrote the book, always reflecting the time of writing in the period written about. But he was not sure that this resulted in a flaw: "Ma jeunesse pénétrant dans ma vieillesse, la gravité de mes années d'expérience attristant mes années légères, les rayons de mon soleil, depuis son aurore jusqu'à son couchant, se croisant et se confondant, ont produit dans mes récits une sorte de confusion, ou, si l'on veut, une sorte d'unité indéfinissable . . ." (Avant-Propos, MOT I, 2).

In attempting to define that "unité indéfinissable" which in the twentieth century has become perhaps the most appealing aspect of the *Mémoires* one may first take account of the basic structure given to the *Mémoires* by their author: four parts, divided into books, divided into chapters.[5] This division into parts is accomplished basically by a chronological scheme of rather remarkable symmetry (1768-1800, 1800-14, 1814-30, 1830-48) that divides the author's life into segments of about fifteen years each (with roughly a fifteen year childhood and a remarkably prolonged fifteen year youth joined in the first part).

Chateaubriand is at pains to show that this chronology is also the mark of another, deeper and personal, division. Thus we find the idea of his "careers," which expresses the equivalency of the parts of his book and the "parties de ma vie":

> Ici se termine ma *carrière politique*. Cette carrière devait aussi clore mes *Mémoires*. . . . Trois catastrophes ont marqué les trois parties précédentes de ma vie: j'ai vu mourir Louis XVI pendant ma carrière de voyageur et de soldat; au bout de ma carrière littéraire, Bonaparte a disparu; Charles X, en tombant, a fermé ma carrière politique.
>
> J'ai fixé l'époque d'une révolution dans les lettres, et de même dans la politique j'ai formulé les principes du gouvernement représentatif; mes correspondances diplomatiques valent, je crois, mes compositions littéraires.

---

[4] See Chateaubriand's manuscript comment in Clarac, "Une version inédite de l'Avant-propos des 'Mémoires,'" BSC, IX (1965-66), 67, reprinted in Clarac, *A la recherche de Chateaubriand*, p. 292: "une publication hachée, donnée successivement par lambeaux, . . . nuit à l'effet général d'un ouvrage."

[5] This division, obscured in early editions, was definitely, at least at one time, intended by Chateaubriand, as can be seen in many places in the text. Thus the "Préface testamentaire" of 1834 speaks of a division "en livres et en parties" (MOT I, 1047); at the beginning of Book III one reads of "le livre précédent" and "le livre actuel" (MOT I, 75); at the beginning of Book XXXV, after the account of the Revolution of 1830, he is "tout étonné d'ouvrir dans un calme profond la quatrième partie de cet ouvrage" (MOT II, 487); etc. On the chapter divisions see Levaillant's introduction to the Edition du Centenaire, I, lxxxvii, and to the Pléiade edition, I, xiv, xvii.

Il est possible que les unes et les autres ne soient rien, mais il est sûr qu'elles sont équipollentes. (MOT II, 482)[6]

And as Chateaubriand takes his place within a national and historical perspective, the history of his epoch, its events and its heroes become too a part of his careers: indeed an additional way to bring a familiar order to a profusion of facts and as well a temptation, frequently indulged, to add to that profusion.

Much might be added, of course, about the specific parallels mentioned in this passage: even more than egocentric they are highly artificial. The death of Louis XVI had a less clear effect on the first career than Chateaubriand sometimes implies, and the fall of Bonaparte and of Charles X mark so naturally the beginning and end points of the political career of a faithful Restoration politician that they are little more than tautology when presented as a supplementary principle of chronological organization. Thus it is not surprising that Chateaubriand backs the presentation of his personal chronology with a historical overview that tries to show the relationship and flow of the different careers. The "carrière mêlée" of the Fourth Part is by definition a blend of what preceded, "n'ayant plus qu'à résumer les expériences de ma course" (XXXIV, 10—last chapter of Part III—MOT II, 482), although even as he is writing it, it will turn out to be a more active "résumé" than he had expected when he penned, under the date of October, 1830, the following introduction to the last part of his *Mémoires*: "Sur la route, que j'ai jadis parcourue conscrit insouciant, je vais cheminer vétéran expérimenté." He expects nevertheless that his last days will show the closing of the "cercle de [ses] jours," and this rounding off is the image that in XXXV, 1, finally takes the place of the linear "carrière" and "course": "Il ne tiendra qu'à moi de renouer les deux bouts de mon existence" (MOT II, 488-89).

He had already presented the Third Part as the outgrowth of his literary career. Not only does Chateaubriand see himself first started on his way into public life almost at the beginning of his literary career because Napoleon recognized the political potential of his literary talents,[7] but also Chateaubriand presents the transition between his second and third careers in a manner, and, indeed, vocabulary that underlines all their relationships: "Ma vie de poésie et d'érudition fut véritablement

---

[6] Note also, ". . . on maintiendra seulement les quatre parties ou *carrières*, ma carrière de soldat, ma carrière littéraire, ma carrière politique, et ma carrière mêlée au delà de la chute de la monarchie." (Note from the Combourg archives published by Madame Durry, *En marge des Mémoires d'Outre-Tombe*, p. 62, and quoted by Levaillant in MOT I, xxvii: the note is in reference apparently to a late desire of the author to reduce the total number of books grouped in the various "parties.")

[7] Cf. *supra*, p. 66, and MOT I, 461-62, 492.

close par la publication de mes trois grands ouvrages, le *Génie du Christianisme*, les *Martyrs* et l'*Itinéraire*. Mes écrits politiques commencèrent à la
Restauration; avec ces écrits également commença mon existence
politique active" (MOT I, 664). "Le *Génie du Christianisme* commence la
révolution religieuse contre le philosophisme du dix-huitième siècle. Je
préparais en même temps cette révolution qui menace notre langue"
(*Ibid.*). His writings are what is common to the two periods; even the
writing of the beginning of the literary period is characterized in the
language of political action.

But it is in the tracing of the movement from the first to the second
career that Chateaubriand uncovers the most secret inner workings of his
mind, as he gives us his own understanding of the relationship between
his imagination and his literary creations: his character and his acts. Book
VII, chapter 8, the chapter describing Niagara Falls, tells us how the
late-blooming literary works that established Chateaubriand's reputation
arose out of the *ennui* and anguish of his solitary and directionless youth:

> Je ne pouvais communiquer les pensées qui m'agitaient à la vue d'un
> désordre si sublime. Dans le désert de ma première existence, j'ai été obligé
> d'inventer des personnages pour la décorer; j'ai tiré de ma propre substance
> des êtres que je ne trouvais pas ailleurs, et que je portais en moi.[8] Ainsi j'ai
> placé des souvenirs d'Atala et de René aux bords de la cataracte de Niagara,
> comme l'expression de sa tristesse. Qu'est-ce qu'une cascade qui tombe
> éternellement à l'aspect insensible de la terre et du ciel, si la nature humaine
> n'est là avec ses destinées et ses malheurs? S'enfoncer dans cette solitude
> d'eau et de montagnes, et ne savoir avec qui parler de ce grand spectacle! Les
> flots, les rochers, les bois, les torrents pour soi seul! Donnez à l'âme une
> compagne, et la riante parure des coteaux, et la fraîche haleine de l'onde, tout
> va devenir ravissement: le voyage du jour, le repos plus doux de la fin de la
> journée, le passer sur les flots, le dormir sur la mousse, tireront du cœur sa
> plus profonde tendresse. J'ai assis Velléda sur les grèves de l'Armorique,
> Cymodocée sous les portiques d'Athènes, Blanca dans les salles de
> l'Alhambra. Alexandre créait des villes partout où il courait: j'ai laissé des
> songes partout où j'ai traîné ma vie. (MOT I, 244)

It is hard not to stop briefly to comment so characteristic a passage.
Stylistically it may be all too characteristic of a silver-age Chateaubriand,
more a tired-out enchanter than the audacious pace-setter so often
quoted in the preceding pages. The opening sentence is not only pomp-

---

[8] The mechanism is reminiscent—for what reasons?—of the one described by Rousseau in
Book IX of the *Confessions*, as he there discusses the creation of Julie and Claire: "L'impossibilité d'atteindre aux êtres réels me jetta dans le pays des chimères, et ne voyant rien
d'existant qui fut digne de mon délire, je le nourris dans un monde idéal que mon imagination créatrice eut bientot peuplé d'êtres selon mon cœur" (J.-J. Rousseau, *Oeuvres complètes*,
"Pléiade," I, 427).

ous but also misleading in its context of the discovery of the "muse inconnue" (MOT I, 242). The language of the paragraph is all too often worn and full of clichés ("le désert de ma première existence," "les flots," "la fraîche haleine de l'onde"); the rhythms of the middle part are somewhat monotonous, and the antitheses rather stilted. Yet the subject is for the author of central importance.

Dissatisfaction with the scenes of nature viewed in solitude runs throughout Chateaubriand's work. The early plaint of the "Lettre à Fontanes sur la campagne romaine," first printed in the *Mercure* in 1804 (". . . *les jardins parlent peu*. Pour que cette nature nous intéresse encore, il faut qu'il s'y attache des souvenirs de la société: nous nous suffisons moins à nous-mêmes; la solitude absolue nous pèse, et nous avons besoin de ces conversations *qui se font le soir à voix basse entre des amis*" [ORV II, 1486-87]), refers directly to his emotion before Niagara Falls: "je doute que la cataracte de Niagara me causât la même admiration qu'autrefois." Almost thirty years later is penned a disabused meditation on mountain scenery, dated 1832 in Book XXXVI of the *Mémoires*: "En définitive, c'est la jeunesse de la vie, ce sont les personnes qui font les beaux sites. Les glaces de la baie de Baffin peuvent être riantes avec une société selon le cœur, les bords de l'Ohio et du Gange lamentables en l'absence de toute affection" (MOT II, 593).[9] In the *Lettre sur la campagne romaine* the recent death of Madame de Beaumont informs the comment; the "absence de toute affection" of Book XXXVI will rapidly be corrected with the arrival of Madame Récamier several chapters later and the ecstatic idyll on Lake Constance (Book XXXVI, 18).

Description of a natural scene, reflections on it, references to his own work and to universal history are for Chateaubriand a continual procedure. The concluding generalizing thought found in this paragraph we have seen to be a frequent trait also, and here it is combined with another: the break (between the gracefully balanced sounds, Alhambra-Alexandre) leading immediately to an opening perspective introduced by a great name. We have seen other uses of the comparison to Alexander the Great. But, more important than these characteristic aspects of the paragraph is its image "en abyme" of the profound structural pattern of the *Mémoires d'Outre-Tombe*, the memoirs that are for Chateaubriand the reflection of the form and order of his own life. For the chronology of Chateaubriand's life implies for him the reiterated fruition of his

---

[9] The sentence "Faites-moi aimer, et vous verrez qu'un pommier isolé. . ." which precedes immediately the two quoted here can be compared usefully to the sentence "Donnez à l'âme une compagne" of the preceding long quotation. The thematic material is very close, but the passage from Book XXXVI is developed with considerably more detail and freshness as well as stylistic grace.

capabilities. Each career is the expected, necessary development of what came before. Of the four great regions of the *Mémoires*, those of the traveller, littérateur, statesman, memorialist, region I, "le désert de ma première existence," is here seen giving birth to the creatures of the fiction of region II: Atala, René, Velléda, Cymodocée, Blanca. They in turn recount their "souvenirs" (region II reflecting region I) of the places the traveller has visited, as the memorialist of region IV now traces back through them the memories of his youth. In so doing he becomes an Alexander-creator of cities: his "songes" may be ironically contrasted to the solidity of "villes," just as his "traîné" is a feeble substitute for Alexander's "courait"; but "laissé" here can only have a meaning comparable to "créait," meaning "established there where I was," not merely "abandoned." And as in the abruptly expanding paragraphs that were examined in earlier chapters of the present study this juxtaposition of Alexander's to Chateaubriand's creativity is not a dispairingly ironic sign of change and contingency, but rather the contrary. Juxtaposition, by the logic of association, implies for Chateaubriand continuity and evolution. Moreover in juxtaposition, whether of "careers" or ambitions, time is suppressed in favor of the unified present of the artistic object. On the level of the author's life this freedom from contingency will finally be developed as one of the *Mémoires'* great themes, the theme of that force finally resistant to Time: Destiny.

The doubled frames of chronology and "careers" that Chateaubriand uses to guide the flow of the *Mémoires d'Outre-Tombe* form, still, an obvious and simple structure for his book. They are a logical and appropriate and indeed customary mechanical ordering of autobiography. But the *Mémoires d'Outre-Tombe* present other structural principles which are often more characteristic of lyrical than narrative form.

Next in obvious importance after the guiding framework of temporal division come the abstract, thematic structures of character and personality. Chateaubriand takes great pains to show his readers that he is always the same, that his life from beginning to end has been shaped by the same forces of race and country, the same energies and passions, the same principles. When his transitions or his passionate outcries have led him into showing the inter-"penetration" of youth and age, he wants us to understand that this method of juxtaposition and confrontation is perfectly adapted to the unity of the character it in turn illustrates. If, as I surmised in Chapter 4, he placed his life against the backdrop of History at least in part to give it reality, breadth, and credibility, reacting to those readers ill-disposed towards him who are only too ready to find him pompous or pretentious, he can now place his life against itself to prove his wholeness to those detractors who would wish to make him appear inconsistent or opportunistic.[10]

The reader of the *Mémoires* notes from the beginning the repetition of certain key words: *fidélité* ("Si jamais les Bourbons remontent sur le trône, je . . . leur demanderai, en récompense de ma fidélité . . ." [etc.] [I, 1, first sentence of second paragraph, MOT I, 6]); *mort* ("J'étais presque mort quand je vins au jour" [I, 2, MOT I, 17] and "Je n'avais vécu que quelques heures, et la pesanteur du temps était déjà marquée sur mon front. Que ne me laissait-on mourir?" [I, 3, MOT I, 19]); *destinées* ("Il n'y a pas de jour où, rêvant à ce que j'ai été, je ne revoie en pensée le rocher sur lequel je suis né, la chambre où ma mère m'infligea la vie, la tempête dont le bruit berça mon premier sommeil, le frère infortuné qui me donna un nom que j'ai presque toujours traîné dans le malheur. Le Ciel sembla réunir ces diverses circonstances pour placer dans mon berceau une image de mes destinées" [end of I, 2, MOT I, 18]); *exil* ("En sortant du sein de ma mère, je subis mon premier exil . . ." [first sentence of I, 3, MOT I, 18[11]]); *religion* ("Ma nourrice . . . me voua à la patronne du hameau, Notre-Dame de Nazareth" [I, 3, MOT I, 18]; "Durant les jours de fête que je viens de rappeler . . . j'éprouvais un sentiment extraordinaire de religion" [I, 4, MOT I, 32]; "C'est de ma mère que je tiens la consolation de ma vie, puisque c'est d'elle que je tiens ma religion . . ." [I, 5, MOT I, 38]); *mélancolie* (. . . la dure éducation que je reçus . . . a imprimé à mes sentiments un caractère de mélancolie née chez moi de l'habitude de souffrir à l'âge de la faiblesse, de l'imprévoyance et de la joie" [I, 5, MOT I, 38]); *mémoire* ("ma mémoire [était] extraordinaire. . . . Une chose m'humilie: la mémoire est souvent la qualité de la sottise. . . . Et néanmoins, sans la mémoire, que serions-nous? . . . notre existence se réduirait aux moments successifs d'un présent qui s'écoule sans cesse; il n'y aurait plus de passé" [II, 1, MOT I, 48-50]); *témoin* ("je suis comme le dernier témoin des mœurs féodales" [II, 2, MOT I, 51]); *vain, vanité* ("j'ai écrit longtemps en vers avant d'écrire en prose: M. de Fontanes prétendait que j'avais reçu les deux instruments. Ce talent que me promettait l'amitié s'est-il jamais levé pour moi? Que de choses j'ai vainement attendues! [III, 7, MOT I, 88]).

Each of these themes is then fully developed, as together they are woven throughout the texture of the autobiography. For example, Chateau-

[10] He is also following the autobiographical example and, to an extent, methods, of Rousseau: see Starobinski, *J.-J. Rousseau, La transparence et l'obstacle*, particularly the chapter, "Les problèmes de l'autobiographie."

[11] Note Chateaubriand's earlier transformation of this biographical situation in *René*, via Rousseau's *Confessions*: "je coûtai la vie à ma mère, et ma naissance fut le premier de mes malheurs" (in *Oeuvres complètes*, "Pléiade," I, 7), in *René*: "J'ai coûté la vie à ma mère en venant au monde" (ORV I, 119).

briand's *fidélité* of character has as its counterpart the tragic and grandiose political infidelity of Napoleon:

> La république de Washington subsiste; l'empire de Bonaparte est détruit. Washington et Bonaparte sortirent du sein de la démocratie: nés tous deux de la liberté, le premier lui fut fidèle, le second la trahit. (Complete paragraph, VI, 8, MOT I, 224)

as well as the burlesque infidelity of a Talleyrand: "J'ai eu des rapports avec M. de Talleyrand; je lui ai été fidèle en homme d'honneur, ainsi qu'on l'a pu remarquer . . ." (XLIII, 8, MOT II, 896). "M. de Talleyrand a trahi tous les gouvernements, et, je le répète, il n'en a élevé ni renversé aucun" (XLIII, 8, MOT II, 904). A less dominant theme, closely related to *fidélité*, is the theme of *honneur*, mentioned in the penultimate quotation and already in I, 5 (MOT I, 35: "Quand quelque polisson me parlait, Gesril me disait: 'Tu le souffres?' A ce mot je croyais mon honneur compromis et je sautais aux yeux du téméraire; la taille et l'âge n'y faisaient rien"; cf. II, 4 [MOT I, 60]: "cet honneur devenu l'idole de ma vie, et auquel j'ai tant de fois sacrifié repos, plaisir et fortune").

There is no need here to trace throughout the *Mémoires* the development of these abstract themes: many excellent studies of such thematic structure already exist, particularly concerning such themes as *mort*. It should be recalled, however, that these are among the sensitive themes that touch off particularly lyrical moments in the *Mémoires*, especially the expanding paragraph form examined earlier.[12] Such is the case perhaps even more when we come to the third structural principle of the *Mémoires d'Outre-Tombe*: the imagistic structure that depends, rather than on character, on the author's sensibility. Three of the major images are *mer*, *tombe*, *printemps*; they too are developed repeatedly and from the beginning in particularly loving passages of the autobiography.

"La chambre où ma mère accoucha domine une partie déserte des murs de la ville, et à travers les fenêtres de cette chambre on aperçoit une mer qui s'étend à perte de vue, en se brisant sur des écueils. . . . Le mugissement des vagues, soulevées par une bourrasque annonçant l'équinoxe d'automne, empêchait d'entendre mes cris" (I, 2, MOT I, 17-18, the same paragraph in which we have just noted the themes of *mort* and *destinées*): this passage introduces the image of the sea which is rapidly picked up and developed in further passages that continue the close association of Chateaubriand with the sea. I have already traced the development[13] of the paragraph of I, 4 (MOT I, 29-30) that tells us "C'est sur la grève de la pleine mer . . . que j'ai été élevé, compagnon des flots et des vents." Soon

[12] Cf. *supra*, p. 45.
[13] *Supra*, p. 35.

after (I, 6, MOT I, 39-40), in the first major interruption of the vicissitudes of the time of writing into the narrative account of the *Mémoires*, Chateaubriand uses the image of the sea to bridge past and present:

> Le 4 septembre 1812, j'ai reçu ce billet de M. Pasquier. . . .
> C'était un ordre de m'éloigner de Paris que M. le préfet de police voulait me signifier. Je me suis retiré à Dieppe . . . du mot anglais *deep*, profond (mouillage). En 1788, je tins garnison ici . . . : habiter cette ville . . . c'était me réfugier auprès de ma jeunesse. . . . Lorsque je restais chez moi, j'avais pour spectacle la mer; de la table où j'étais assis, je contemplais cette mer qui m'a vu naître, et qui baigne les côtes de la Grande-Bretagne, où j'ai subi un si long exil: mes regards parcouraient les vagues qui me portèrent en Amérique, me rejetèrent en Europe et me reportèrent aux rivages de l'A-frique et de l'Asie. Salut, ô mer, mon berceau et mon image! Je te veux raconter la suite de mon histoire: si je mens, tes flots, mêlés à tous mes jours, m'accuseront d'imposture chez les hommes à venir.

The third paragraph following this begins the *printemps en Bretagne* discussed at the end of Chapter 3, and the motif of the sea returns in connection with the theme of death in a discontinuous expanding paragraph describing Saint-Pierre island, "Plante voyageuse, j'ai pris mes précautions pour disparaître au bord de la mer, mon site natal" (VI, 5, MOT I, 213).

Not only is the sea repeatedly associated with the man; it is also, as in the "campagnes pélagiennes" of the "printemps en Bretagne" associated with fertility, and more specifically the creativity of the writer. In November 1802, continuing a trip to the south of France occasioned by the appearance in Avignon of a pirated edition of the *Génie du christianisme*, Chateaubriand visits Marseilles (XIV, 2). His first sight of a new *mer* is thus from the very beginning presented in a literary context, and Chateaubriand emphasizes that context: "J'allais voir le soleil de Provence, ce ciel qui devait me donner un avant-goût de l'Italie et de la Grèce, vers lesquelles mon instinct et la muse me poussaient" (MOT I, 476-77). En route, by boat on the Rhône ("Je me croyais en Amérique: le Rhône me représentait mes grandes rivières sauvages"—water thus affiliated with another motif of his creativity, the New World, where [MOT I, 242] "m'apparut une muse inconnue"), he is writing an article for the *Mercure* on Bonald's *Législation primitive*: "Au moment même où [l'auteur de cet article] écrit ces derniers mots, il descend un des plus grands fleuves de France." On arriving in Marseilles:

> Je me hâtai de monter à *Notre-Dame de la Garde*, pour admirer la mer que bordent avec leurs ruines les côtes riantes de tous les pays fameux de l'antiquité. La mer, qui ne marche point, est la source de la mythologie, comme

l'océan, qui se lève deux fois le jour, est l'abîme auquel a dit Jéhovah: "Tu n'iras pas plus loin." (MOT I, 482)[14]

Immediately after this Chateaubriand jumps forward to 1838, the very year in which he is writing, to another visit to Marseilles when the sound of the *mistral* brought back to his mind the Ocean he knew in his childhood and the *"Etoile des mers*, à laquelle j'avais été voué." He then recalls a literary experience, so completing another expanding paragraph with a reference to two of the greater poets of his pantheon:

> Lorsque je contemplais ces *ex-voto*, ces peintures de naufrages suspendues autour de moi, je croyais lire l'histoire de mes jours. Virgile place sous les portiques de Carthage un Troyen, ému à la vue d'un tableau représentant l'incendie de Troie, et le génie du chantre d'Hamlet a profité de l'âme du chantre de Didon. (MOT, *ibid.*)

The motif of the *tombe* is affiliated as powerfully with Chateaubriand's sensibility as the *mer*, but it represents the end and ultimate powerlessness of creativity. A paragraph almost at the end of II, 4, recounts thus the results of a childhood fever:

> On arrêta les effets de cette trop forte dose d'émétique, et je fus remis sur pied. Toute notre vie se passe à errer autour de notre tombe; nos diverses maladies sont des souffles qui nous approchent plus ou moins du port. Le premier mort que j'aie vu, était un chanoine de Saint-Malo; il gisait expiré sur son lit, le visage distors par les dernières convulsions. La mort est belle, elle est notre amie: néanmoins, nous ne la reconnaissons pas, parce qu'elle se présente à nous masquée et que son masque nous épouvante. (MOT I, 62)

---

[14] This passage is a curious variant of a remark made in the description of the voyage from Trieste to Greece that occurs at the beginning of the *Itinéraire*. There the sea and the ocean are again compared and contrasted, but this time both receive literary attributes: "La Méditerranée, placée au centre des pays civilisés, semée d'îles riantes, baignant des côtes plantées de myrtes, de palmiers et d'oliviers, donne sur-le-champ l'idée de cette mer où naquirent Apollon, les Néréides et Vénus, tandis que l'Océan, livré aux tempêtes, environné de terres inconnues, devait être le berceau des fantômes de la Scandinavie, ou le domaine de ces peuples chrétiens, qui se font une idée si imposante de la grandeur et de la toute-puissance de Dieu" (ORV II, 772). Both passages in turn may be usefully compared to Chateaubriand's very different contrast of sea and ocean in connection with Napoleon's final exile on Saint Helena: "La mer que Napoléon franchissait n'était point cette mer amie qui l'apporta des havres de la Corse, des sables d'Aboukir, des rochers de l'île d'Elbe, aux rives de la Provence; c'était cet océan ennemi qui, après l'avoir enfermé dans l'Allemagne, la France, le Portugal et l'Espagne, ne s'ouvrait devant sa course que pour se refermer derrière lui" (MOT I, 1012). In that paragraph also it seems quite clear that the "océan ennemi" is associated with divine judgment; the "mer amie" on the other hand is the site of Napoleon's achievements, which are related for Chateaubriand, as we know, to the emperor's boundless imagination.

Here Chateaubriand presents under the sign of strong emotion (the verb "épouvanter" has appeared already in the preceding paragraph) the encounter and opposition of the essential motifs of sea ("souffles" and "port") and voyage and tomb and mask, under the broader theme of *la mort*. Chateaubriand's own tomb will be by the sea at Saint-Malo, at the end of his travels (VI, 5, MOT I, 213, final sentence in a paragraph): "Plante voyageuse, j'ai pris mes précautions pour disparaître au bord de la mer, mon site natal," and his memories as well as his *Mémoires* are filled with other tombs: the royal tombs desecrated during the Revolution, so unforgettably described in the passages quoted in notes to the *Génie du christianisme*, the royal exhumations of 1815, Napoleon's tomb on Saint Helena which Chateaubriand never saw, and Madame de Beaumont's tomb, which marked for him, right at the beginning of his literary career, the finality of death, which even the writer of Mémoires d'Outre-*Tombe* does not then contest:

> . . . depuis que je l'ai perdue, non loin de son tombeau, à Rome, j'ai plusieurs fois, du milieu de la campagne, cherché au firmament les étoiles qu'elle m'avait nommées; je les ai aperçues brillant au-dessus des montagnes de la Sabine; le rayon prolongé de ces astres venait frapper la surface du Tibre. Le lieu où je les ai vus sur les bois de Savigny, et les lieux où je les revoyais, la mobilité de mes destinées, ce signe qu'une femme m'avait laissé dans le ciel pour me souvenir d'elle, tout cela brisait mon cœur. Par quel miracle l'homme consent-il à faire ce qu'il fait sur cette terre, lui qui doit mourir? (MOT I, 455)[15]

And yet the *Mémoires* do suggest a tie, however tenuous, between death, in particular the death of Madame de Beaumont, and the origin of the autobiography. Immediately after quoting from the *Lettre à Fontanes sur la campagne romaine*, in reference to the foreign visitor who "a mêlé les cendres qu'il aima à tant de cendres illustres, avec quel charme ne passera-t-il pas du tombeau de Cecilia Metella au cercueil d'une femme infortunée," he begins a new paragraph with the statement, "C'est aussi à Rome que je conçus, pour la première fois, l'idée d'écrire les *Mémoires de ma vie* . . ." (MOT I, 525). For the *Mémoires* themselves may prove a lasting monument, a "tombeau" "outre tombe," like the "chapelle expiatoire," "le

---

[15]   In a passionate and moving passage which concludes the description of the exhumation of Louis XVI and Marie-Antoinette in 1815, a movement that begins with the "morale vulgaire" of the thought of "la vanité des grandeurs humaines," Chateaubriand is led to inquire into the finality of death: "N'y a-t-il rien dans ce rien?" and concludes in a manner I find less than convincing. "Dans votre éternel silence, ô tombeaux, si vous êtes des tombeaux, n'entend-on qu'un rire moqueur et éternel? Ce rire est-il le Dieu, la seule réalité dérisoire, qui survivra à l'imposture de cet univers? Fermons les yeux; remplissons l'abîme désespéré de la vie par ces grandes et mystérieuses paroles du martyr: 'Je suis chrétien' " (MOT I, 907-8: end chap. XXII, 25).

monument peut-être le plus remarquable de Paris. Ce cloître, formé d'un enchaînement de tombeaux, saisit l'imagination et la remplit de tristesse" (MOT I, 905-6), a monument which unites, like a metaphor, the forever past historical time, imprisoned in the "tombeaux," and the eternal present ("saisit," "remplit") of art.

The motif of the spring of the year is the last of the structural images established early in the *Mémoires* that I shall examine here. A long paragraph from X, 3, which occurs in the description of Chateaubriand's 1793 emigration to the island of Jersey, establishes with great clarity how central an image the *printemps* is for the author's sensibility. Jersey, like the Brittany of "le printemps en Bretagne," is insular and productive under the protection of the sea: "L'île est féconde. . . . Le vent de l'océan, qui semble démentir sa rudesse, donne à Jersey du miel . . . de la crème . . . du beurre . . ." (MOT I, 346). "Le printemps conserve à Jersey toute sa jeunesse; il pourrait encore s'appeler *primevère* comme autrefois . . ." (*ibid.*). The paragraph in question follows the mention of all those whom Chateaubriand has left or is leaving behind, never to see again, his mother, sister, and brother, and now his uncle Bedée; it precedes the description of his voyage to Southampton.

> Si l'on pouvait dire au temps: "Tout beau!" on l'arrêterait aux heures des délices; mais comme on ne le peut, ne séjournons pas ici-bas; allons-nous-en, avant d'avoir vu fuir nos amis, et ces années que le poète trouvait seules dignes de la vie: *Vita dignior aetas.* Ce qui enchante dans l'âge des liaisons devient dans l'âge délaissé un objet de souffrance et de regrets. On ne souhaite plus le retour des mois riants à la terre; on le craint plutôt: les oiseaux, les fleurs, une belle soirée de la fin d'avril, une belle nuit commencée le soir avec le premier rossignol, achevée le matin avec la première hirondelle, ces choses qui donnent le besoin et le désir du bonheur, vous tuent. De pareils charmes, vous les sentez encore, mais ils ne sont plus pour vous: la jeunesse qui les goûte à vos côtés et qui vous regarde dédaigneusement, vous rend jaloux et vous fait mieux comprendre la profondeur de votre abandon. La fraîcheur et la grâce de la nature, en vous rappelant vos félicités passées, augmentent la laideur de vos misères. Vous n'êtes plus qu'une tache dans cette nature, vous en gâtez les harmonies et la suavité par votre présence, par vos paroles, et même par les sentiments que vous oseriez exprimer. Vous pouvez aimer, mais on ne peut plus vous aimer. La fontaine printanière a renouvelé ses eaux sans vous rendre votre jouvence, et la vue de tout ce qui renaît, de tout ce qui est heureux, vous réduit à la douloureuse mémoire de vos plaisirs. (MOT I, 349)

The sweet bitterness of a page such as this is unmistakably characteristic of Chateaubriand, from his resentful jealousy of the younger lovers all around him to his sentimental evocation of a better, other time and place. The spring motif picks up here not only the motif of fecund waters and the idea of imminent death, not only the themes of destiny, exile, melancholy, memory, and vanity, by reference if not directly, but also leads the reader into the great theme of Time, perhaps the dominant theme of the *Mémoires d'Outre-Tombe*. Time, which is inevitable passing, which takes away from us, which forces comparison of a better past to a less perfect present, which "kills"; Time, which forces us to the realization that, unlike Nature, man is not cyclical in his creativity; Time forces one's "words" and "expressions" into the form of a painful memory of happiness past.

To hold the *Mémoires d'Outre-Tombe* together, to counter-balance the strains of discontinuity that are the result of various juxtapositions and extraordinary richness and diversity of materials, one finds then a chronological and historical structure, a narrative thematic structure, and an imagistic structure reminiscent of lyrical forms. Still there remains to be examined the structural principle most peculiar to the *Mémoires d'Outre-Tombe*. The major themes of the *Mémoires*, like Time just mentioned, are brought into full development by a method which is almost musical in nature. Like a theme first announced in an overture, or the arrival of Vinteuil's "petite phrase" in Proust, a theme to be developed is referred to casually, then mentioned as a matter for later development, then partially expressed, then developed fully, directly and in variations; then it is used in counterpoint or at least leaves a trail of brief references throughout the rest of the work. These major themes can be developed in the form of almost allegorical images: such is the case of the sylphide. They can be historical accounts, like the history of Napoleon in the *Mémoires d'Outre-Tombe*. They can be abstractions, as Time, Imagination, and, indeed, the "Avenir du Monde."

The introduction and assimilation of the story of Napoleon into the autobiography of Chateaubriand was examined in Chapter 4. The theme of Imagination will be considered in the following chapter. Here let us look at the development of the image of the sylphide and the great abstraction Time. Both are orchestrated in a musical fashion, but because of their divergent nature the precise kind of development is necessarily different.

The presentation of the sylphide is not unlike the incorporation of the story of Napoleon in the *Mémoires*; the story of the sylphide is, however, worked out on a smaller scale even if it is much more immediately a part of Chateaubriand's life. The sylphide receives her fullest description in Chapter 10 of Book III: "Fantôme d'amour," a one-page, five paragraph, elegantly assembled chapter; Levaillant's notes[16] suggest the richness and complexity of its evolution. The chapter presents a remarkable study of adolescence; it is one of several chapters in which Chateaubriand de-

[16] See MOT I, 1133-34.

scribes the anguish of puberty, descriptions that have not yet received sufficient critical attention. It is also a rather remarkable example of composition by juxtaposition. Its principal effects result from a very careful balancing of parts.

The "narrative" structure of the passage might be usefully compared to the structure of another great adolescence poem, Rimbaud's "Bateau ivre": a flight into fancy, a movement into increasingly exotic and wondrous dream, interrupted by an abrupt return to a sordid, everyday reality. The abruptness of the fall, however, is considerably greater in the sylphide passage, where it is less prepared by disquieting elements such as those that appear among more beautiful visions in the Rimbaud lyric.

"Comme je descendais des fleuves impassibles": the first paragraph of the "Fantôme d'amour" is a direct statement, like Rimbaud's in the past tense, pointing out the relationship between the idealistic dream and the reality of life surrounding its creation. The sylphide is a composition, "une femme de toutes les femmes que j'avais vues." Chateaubriand blends in her creation real people ("l'étrangère qui m'avait pressé contre son sein," "telle jeune fille du village"), the paintings of the mysterious château that symbolizes his family and France and the monarchy ("les portraits des grandes dames du temps de François Ier, de Henri IV et de Louis XIV, dont le salon était orné"), even the sensuous charms of religion ("j'avais dérobé des grâces jusqu'aux tableaux des Vierges suspendus dans les églises"). The sylphide is only a "femme" in the first paragraph; she is the focus of sexual, artistic, religious yearnings.

"Cette charmeresse"—already the first two words of the second paragraph reveal that the "fantôme d'amour" is other than an "être réel." Though she is still dressed in finery of "tous les pays . . . tous les siècles . . . tous les arts . . . toutes les religions," her character now reflects particularly the literary imagination of her creator: "Aphrodite . . . Diane . . . Thalie . . . Hébé." The grammatical subject of the first paragraph had been the desiring boy: "Je me composai . . . je lui donnai . . . j'avais dérobé"; now the subject is first and last the creature who, come alive, has escaped the complete control of the creator: "Cette charmeresse me suivait . . . elle devenait une fée qui me soumettait la nature . . . ma femme unique se transformait en une multitude de femmes." Still in the middle of this transformation—and this paragraph—our attention is called to the young man, who now presents himself as a painter: "Sans cesse, je retouchais ma toile. . . . Puis, quand j'avais fait un chef-d'œuvre, j'éparpillais de nouveau mes dessins et mes couleurs. . . ."

The myth of "Pygmalion," subject and first word of the opening sentence of paragraph three, has already been suggested in the preceding paragraph by a certain independence of the creation from her maker.

The image of the statue is quickly dropped, however, and the dominant metaphor becomes that of fiction, introduced through myth. Attention is once again deflected from the creature herself to the creator, who sees himself as Castor and Pollux, Apollo, Mars, Ossian, a sultan, a châtelain: "héros de roman ou d'histoire, que d'aventures fictives j'entassais sur des fictions!" But like the "noyé pensif [qui] parfois descend" ominously in Rimbaud's poem, here, right in the middle of the middle paragraph is a warning, insufficiently heeded, of disaster ahead: "mon embarras était de plaire à [ma statue]. Ne me reconnaissant rien de ce qu'il fallait pour être aimé, je me prodiguais ce qui me manquait."

The sylphide, this time so named, is the subject of paragraph four, "Voici venir une jeune reine," a paragraph again quite Rimbaldian, but this time paralleling in movement the Illumination, "Aube." Chateaubriand's queen searches for him through a landscape of natural beauty and art; he finally falls at her knees, as the "ondes de soie de son diadème dénoué viennent caresser [son] front." The longest of the paragraphs in the chapter, it picks up in its details the outstanding images of the preceding paragraphs, always transforming them into something superior. The "jeune reine" who now enters—in the present tense, after the simple past of the first and the imperfects of the second and third paragraphs—is the metamorphosis of the "grandes dames" of the days of the kings. The diamonds and flowers with which she is bedecked are the first precision of the "parures" the painter of paragraph two kept changing. The sylphide "me cherche," while the "charmeresse" of paragraph two only "me suivait partout invisible"; pleasant places like Bagdad, Granada, old manors, Asia were only mentioned in paragraph three, and they are now described, but the palaces of medieval romance have become magnificent classical palaces, the palaces of Italy and Sicily, the palaces of the arts, the domain of the artist once more and not just the hero: "à minuit, au travers des jardins d'oranger, dans les galeries d'un palais baigné des flots de la mer, au rivage embaumé de Naples ou de Messine, sous un ciel d'amour que l'astre d'Endymion pénètre de sa lumière; elle s'avance, statue animée de Praxitèle, au milieu des statues immobiles, des pâles tableaux et des fresques silencieusement blanchies par les rayons de la lune: le bruit léger de sa course sur les mosaïques des marbres se mêle au murmure insensible de la vague." Fiction reasserts its presence, however, in the menacing sentence that interrupts the movement: "La jalousie royale nous environne."

The final paragraph represents an abrupt interruption in many respects. After the long paragraph in the present tense it jumps back to the imperfect. The subject of the paragraph is a new subject in the chapter, "un pauvre petit Breton obscur, sans gloire, sans beauté, sans talents, qui n'attirerait les regards de personne, qui passerait ignoré, qu'aucune femme n'aimerait jamais," the inverse of all preceding subjects. The grammatical subject of the first part of the single sentence, "le désespoir," is likewise the negation of everything preceding. After the ecstasy building throughout to its climax in paragraph four, paragraph five would seem to represent a post-masturbatory depression. The sentence begins with an adverbial phrase, "Au sortir de ces rêves," marking at the same time a contrast in message and manner: each preceding paragraph had begun with the pronoun or noun (or "voici venir une jeune reine") that was one of its subjects at least. But this juxtaposition is not for purposes of expansion and reverie, like those examined in the early chapters of this study. It presents instead an ironic fall such as those the author has characteristically used in his political satire.

The sylphide had already been introduced, before she made her first major appearance in III, 10. She was first announced in the third paragraph of the "printemps en Bretagne," in a clause added between two sentences of the "Manuscrit de 1826":[17] "c'était le séjour des fées, et vous allez voir qu'en effet j'y ai rencontré ma sylphide" (MOT I, 41). The final versions of both these carefully elaborated passages would thus seem to date from the period shortly before 1834. Several imprecise references to the author's sexual awakening (MOT I, 57, 65-66, 71) then lead the reader to the admirable middle chapters of Book III that describe Chateaubriand's early adolescent yearnings: 4, "Mon donjon," 5, "Passage de l'enfant à l'homme," 9, "Révélation sur le mystère de ma vie." The final paragraph of the latter, which precedes immediately the chapter of the sylphide, introduces the "Fantôme d'amour" in a way that stresses how she is created out of the boy's desires. Chateaubriand has just recounted how one day, in the midst of his adolescent turmoil, he found himself squeezed in a narrow window opening next to a very pretty woman. His expression of amazement at the uniqueness of his emotion is very reminiscent of Rousseau, as is his description of the mechanism of the creation of fiction.[18]

---

[17] Cf. *supra*, pp. 60-62.

[18] Note the passage quoted *supra*, n. 8; the whole elaboration of the "fantôme d'amour" recalls also Rousseau's analysis of his adolescence and awakening desires: "Mes sens émus depuis longtems me demandoient une jouissance dont je ne savois pas même imaginer l'objet. . . . Dans cette étrange situation mon inquiete imagination prit un parti. . . . Ce fut de se nourrir des situations qui m'avoient intéressé dans mes lectures, de les rappeler, de les varier, de les combiner, de me les approprier tellement que je devinsse un des personnages que j'imaginois . . . enfin que l'état fictif où je venois à bout de me mettre me fit oublier mon état réel dont j'étois si mécontent" (*Confessions*, in *Oeuvres complètes*, "Pléiade," I, 41). Despite the many profound differences that separate him from Rousseau, in this precise situation Chateaubriand does not seem to be quite so "extraordinaire" as he claims. In his

Dès ce moment, j'entrevis que d'aimer et d'être aimé d'une manière qui m'était inconnue, devait être la félicité suprême. Si j'avais fait ce que font les autres hommes, j'aurais bientôt appris les peines et les plaisirs de la passion dont je portais le germe; mais tout prenait en moi un caractère extraordinaire. L'ardeur de mon imagination, ma timidité, la solitude firent qu'au lieu de me jeter au dehors, je me repliai sur moi-même; faute d'objet réel, j'invoquai par la puissance de mes vagues désirs un fantôme qui ne me quitta plus. Je ne sais si l'histoire du cœur humain offre un autre exemple de cette nature. (MOT I, 92)

After her presentation in III, 10, the sylphide returns, at first frequently, and then from place to place, throughout the rest of the *Mémoires*. She appears sometimes under her own name, sometimes in disguise. These appearances are traced well and compendiously by Levaillant in his notes to the Pléiade edition of the *Mémoires* (MOT I, 1134). She is associated with the motif of spring ("J'associais. . . . son image à la beauté de ces nuits de printemps," MOT I, 95) and like spring is associated with the idea of fecundity, and, particularly, Chateaubriand's literary production.

. . . j'écoutais les bruits qui sortent des lieux infréquentés; je prêtais l'oreille à chaque arbre; je croyais entendre la clarté de la lune chanter dans les bois: je voulais redire ces plaisirs, et les paroles expiraient sur mes lèvres. Je ne sais comment je retrouvais encore ma déesse dans les accents d'une voix, dans les frémissements d'une harpe, dans les sons veloutés ou liquides d'un cor ou d'un harmonica. Il serait trop long de raconter les beaux voyages que je faisais avec ma fleur d'amour; comment main en main nous visitions les ruines célèbres, Venise, Rome, Athènes, Jérusalem, Memphis, Carthage. . . . (MOT I, 95)

Her appearance thus seems to coincide with the awakening of the muse;[19] she leads the future voyager precisely on the "itinéraire" of Chateaubriand. The sylphide is associated also with "Mes joies de l'automne":

Je voyais avec un plaisir indicible le retour de la saison des tempêtes. . . . Rencontrais-je quelque laboureur au bout d'un guéret? je m'arrêtais pour regarder cet homme germé à l'ombre des épis parmi lesquels il devait être moissonné, et qui retournant la terre de sa tombe avec le soc de la charrue, mêlait ses sueurs brûlantes aux pluies glacées de l'automne: le sillon qu'il creusait était le monument destiné à lui survivre. Que faisait à cela mon élégante démone? Par sa magie, elle me transportait au bord du Nil, me montrait la pyramide égyptienne noyée dans le sable, comme un jour le sillon armoricain caché sous la bruyère: je m'applaudissais d'avoir placé les fables de ma félicité hors du cercle des réalités humaines. (MOT I, 96-97)

claim to uniqueness, however, he does of course recall Rousseau's "j'ose croire n'être fait comme aucun de ceux qui existent" (*ibid.*, I, 5).

[19] Note the close proximity of III, 7 ("Premier souffle de la muse") and 9-10, which initially describe the sylphide; note also, III, 15, the reference to the "tourments par qui m'arrivèrent les premières inspirations de la muse et les premières attaques des passions" (MOT I, 101).

And so the sylphide, too, comes to be associated with death and the enduring tomb. If the sylphide is most simply a woman whom he loves passionately, "à la fois vierge et amante, Eve innocente, Eve tombée, l'enchanteresse par qui me venait ma folie était un mélange de mystères et de passions," his passion takes the form of words—words that can conquer death: "Les paroles que j'adressais à cette femme auraient rendu des sens à la vieillesse, et réchauffé le marbre des tombeaux" (MOT I, 97-98).

When Chateaubriand endeavors in going to America to flee the disturbed and unsettling inactivity imposed on him by the onset of the Revolution, the sylphide accompanies him. She is there at sea in the form of the "femme inconnue": "Je me figurais qu'elle palpitait derrière ce voile de l'univers qui la cachait à mes yeux. Oh! que n'était-il en ma puissance de déchirer le rideau pour presser la femme idéalisée contre mon cœur, pour me consumer sur son sein dans cet amour, source de mes inspirations, de mon désespoir et de ma vie!" (MOT I, 215). She is there in the American wilds, where all the verbal poetry latent in her finally assumes literary form: "Or, ne m'étant attaché à aucune femme, ma sylphide obsédait encore mon imagination. Je me faisais une félicité de réaliser avec elle mes courses fantastiques dans les forêts du Nouveau-Monde. Par l'influence d'une autre nature, ma fleur d'amour, mon fantôme sans nom des bois de l'Armorique, est devenue *Atala* sous les ombrages de la Floride" (MOT I, 188). After the tragi-comic episode of the Floridiennes the sylphide reappears, once more described in a context of literature: "Je reçus mal ma sylphide généreusement accourue pour consoler un infidèle, comme Julie lorsqu'elle pardonnait à Saint-Preux ses Floridiennes de Paris" (MOT I, 267). Later, during his emigration in England, the memory of his brief encounter with Charlotte Ives does however counter for a moment the magic of the sylphide: "attachée à mes pas par ma pensée, Charlotte gracieuse, attendrie, me suivait, en les purifiant, par les sentiers de la sylphide . . . ma démone, comme un mauvais génie, se replongea dans l'abîme,"(MOT I, 372, 377) for Charlotte represents the temptation for the creator to abandon his muse:

> Au reste, en épousant Charlotte Ives, mon rôle changeait sur la terre: enseveli dans un comté de la Grande-Bretagne, je serais devenu un *gentleman* chasseur: pas une seule ligne ne serait tombée de ma plume. . . . Mon pays aurait-il beaucoup perdu à ma disparition? . . . Est-il certain que j'aie un talent véritable et que ce talent ait valu la peine du sacrifice de ma vie? Dépasserai-je ma tombe? . . . Mon ombre pourra-t-elle dire comme celle de Virgile à Dante: *"Poeta fui e cantai,* je fus poète, et je chantai!" (MOT I, 370-71, beginning, middle, end of final paragraph, X, 9)

The sylphide is clearly associated with a poetic ambition that Chateaubriand rarely expresses (even if negatively and interrogatively) with so daring a comparison. The "chœur féminin" that surrounds him after the publication of *Atala* and the *Génie du christianisme* "était mon ancienne sylphide réalisée" (MOT I, 447).

The inspiring presence of the sylphide leads Chateaubriand to an artistic ambition if anything even greater than that we see in the apposition of his aspirations as a writer and the reference to Vergil and Dante; in a parallel development, in reference to the writing of the *Martyrs*, Chateaubriand very precisely points out that he is comparing himself, as artist, to Raphael:

> Ma vie, creusée par la mort de madame de Beaumont, était demeurée vide: des formes aériennes, houris ou songes, sortant de cet abîme, me prenaient par la main et me ramenaient au temps de la sylphide. Je n'étais plus aux lieux que j'habitais, je rêvais d'autres bords. Quelque influence secrète me poussait aux régions de l'Aurore, où m'entraînaient d'ailleurs le plan de mon nouveau travail et la voix religieuse qui me releva du vœu de la villageoise, ma nourrice. Comme toutes mes facultés s'étaient accrues, comme je n'avais jamais abusé de la vie, elle surabondait de la sève de mon intelligence, et l'art, triomphant dans ma nature, ajoutait aux inspirations du poète. J'avais ce que les Pères de la Thébaïde appelaient des *ascensions* de cœur. Raphaël, (qu'on pardonne au blasphème de la similitude), Raphaël devant *la Transfiguration* seulement ébauchée sur le chevalet, n'aurait pas été plus électrisé par son chef-d'œuvre que je ne l'étais par cet Eudore et cette Cymodocée, dont je ne savais pas encore le nom et dont j'entrevoyais l'image au travers d'une atmosphère d'amour et de gloire. (MOT I, 585)

Down to his last voyages the sylphide will return, to receive in turn from the writer his passionate language, his ever greater achievements. At Altorf in 1832:

> Ces montagnes, cet orage, cette nuit sont des trésors perdus pour moi. Que de vie, cependant, je sens au fond de mon âme! Jamais, quand le sang le plus ardent coulait de mon cœur dans mes veines, je n'ai parlé le langage des passions avec autant d'énergie que je le pourrais faire en ce moment. Il me semble que je vois sortir des flancs du Saint-Gothard ma sylphide des bois de Combourg. Me viens-tu retrouver, charmant fantôme de ma jeunesse? as-tu pitié de moi? Tu le vois, je ne suis changé que de visage; toujours chimérique, dévoré d'un feu sans cause et sans aliment. Je sors du monde, et j'y entrais quand je te créai dans un moment d'extase et de délire. . . . Si tu n'es pas contente des grâces que je t'avais prodiguées, je te ferai cent fois plus séduisante; ma palette n'est pas épuisée; j'ai vu plus de beautés et je sais mieux peindre. . . . (MOT II, 581-82)

He will keep his promise to make the sylphide "cent fois plus séduisante," when he comes the next year to paint Cynthie, the last incarnation of the sylphide, the best poem Chateaubriand ever wrote.

The major theme of Time is even more frequently present throughout the *Mémoires* than the sylphide. Rather than as a fairly rigorous theme and variations it is developed in a manner that evokes the technique of the leitmotif; many of the appearances of the motif have already been noted in passages examined under other headings. One of the very few passages concerning Time that is elaborated at length is the paragraph of X, 3 (MOT I, 349) already examined in the discussion of the image of spring,[20] a paragraph dignified but bitter, elegiac and disabused; Time appears there not only with the motifs of death and love and nature but also as the inherent contradiction of the theme of spring.

Time is present from the opening of the *Mémoires d'Outre-Tombe*; already in the very title Time is related to the same yearning for death as is stressed in the paragraph just referred to. Time is implicit in the epigraph—"Sicut nubes . . . quasi naves . . . velut umbra"—as in all the motifs of passage strewn, as in Chateaubriand's other works, throughout his autobiography. The very first words of the text, "Il y a quatre ans," are a temporal marker. From his birth Chateaubriand's forehead has marked on it "la pesanteur du temps."[21] The rapid disappearance of the society and family that surrounded his childhood announces what he will note twenty times after: the rapidity with which in time all human relationships dissolve: "cette impossibilité de durée et de longueur dans les liaisons humaines," "vingt fois des sociétés se sont formées et dissoutes autour de moi" (MOT I, 24). One of the most memorable early scenes in the *Mémoires* shows the young boy suffering with his mother and sister the gloomy, mechanical, clockwork rhythm of his father's taciturn and unsociable style of life. "Je n'avais aucune heure fixe, ni pour me lever, ni pour déjeuner; j'étais censé étudier jusqu'à midi: la plupart du temps je ne faisais rien," while his father got up at 4:00, had his coffee at 5:00, worked and ate at appointed times, and in the winter evenings walked back and forth in the somber *grand'salle*, like a ghost:

> Dix heures sonnaient à l'horloge du château: mon père s'arrêtait; le même ressort, qui avait soulevé le marteau de l'horloge, semblait avoir suspendu ses pas. Il tirait sa montre, la montait, prenait un grand flambeau d'argent surmonté d'une grande bougie, entrait un moment dans la petite tour de l'ouest, puis revenait, son flambeau à la main, et s'avançait vers sa chambre à coucher, dépendante de la petite tour de l'est. Lucile et moi, nous nous tenions sur son passage; nous l'embrassions, en lui souhaitant une bonne nuit. Il penchait vers nous sa joue sèche et creuse sans nous répondre, continuait sa route et se retirait au fond de la tour, dont nous entendions les portes se refermer sur lui. (MOT I, 83)

---

[20] *Supra*, p. 109.
[21] MOT I, 19, quoted *supra*, p. 104.

Time in all its aspects—passage, dates, duration, the clock—is thus noted from the earliest books. More profoundly Chateaubriand casts his definition of his own being in temporal terms. When he tries to find in his childhood experience the traces of his basic qualities he comes upon his extraordinary memory. I have already referred to his humiliation at having to characterize himself by a good memory, "souvent la qualité de la sottise. . . . Et néanmoins, sans la mémoire, que serions-nous? Nous oublierions nos amitiés, nos amours, nos plaisirs, nos affaires; le génie ne pourrait rassembler ses idées; le cœur le plus affectueux perdrait sa tendresse, s'il ne s'en souvenait plus; notre existence se réduirait aux moments successifs d'un présent qui s'écoule sans cesse; il n'y aurait plus de passé. O misère de nous! notre vie est si vaine qu'elle n'est qu'un reflet de notre mémoire" (MOT I, 49-50). To a sensitive man who so obviously treasures all that is here mentioned, and particularly the past, it is of crucial importance to remain fully conscious of Time and how the very modifications brought to us by the erosion as well as the alluvion of its flow affect our existence. More than any mere accretion of successive moments he wants to be a reflection of the relationship or evolution of those moments: it is in coming to understand how Time has affected him that he can seize his own coherence, his own identity.

As he comes to understand himself existing and changing in Time so he understands his own works. They too are the result of one temporal development and simultaneously the beginning of another. If they "matter" it is because they have marked their moment in time: "A mesure que ces *Mémoires* se remplissent de mes années écoulées, ils me représentent le globe inférieur d'un sablier constatant ce qu'il y a de poussière tombée de ma vie" (MOT I, 134-35): as memory retrospectively transforms moments into a life, so the metaphor for the *Mémoires* transforms grains of sand into significant parts of a whole. "En supposant que l'opinion religieuse existât telle qu'elle est à l'heure où j'écris maintenant, le *Génie du Christianisme* étant encore à faire, je le composerais tout différemment qu'il est: au lieu de rappeler les bienfaits et les institutions de notre religion au passé, je ferais voir que le christianisme est la pensée de l'avenir" (MOT I, 468)—that "Avenir du monde" towards which, one may add, the whole of the *Mémoires d'Outre-Tombe* is directed. Chateaubriand sees his own being and creative activity as something that takes its meaning in time even as it becomes part of time; so also he sees others. Napoleon, Talleyrand, Madame Récamier, and later Rancé: all will be examined and evaluated, biographically, in terms of their own historical, dated, measurable evolution in a parallel, ironical, or some other relationship with the autobiographer. For to Chateaubriand Time is that essential perspective that Pascal sought: "Le temps fait pour les hommes ce que l'espace fait pour les monuments; on ne juge bien des uns et des autres qu'à distance et au point de la perspective; trop près on ne les voit pas, trop loin on ne les voit plus" (MOT II, 243).

Time comes to assume a central place in Chateaubriand's expression of his understanding of himself and the world. How did he explain the particular struggle of sensuality and religion in his novels? By a temporal coincidence, a "hasard [qui] fit tomber entre mes mains deux livres bien divers, un *Horace* non châtié et une histoire des *Confessions mal faites* . . . hasard qui me fit connaître au même moment deux empires ennemis" (MOT I, 56, 57). Why did he leave the collège at Rennes with less regret than the collège at Dol? "Peut-être n'avais-je plus cette innocence qui nous fait un charme de tout: ma jeunesse n'était plus enveloppée dans sa fleur, le temps commençait à la déclore" (MOT I, 71). How does he understand an event of historical import like the "Etats de Bretagne" just before the Revolution? In a temporal framework of history, and so the opening pages of Book V will be strewn with dates and other temporal indications: "1787 et 1788," "depuis deux cents ans," "le dix-huitième siècle," "Louis XVI," "l'année 1786," "1614," "1651," "1614," "1786, 1787 et 1788," "1491," "1532," "1630," "1793"; everywhere it is a question of "transformation," "terme," "tendait," "convergeant," "devinrent," "hâtaient," "allait" (MOT I, 147-54). For Chateaubriand history is cyclical, and that is why his temporal juxtapositions will seem to him so normal: "l'histoire n'est qu'une répétition des mêmes faits appliqués à des hommes et à des temps divers" (MOT I, 877). "L'homme est placé dans un tableau dont le cadre ne change point, mais dont les personnages sont mobiles" (MOT II, 243).

It is not very surprising that Chateaubriand sees history in a temporal framework; but he also sees landscape that way, and his descriptions are just as temporally layered as his historical panoramas. When he describes his visit of 1802 to Marseilles he interrupts himself with a reference to another visit there, closer to the time of writing, "cette année même, 1838":

> Au bas de ce rocher, couvert autrefois d'une forêt chantée par Lucain, je n'ai point reconnu Marseille: dans ses rues droites, longues et larges, je ne pouvais plus m'égarer. Le port était encombré de vaisseaux; j'y aurais à peine trouvé, il y a trente-six ans, une *nave*, conduite par un descendant de Pythéas, pour me transporter en Chypre comme Joinville: au rebours des hommes, le temps rajeunit les villes. J'aimais mieux ma vieille Marseille, avec ses souvenirs des Bérenger, du duc d'Anjou, du roi René, de Guise et d'Epernon, avec les monuments de Louis XIV et les vertus de Belzunce; les rides me plaisaient sur son front. Peut-être qu'en regrettant les années qu'elle a perdues, je ne fais que pleurer celles que j'ai trouvées. Marseille m'a reçu

gracieusement, il est vrai; mais l'émule d'Athènes est devenue trop jeune pour moi. (MOT I, 482-83)

The basic sense of the description (in some ways comparable to Baudelaire's observation of several years later that "la forme d'une ville / Change plus vite, hélas! que le cœur d'un mortel"), the contrasting changes in observed and observer, 1802 and 1838, is reinforced, positively ("le port encombré de vaisseaux") and negatively ("je ne pouvais plus m'égarer"), by the rude juxtaposition and confusion of at least ten periods: 1838—"ce rocher," first century—"Lucain," 1802—"il y a trente-six ans," fourth century B.C.—"Pythéas," thirteenth century—"Joinville," "le duc d'Anjou," fourteenth century—"Bérenger," fifteenth century—"le roi René," sixteenth century—"Guise," "Epernon," seventeenth century—"Louis XIV," eighteenth century—"Belzunce":[22] this is a remarkable descriptive stratification or "alluvionnement," as Jean-Pierre Richard has used the term.[23]

The bravura of this description may be usefully compared to the temporally much simpler but perhaps—for that simplicity itself—more evocative passage, "Qu'arriva-t-il, il y a dix-huit siècles, à pareille heure et aux mêmes lieux" (MOT I, 500), studied in Chapter 2:[24] in that paragraph the temporal juxtapositions of two chronological layers that split into five have been made to form a more unified impression of disappearances.

Even in the detail of style the importance of Time as a way of understanding is emphasized, such as when "le temps" is used as the subject of a verb of action. In the passage quoted three paragraphs above, "le temps commençait à . . . déclore [la fleur de ma jeunesse]" (MOT I, 71); "le temps jette une obscurité inévitable sur les chefs-d'œuvre dramatiques vieillissants" (MOT I, 459); "le temps m'avait ravagé comme le reste" (MOT I, 928).[25] Similarly, among other cases in which an expression signifying Time stands, personified, as the subject of the verb: "Les siècles s'asseyent d'ordinaire devant le portrait d'un grand homme, ils l'achèvent par un travail long et successif" (MOT I, 1009); or, much further on, "Il sort de notre vie un gémissement indéfinissable: les années sont une complainte longue, triste et à même refrain" (MOT II, 891).

The idea of temporal accretions or destruction is so readily an aspect of

[22] May I express my indebtedness here once for all to the wonderful Indexes in the Pléiade MOT.

[23] *Paysage de Chateaubriand*, pp. 104-5.

[24] Cf. *supra*, p. 28 and n. 15.

[25] Cf. this sentence from the "Avenir du monde" which does not seem to have been kept in the final version of the Conclusion of the *Mémoires*: "Tandis qu'ils [les Français impatients] bouleversent, le temps arrange, il met de l'ordre dans le désordre, rejette le fruit vert, détache le fruit mûr, sasse et crible les hommes, les mœurs et les idées (MOT II, 1051).

Chateaubriand's way of looking at and understanding things that he rather automatically inserts such considerations even when they are not really related to the idea he is developing:

> Si je revoyais aujourd'hui les Etats-Unis, je ne les reconnaîtrais plus: là où j'ai laissé des forêts, je trouverais des champs cultivés. . . . Chactas pourrait être aujourd'hui député au Congrès. . . .
>
> La population des Etats-Unis s'est accrue de dix ans en dix ans, depuis 1790 jusqu'en 1820, dans la proportion de trente-cinq individus sur cent. On présume qu'en 1830, elle sera de douze millions huit cent soixante-quinze mille âmes. En continuant à doubler tous les vingt-cinq ans, elle serait en 1855 de vingt-cinq millions sept cent cinquante mille âmes, et vingt-cinq ans plus tard, en 1880, elle dépasserait cinquante millions.[26] (MOT I, 269-71; in a section of Book VIII dated 1822)

Under the general heading, "le Temps," there are many subdivisions one might make, many lesser themes that represent one aspect or another of Time. Hours: not so much clock time as the rapid markers of an inevitable passing. "Les heures fuient et m'entraînent; je n'ai pas même la certitude de pouvoir achever ces *Mémoires*" (passage dated 1817, Book III, 1, MOT I, 76-77).[27] Or, at the end of a paragraph and chapter mentioning the later death of Fontanes while introducing young Chateaubriand's literary acquaintances in revolutionary Paris, we find a veritable little anthology of time-related expressions: "Notre existence est d'une telle fuite, que si nous n'écrivons pas le soir l'événement du matin, le travail nous encombre et nous n'avons plus le temps de le mettre à jour. Cela ne nous empêche pas de gaspiller nos années, de jeter au vent ces heures qui sont pour l'homme les semences de l'éternité" (MOT I, 143). After the hours of the day, then, the years of a lifetime that they represent; the years will destroy Chateaubriand as surely as the Revolution destroyed his brother. Here is a striking literary image that again ends a paragraph and a chapter: "Mais si les hommes ont fait tomber la tête de mon aîné, de mon

---

[26] Chateaubriand's prediction is quite accurate. The census of the population of the continental United States (quoted in the 1946 edition of the *Encyclopedia Americana*) for this period is as follows:

1790:	3,929,214	1810:	7,239,881	1840:	17,069,453	1870:	39,818,449
1800:	5,308,483	1820:	9,638,453	1850:	23,191,876	1880:	50,155,783
		1830:	12,866,020	1860:	31,443,321		

A comic passage that may be compared to this one in its relatively irrelevant use of dates is in Book IX, 7, MOT I, 310-11, where the author, emigrating with his brother, visits the Tournay cathedral and recounts various amusing legends.

[27] A parallel juxtaposition of the flight of the Hours and the fate of his writings appears in the "Avenir du monde" of 1834 (MOT II, 1052): "Prophète, en quittant le monde, je trace mes prédictions sur mes heures tombantes; feuilles séchées et légères que le souffle de l'éternité aura bientôt emportées." A variant of this sentence, slightly less pessimistic ("dispersées" replacing "emportées"), occurs in XXXVIII, 14 (MOT II, 707).

parrain, avant l'heure, les ans n'épargneront pas la mienne: déjà mon front se dépouille; je sens un Ugolin, le temps, penché sur moi qui me ronge le crâne: . . . *como'l pan per fame si manduca*" (MOT I, 343). And Chateaubriand sees the flow of Time in political history, where "siècles" replace "ans," to be as irreversible and uncontrollable as in his own personal life; his political conservatism, he will often tell us, is anything but reactionary:

> J'ai peur que la Restauration ne se perde par les idées contraires à celles que j'exprime ici; la manie de s'en tenir au passé, manie que je ne cesse de combattre, n'aurait rien de funeste si elle ne renversait que moi en me retirant la faveur du prince; mais elle pourrait bien renverser le trône. L'immobilité politique est impossible; force est d'avancer avec l'intelligence humaine. Respectons la majesté du temps; contemplons avec vénération les siècles écoulés, rendus sacrés par la mémoire et les vestiges de nos pères; toutefois n'essayons pas de rétrograder vers eux, car ils n'ont plus rien de notre nature réelle, et si nous prétendions les saisir, ils s'évanouiraient. . . . (MOT I, 251-52)

The paragraph continues to its conclusion with a description of the opening of Charlemagne's tomb in 1450: "On toucha le fantôme; il tomba en poussière."[28] (Yet just as Chateaubriand's whole presentation of his childhood and youth in the *Mémoires d'Outre-Tombe* is filled with nostalgia, this plea for political progress and advance towards the future occurs abruptly right in the middle of a chapter devoted principally to regretting the disappearance of those American "colonies, qui seraient aujourd'hui pour nous une source inépuisable de prospérité." There are times when one understands the exasperation of certain contemporaries of Chateaubriand the politician!)

Although Time is in constant flight, many of its manifestations are cyclic: so the Seasons, which young Chateaubriand associates closely with his moods and states of consciousness. Chapter 12 of Book III is devoted to "Mes joies de l'automne":

> Plus la saison était triste, plus elle était en rapport avec moi. . . .
> Un caractère moral s'attache aux scènes de l'automne: ces feuilles qui tombent comme nos ans, ces fleurs qui se fanent comme nos heures, ces nuages qui fuient comme nos illusions, cette lumière qui s'affaiblit comme

[28] The same respect for "la majesté du temps" coupled with a similar appreciation of the inescapability of the changes brought to the social order by Time's passing can be seen at the other end of the *Mémoires* (XXXVIII, 14, MOT II, 707-8, a passage dated eleven years later): "Si les hautes races approchaient de leur terme . . . ne serait-il pas mieux que, par une fin digne de leur grandeur, elles se retirassent dans la nuit du passé avec les siècles? Prolonger ses jours au delà d'une éclatante illustration ne vaut rien. . . . Pour mourir beau, il faut mourir jeune . . ." for otherwise one risks being mocked by the "enfants du printemps."

notre intelligence, ce soleil qui se refroidit comme nos amours, ces fleuves qui
se glacent comme notre vie, ont des rapports secrets avec nos destinées.
  Je voyais avec un plaisir indicible le retour de la saison des tempêtes. . . .
(MOT I, 96)

The "retour" is of a particular kind, however: the turn of a spiral rather
than a circle for the Chateaubriand to whom autumn represents more
another turn of the screw than a renewal. Spring, as was noted earlier, also
leads from the idea of fecundity to vanity, passage, death, although even
in his later years Chateaubriand can associate spring with love and hope:
in April 1829, at the beginning of Holy Week, he writes to Madame
Récamier from Rome, "Que n'êtes-vous ici pour entendre avec moi les
beaux chants de douleur! Nous irions nous promener dans les déserts de
la campagne de Rome, maintenant couverts de verdure et de fleurs.
Toutes les ruines semblent rajeunir avec l'année: je suis du nombre"
(MOT II, 339).

  Time is then a fact of life to which Chateaubriand is particularly sensitive. Though he tends to submit himself to its inevitability, Time is occasionally, and to a certain extent, dominated by Chateaubriand the Wit-
ness, who because of his very continuity can assume and unite in himself
diverse moments of Time:

> Ainsi, j'ai été placé assez singulièrement dans la vie pour avoir assisté aux
> courses de la *Quintaine* et à la proclamation des *Droits de l'Homme*; pour avoir
> vu la milice bourgeoise d'un village de Bretagne et la garde nationale de
> France, la bannière des seigneurs de Combourg et le drapeau de la Révolu-
> tion. Je suis comme le dernier témoin des mœurs féodales. (II, 2, MOT I, 51)

In a passage such as this one can see just how, finally, the great theme of
Time is related to the question of unity and diversity, confrontation,
juxtaposition,[29] and assimilation in the *Mémoires d'Outre-Tombe*. To each
man is allotted a certain portion of Time. It was Chateaubriand's destiny
to have his Time correspond to a period of divergencies in society so great
as to be practically irreconcilable. They are reconciled, however, to the
extent that they did come all in his lifetime, that he did contemplate them
all.

> Je me suis rencontré entre deux siècles, comme au confluent de deux
> fleuves; j'ai plongé dans leurs eaux troublées, m'éloignant à regret du vieux
> rivage où je suis né, nageant avec espérance vers une rive inconnue. (end
> XLIV, 8, MOT II, 936)

This temporal advantage that has fallen to Chateaubriand not only en-

---

[29] (Among notable juxtapositions of an historical order see those bird's-eye surveys scat-
tered through the MOT under the title, "Incidences.")

courages him to extend into the past and future, beyond the bounds of his own life, his search for traces of himself, but also permits him to associate himself with history, to sense that his own history is parallel to the development of human society.

> J'étais né pendant l'accomplissement de ces faits. Deux nouveaux empires, la Prusse et la Russie, m'ont à peine devancé d'un demi-siècle sur la terre; la Corse est devenue française à l'instant où j'ai paru; je suis arrivé au monde vingt jours après Bonaparte. Il m'amenait avec lui. J'allais entrer dans la marine en 1783 quand la flotte de Louis XVI surgit à Brest: elle apportait les actes de l'état civil d'une nation éclose sous les ailes de la France. Ma naissance se rattache à la naissance d'un homme et d'un peuple: pâle reflet que j'étais d'une immense lumière. (first paragraph of XLIV, 2, MOT II, 916)

However pale he might allow that his "reflection" is, this simultaneity of his with the History of France gives him a privileged position of observer and knower, from a perspective that, in a somewhat different context, he will not hesitate to compare with God's: ". . . la politique fait des solitaires, comme la religion fait des anachorètes. Quand l'homme habite le désert, il trouve en lui quelque lointaine image de l'être infini qui, vivant seul dans l'immensité, voit s'accomplir les révolutions des mondes" (MOT II, 86).

But just as, ruthlessly, the seasons return, this consolation of being the observer will not eliminate the basic suffering of continual loss, brought by Time, the Time this time of Ecclesiastes (3:2, 6), "A time to be born, and a time to die . . . a time to get, and a time to lose," "tempus nascendi, et tempus moriendi . . . tempus acquirendi, et tempus perdendi": "Combien rapidement et que de fois nous changeons d'existence et de chimère! Des amis nous quittent, d'autres leur succèdent; nos liaisons varient: il y a toujours un temps où nous ne possédions rien de ce que nous possédons, un temps où nous n'avons rien de ce que nous eûmes. L'homme n'a pas une seule et même vie; il en a plusieurs mises bout à bout, et c'est sa misère" (MOT I, 103). The continuity of a single life is eventually not strong enough to stand up under the demands of Life, and the unity imposed on diversity becomes a new fragmentation, united only by the repetitious suffering of loss after loss. Chateaubriand's confidence on beginning Part IV, "Il ne tiendra qu'à moi de renouer les deux bouts de mon existence" (MOT II, 489), cannot go far beyond his prose (where he does have the power to "confondre des époques éloignées" and "mêler des illusions d'âges divers") in order to encompass his existence: like Lafayette in 1815, "il n'était pas en son pouvoir de souder les deux bouts de la chaîne rompue du temps" (MOT I, 968-69).

The same was after all true of Napoleon, whose life is, in terms of Time as well, correlative to Chateaubriand's. "L'Homme du temps" (MOT I,

490)—even "ce premier homme des temps modernes, cet homme de tous les siècles" (MOT I, 1021); the emperor by whose second marriage "le passé se réunit à l'avenir" (MOT I, 776); the Napoleon who "a dérangé jusqu'à l'avenir," who "est un obstacle aux événements futurs" (MOT I, 1007, 1008)—even Napoleon was destroyed by Time: "Pour la vengeance, il ne s'agissait que de gagner un mois, que d'attendre les premiers frimas. . . . Durant trente-cinq jours . . . il s'était oublié: c'était apparemment les jours nécessaires pour changer le sort d'un homme pareil. Pendant ce temps-là l'astre de sa destinée s'inclinait. . . . Cependant Kutuzoff nous poursuivait mollement. Wilson pressait-il le général russe d'agir, le général répondait: 'Laissez venir la neige'" (MOT I, 810, 813, 816). One knows how Victor Hugo was drawn to this description.

For the autobiographer there is then a certain hope in art, which is timeless, whether it be the art of a Titian, holding "encore d'une main ferme, à Venise, son pinceau d'un siècle, vainqueur des siècles" (MOT II, 240), or of the epic poem that is simply "detached"[30] from the subservience of history to Time. But for Chateaubriand, even Chateaubriand Memorialist, Time is still indifferent ("Le temps nous engloutit et continue tranquillement son cours" [MOT I, 847]) and relentless ("Mais tandis que j'écrivais ceci le temps a marché" [MOT I, 1029]); life in Time is at best a doubtful struggle:

> Et moi qui me débats contre le temps, moi qui cherche à lui faire rendre compte de ce qu'il a vu, moi qui écris ceci si loin des événements passés, sous le règne de Philippe, héritier contrefait d'un si grand héritage, que suis-je entre les mains de ce Temps, de ce grand dévorateur des siècles que je croyais arrêtés, de ce Temps qui me fait pirouetter dans les espaces avec lui? (MOT I, 878: end XXII, 16)

---

[30] Near the end of his *Life of Napoleon* Chateaubriand writes, "Ores donc que, détaché de son temps, son histoire est finie et que son épopée commence, allons le voir mourir: quittons l'Europe; suivons-le sous le ciel de son apothéose!" (MOT I, 1010.)

The grandest efforts of poetry are where the imagination
is called forth, not to produce a distinct form, but a strong
working of the mind . . . ; the result being what the poet
wishes to impress, namely, the substitution of a sublime
feeling of the unimaginable for a mere image.

Coleridge, "The Grandest Efforts of Poetry"

7 Chateaubriand's Poetry

"Nos ans et nos souvenirs sont étendus en couches régulières et parallèles,
à différentes profondeurs de notre vie, déposés par les flots du temps qui
passe [*sic*] successivement sur nous" (MOT II, 746).

Chateaubriand's poetry is a poetry of parallels. His subjects are "parallel
lives": "Caractère des Athéniens et des Français," "Parallèle de Virgile et
de Racine," the Life of Napoleon in the *Mémoires d'Outre-Tombe*,
Chateaubriand at Chambord in the *Vie de Rancé*. He makes of his autobiography a set of parallels. His repeated motifs—the waves of the sea,
the clouds in the sky, echoes and reverberations—are composites of
parallel pulsations and movements. He favors metaphors and images
whose sense is determined by parallel analogy.

Chateaubriand's parallels are poetry, if poetry can be considered the art
of the suggested, not spoken; of the evoked, not described; of the hinted,
not demonstrated. For when Chateaubriand traces parallels he usually
leaves it to his reader to find the shape, the picture.[1] Parallels are the lines
that meet only at infinity, and it is that infinity which more often than not
Chateaubriand finds in himself. Where Rancé's worldly past and Rancé's
austerity, Chateaubriand's flesh and Chateaubriand's ideal, come to-

[1] Cf. Cohen, *Structure du langage poétique*, pp. 179, 182, *et passim*: ". . . cette unité émotion-
nelle que la prose ignore et que la poésie suscite, ce 'sens atmosphérique' qui est le sens de
tout poème . . . c'est dans et par l'inconséquence qu'elle apparaît." "La poétisation est un
processus à deux faces, corrélatives et simultanées: écart et réduction, déstructuration et
restructuration. Pour que le poème fonctionne poétiquement, il faut que dans la *conscience du
lecteur la signification soit à la fois perdue et retrouvée*." Cohen calls the resulting meaning
"l'analogie subjective, le signifié émotionnel ou sens poétique" (p. 215).

gether, there we find the Chateaubriand who is painted in *La Vie de Rancé*. Chateaubriand is not the voyager, not the writer, not the statesman, not the elder statesman of the opposition: he is the convergence of the four careers. Chateaubriand is not the splendid ambassador in London, nor is he the starving émigré he there recalls: he is the *Mémoires d'Outre-Tombe* altogether which includes everything: "Quand ne m'occuperai-je plus que d'achever les mémoires de ma vie et ma vie aussi, comme dernière page de mes *Mémoires?*" (MOT II, 332).

But those *Mémoires d'Outre-Tombe*, the book, only become a whole, a unity, an existence, when they have been read and assimilated by the reader. It is the reader only who learns to know the Chateaubriand described by Chateaubriand under the name of Napoleon, or of Chactas who is the hater and admirer of Christianity, or of Rancé who is first the reformed and then the reformer. Chateaubriand the poet sings but it is for us to hear. He evokes, we see. He suggests, we understand.

Chateaubriand is one of the first modern poets to make the demands on his readers that the poets of the end of his century are more famous for.[2] His contemporaries in literature will come later. Stendhal was wrong: instead of not being read at all a hundred years after,[3] Chateaubriand was then read better—as of course Stendhal was himself. Chateaubriand is a perfect example of what Gertrude Stein spoke about in "How Writing Is Written":[4] the truly creative writer's great work is what is "perfectly easy to see"—two generations later. Chateaubriand the great "pre-Romantic" may well turn out to have been more significantly a pre-"post-Romantic."

For he developed a new way of writing about his themes, a way that, partially, becomes his theme. I do not refer to his statement that the *Génie du christianisme* began, as well as a religious revolution, a "révolution qui menace notre langue, car il ne pouvait y avoir renouvellement dans l'idée qu'il n'y eût innovation dans le style" (MOT I, 664): there he was speaking of the new harmony, color, vivacity, and exoticism of his prose which he always felt his imitators and followers developed further to the disaster point.[5] I refer rather to his choice of the abrupt, changing, juxtaposed, dissonant, and discontinuous as a method for presenting parallels: those structures that have been the subject of the preceding chapters.

---

[2] Cf. Cohen, *op. cit.*, p. 172: "C'est à partir du romantisme que la grande poésie a commencé d'user de l'inconséquence comme procédé systématique." For his example he takes Hugo's "Booz endormi"; but much of his analysis would apply admirably to Chateaubriand, according to Cohen's own (p. 149) claim that "la prose littéraire n'est qu'une poésie modérée."

[3] Stendhal, *Vie de Henry Brulard*, p. 194, and *Journal*, p. 1212, in *Oeuvres intimes*, "Pléiade."

[4] Reprinted in Maugham's *Introduction to Modern English and American Literature*, pp. 356-65.

[5] For a useful summary of his views on this matter see Lynes, *Chateaubriand as a Critic of French Literature*, pp. 84-98.

Four particularly subtle and penetrating twentieth-century readers of Chateaubriand's work have commented on these structures from four rather different and complementary perspectives; though they are all referring to parts of Chateaubriand's last works, they may appropriately be recalled here in the discussion of the unity of Chateaubriand's literary work, since they suggest to us how the writer, through divergence, has found unity. These critics speak of rupture, of superposition, of richness, of spontaneity as maps to the perspectives of Chateaubriand's literary landscape.

For Jean-Pierre Richard, in *Paysage de Chateaubriand*, "A mesure que Chateaubriand vieillit, dans les *Mémoires*, et surtout dans la *Vie de Rancé*, il découvre la puissance d'une rhétorique de l'abrupt, liée à une littérature du fragment, et . . . à un fantastique de l'hétérogène. C'est désormais la rupture qui commande, non l'écho: ou plutôt l'écho devra naître indirectement, quasi obliquement, de la rupture même."[6] Richard finds the resulting "correspondances" evolving "à travers des espaces de plus en plus scandaleusement raréfiés." Indeed if we find Chateaubriand's a poetry of parallels, "rupture," separation, is a sine qua non: parallels cannot be superimposed. To achieve variety in parallels, however, the writer experiments with seeing how far they can be spaced without the reader losing consciousness of their relationship. And this is how it becomes possible for Chateaubriand to become contemporary with later readers, whose eyes have become accustomed to more "scandalously" wide spaces.

Julien Gracq, in a remarkable short essay of 1960,[7] uses a different metaphor; by speaking in terms of planes rather than lines, he can use the image of superposition to evoke, not as much this time the act of tracing the structures we examined as the result of viewing them.

> Un monde . . . où tout ce qui est . . . se voit contesté, mordu au cœur par ce qui a été. Le mouvement de l'imagination de Chateaubriand est toujours commandé par la même pente: sur toute scène, sur tout paysage, sur tout haut lieu affectif qu'elle se propose, elle fait glisser successivement, comme autant de *négatifs*, une, puis deux, trois, quatre lames superposées aux couleurs du souvenir,—et, comme quand on fait tourner rapidement un disque peint aux couleurs du spectre, elle obtient par cette rapide superposition tonale une espèce d'annulation qui reste vibrante, un *blanc* tout frangé d'une subtile irisation marginale qui est la couleur du temps propre aux *Mémoires*, et qui fait d'elles et de la *Vie de Rancé* le plus chatoyant hymne à l'impermanence qui soit dans notre littérature.

---

[6]   Richard, *Paysage de Chateaubriand*, p. 139.
[7]   Gracq, "Le grand Paon," in *Préférences*, p. 157.

The procedure that is "rupture," the effect that is the "couleur du temps," are the medium and the message that furnish unity in impermanence, stability in plurality. Gracq's image is a suggestive one, and one may turn momentarily from the resultant white of his experiment on light and color to the "irisation marginale" that he does not fail to evoke as well. For there is the abundance, there is the richness that Marie-Jeanne Durry wrote about with such sympathy in *La Vieillesse de Chateaubriand*. Noting the diversity brought into the *Mémoires* by constant retouching and additions over forty years, she notes that as the partial result of such a method the *Mémoires* seem written from beginning to end by a man who remains the same age.[8] And then she notes (referring more particularly, it is true, to the *Vie de Rancé* and the *Essai sur la littérature anglaise*—but the latter work especially and the later parts of the *Mémoires* have much in common):

> Osons lâcher le mot: ces livres sont amusants; leur pêle-mêle de richesse offre à l'esprit un perpétuel divertissement. . . . Qu'on s'y résigne: de plus en plus Chateaubriand édifie en juxtaposant. . . . Il cultive toutes les formes de la discontinuité, les digressions, les développements auxquels un mot sert de prétexte, les grosses transitions, passerelles de fortune sur un hiatus, et l'absence de transitions. On y éprouve un plaisir de saveur un peu sauvage. Moins de fondu, plus d'imprévu. Jamais on ne se noie dans la fadeur. . . . Cette grande allure saccadée, cette composition à surprises et à foucades n'a jamais pour rançon l'incohérence. Jamais Chateaubriand ne cesse de savoir où il va. Ni il ne se livre les yeux bandés et la bouche béante à des vociférations pythiques, ni il ne permet à son œuvre la plus disloquée d'être cohue ou chaos. . . . Il garde le contrôle littéraire de son plus réel délire. Et de même, il est un conscient organisateur de désordre.[9]

Richness is a quality at all points apparent in Chateaubriand's work: he is one of the generous, the abundant writers. His first great new style, the style of *Atala* and the *Génie*, proposed a diversity and high color instantly famous. The firmness and leanness of his polemical writings are a field for learned investigation still largely unexplored. The variety and daring of his word play in the writings of his old age is stunning for new admirers in each generation of readers. The breadth of his subjects and encyclopedic nature of his literary interests (turned, it is true, largely to the past, and to historical or "philosophique" writings rather than belles-lettres) are considerable. Then when he concocts from all this a pot-pourri of themes, ideas, notions, motifs, the richness is multiplied in a way powerfully pleasing to readers willing to accept a mixture that may tend dangerously towards the indigestible, that is clearly heady, that will never please all

---

[8] Durry, *La Vieillesse de Chateaubriand*, I, 527.
[9] *Ibid.*, pp. 529-30.

partakers. There is in Chateaubriand a distant cousin of Rabelais as well as Rimbaud.

And the concoction is at once spontaneous and contrived with infinite care. Gilbert Boutet has written passionately, about the "Invocation à Cynthie," the following characterization, quite applicable to all the impassioned and evocative passages that have been the special concern of the present study:

> Si les *Mémoires* s'établissaient d'emblée et définitivement dans le passé pour redescendre au fil du temps, ils seraient linéaires et plats. La profondeur, le volume de l'œuvre sont créés par les communications qui s'établissent entre les plans temporels. . . . On sait que Proust . . . retrouvait [dans certains passages] ce 'saisissement' immédiat et cette présence totale de la réminiscence, qui sont, pour lui, les signes de sa nécessité et garantissent la vérité de sa révélation.
>
> Ces caractères n'apparaissent-ils pas, [dans "Cynthie"], dans leur extrême dépouillement? Le souvenir semble surgir avec une spontanéité absolue, sans lien avec les circonstances biographiques du moment, et n'en laisser dans l'esprit aucun vestige. Il y retombe et s'y éteint tout aussi brusquement. Il y a la gratuité, la certitude et la fragilité d'une extase. . . . c'est encore affaire de composition que de montrer l'étrangeté réciproque de deux mondes. Composer, c'est supprimer et l'indifférent et l'insignifiant.[10]

"Gratuitousness" and "spontaneity" are another way of considering the impressions that result from the abruptness of the "ruptures" and the "superposition" we have been examining; they are a major source of the pleasing diversity or richness that is the subject of the present analysis. Boutet's term "extase" is appropriate to the degree that it characterizes all true lyric poetry, and here it places a premium on the fanciful flight shown in the many passages and compositions that have been under discussion. The word must not, however, blur the fact that any "ecstasy" in Chateaubriand is always solidly and continuously tied to earthly reality.

In whichever manner, or manners, the reader may choose to look at Chateaubriand's poetry, as a lyricism of abrupt discontinuity, of accretion, of divergent richness, of a truly free association of images, it should be apparent that, through its diversity, Chateaubriand's work is remarkably unified. It is instructive to note the convergence of the four otherwise quite different analyses that have just been cited. In the preceding chapters I have tried to suggest a parallel between the evocative stylistic discontinuity developed in a characteristic kind of paragraph, particularly in the later works that those critics referred to, and the more general effects of discontinuity apparent and resulting from juxtaposition of

[10] Boutet, "Un 'Art Poétique' de Chateaubriand, *Cynthie*," *Les Lettres romanes*, XXII, 1 (Feb. 1968), 29-30.

larger masses of material in works as different as *Atala* and the *Mémoires d'Outre-Tombe*. One could easily find a use of dissonance in the sentence or in the fabrication of images that would be a further parallel on a yet smaller scale, and even a use of discordant sounds.[11] It seems clear that on a larger scale than that of the individual work, that of the writer's work in general, one can sense the juxtaposition of pagan-inspired and Christian-inspired works, or literary and polemical works, and such juxtaposition could lead quite directly to the still larger-scale juxtapositions of Chateaubriand's private life and public career, historically, politically, and perhaps even psychoanalytically viewed.

For the essential unity of Chateaubriand's poetic achievement must, I think, be sought in discontinuity, and a surprising number of his critics from his time to ours have found it there. It is a discontinuity of perception, of character, and of method.

Chateaubriand does not tend to perceive continuities but rather reflections in mirrors facing each other on two sides of the object. This is a principal source of the parallels, contrasts, oppositions so common in his works. In the projected *Natchez* a primitive pagan society stands facing foreign and Christian civilization; in the finished *Atala* an Indian brave hates Christianity for stealing Atala from him (as does she) and succumbs (without becoming, nevertheless, until much later a convert) to the beauty and poetry of Père Aubry's Mission: there is no more continuity between the two attitudes of Chactas than there is between what we understand of the earliest *Natchez* and what we read in its most complete parts. We have examined the similar double and contrary point of view in *René*. "Toutes les grandes œuvres de Chateaubriand sont en réalité des compromis entre ce démon si prodigieusement fécond et inspiré, d'où vient la matière, et l'ambassadeur qui va ensuite s'efforcer de maquiller, de baptiser cette progéniture demi-sauvage. L'exemple le plus clair d'un tel baptême est évidemment l'utilisation dans *Le Génie du Christianisme* des deux épisodes des *Natchez*. . . ."[12]

Chateaubriand is as conscious as his critics of his perception of opposites, making already in the *Essai sur les révolutions* a clear and lucid statement of it. When he defended there, in the paragraph quoted above in Chapter 2,[13] one of his famous "rapprochements," that of the reforms of Lycurgus compared to those of the French Revolution, he argued first that his method of comparison gave the reader the facts he needed to draw

---

[11] See, for instance, Mourot, *Rythme et sonorité dans les Mémoires d'Outre-Tombe*, pp. 139-41 and n. 3 on pp. 235-36; Lehtonen, *L'Expression imagée dans l'œuvre de Chateaubriand*, pp. 499-500.

[12] Butor, "Chateaubriand et l'ancienne Amérique," in *Répertoire II*, p. 154.

[13] *Supra*, p. 39.

his own conclusions; after this logical defence of a *rapprochement* he gave stylistically another one with the sudden expanding concluding image of the reader of history who "ressemble à un homme voyageant dans le désert, à travers ces bois fabuleux de l'antiquité qui prédisoient l'avenir."[14] He saw his readers facing two sets of facts; he saw himself facing the oracle. In commenting the *Essai* Sainte-Beuve exclaimed over the abuse of "rapprochements," "l'antithèse historique," "le parallèle." "L'abus porté à ce point est plus qu'un accident, et trahit un tour d'esprit, un pli bien marqué: il lui en restera toujours quelque chose."[15] And it did remain through to the end, although the confrontations were especially developed, as has been seen even in the structure of the paragraph, in the later works. Michel Butor in turn[16] has pointed out a model of narrative structure that, as easily noted in *Atala*, forms another kind of discontinuity of perception: the structure in which religion snatches the beloved from the lover just when he is about to possess her at last. In the *Martyrs*, Butor points out, the saints descending from heaven play the same rôle as Père Aubry; he finds more dramatic yet the death of Madame de Montbazon, a death that Chateaubriand suggested so delicately in the following brief paragraph of the *Vie de Rancé*, opening out characteristically by juxtaposed quotation and metaphor towards a world of legend and allegory:

> Madame de Montbazon fut l'objet de la passion de Rancé jusqu'au jour où il vit flotter un cilice parmi les nuages de la jeunesse. "Tandis que je m'entretiens de ces choses criminelles, dit un anachorète, les abeilles volent le long des ruisseaux, pour ramasser le miel si doux à ma langue qui prononce tant de paroles injustes."[17]

Discontinuity in perception is again an important aspect of Chateaubriand as descriptive writer. Learned editions of his travel writings make it quite clear that in America as in the Near East he sees partly with his own eyes and partly with the eyes of former describers, and that he alternates or combines the two witnesses by means of a style that is often more persuasive than any objective truth. On rare occasions we are able to observe him struggling to unify the two. Jean Thoraval, in an article entitled "Chateaubriand Paysagiste d'après ses variantes,"[18] traces the development of his famous description in the *Itinéraire de Paris à Jérusalem* of the River Jordan, from the state where "ce descriptif . . . en même temps un imaginatif . . . ne sauroit s'empêcher d'évoquer spontanément des prolongements et des perspectives qui débordent le cadre de la chose

[14] *Essai sur les révolutions*, in *Oeuvres*, ed. Ladvocat, I, 86.
[15] Sainte-Beuve, *Chateaubriand et son groupe littéraire*, I, 122-23.
[16] Butor, *Répertoire II*, p. 192.
[17] *Vie de Rancé*, ed. Letessier, p. 80.
[18] In BSC, I (1957), 32.

vue. Lorsqu'il se trouve en face du Jourdain, son imagination l'entraîne vers le spectacle qu'il n'a pu aller contempler par suite du refus de ses guides: l'embouchure du fleuve se jetant dans la mer Morte," to a state, no longer expressible in a characteristic period, in which a series of short, lean phrases depict exactly his astonishment at the sight:

Journal de Jérusalem

Je m'approchai et j'aperçus couler, profondément encaissé entre deux rives de sable, un fleuve jaune, presque sans mouvement, roulant avec lenteur une eau épaisse, dans un lit de 400 à 500 pieds de largeur, et se traînant comme à regret vers le lac empoisonné où il allait s'engloutir.

Itinéraire de Paris à Jérusalem

. . . je vis un fleuve jaune que j'avais peine à distinguer de l'arène de ses deux rives. Il était profondément encaissé, et roulait avec lenteur une onde épaissie: c'était le Jourdain. (ORV II, 1006)

"Un véritable tic d'imagination et de pensée," "une figure, à la fois de rhétorique et d'existence,"[19] is Jean-Pierre Richard's summation of Chateaubriand's tendency toward "rapprochements." The *rapprochement* is the literary structure related to the mechanism of the "écho" that Richard analyses, echo which permits Chateaubriand to find himself resounding throughout all historical and geographical space. This space of resonance is the particular domain of memory that can visit and vivify, that excellent memory "étonnante et cruelle à la fois" that we earlier saw Chateaubriand marveling at.[20] Chateaubriand himself marked the point of contact between his perception of nature and his character in those earlier quoted remarks about memory, "sans la mémoire, que serions-nous? . . . le génie ne pourrait rassembler ses idées" (MOT I, 49-50)— words that receive an added emphasis from the fact that they appear in an addition between two paragraphs of the text of the "manuscript of 1826." The cliché expression "rassembler ses idées" takes its full meaning here: at the moment of perception ideas are separated, disunited; the "génie" must bring them together again.

It is in connection with this rôle that we can also speak of discontinuity in relation to the character of Chateaubriand the writer. Having perceived discontinuity in himself and in the world outside, he makes his life the process of trying to reunite. Certain human abilities, like memory, certain moral qualities, like fidelity, become all-important. When, as in the quota-

---

[19] Richard, *Paysage de Chateaubriand*, p. 121. Cf. Lehtonen, *L'Expression imagée dans l'œuvre de Chateaubriand*, p. 122: "Dans *René*, l'antithèse n'est pas une simple figure de rhétorique: elle traduit les contradictions et les paradoxes d'une âme qui prend conscience de son propre mystère. . . . Son règne dans l'œuvre de Chateaubriand semble commencer avec *René*."
[20] *Supra*, pp. 44, 104, 118.

tion, "sans la mémoire . . . il n'y aurait plus de passé," the discontinuity is in time, memory is the reuniting principle in life and analogy the principle in writing. Discontinuity in space is satisfied by the voyage; in writing this discontinuity is overcome by "rapprochement." The metaphor which results from a juxtaposition is the stylistic equivalent of the "reassembling" of separate ideas; metaphor is the distant brought close, time-as-separation capsized.

Chateaubriand often writes of the discontinuities in his own being that are reflected in his writings. "Si mon imagination était naturellement religieuse, mon esprit était sceptique," he writes in the "Digression Philosophique" of the *Mémoires d'Outre-Tombe* (I, 1070) that about 1840 he removed from the section speaking of the *Génie du christianisme*. While openness to the charms of religious art and philosophical skepticism are by no means necessarily contrary, they can be used as the banners of opposing armies; it must be admitted that in his early works, including the *Génie*, Chateaubriand did fly them in such a manner. "Dans l'*Essai* [*sur les révolutions*], mon indépendance en religion et en politique est complète; j'examine tout: *républicain*, je sers la monarchie; *philosophe*, j'honore la religion. Ce ne sont point là des contradictions, ce sont des conséquences forcées de l'incertitude de la théorie et de la certitude de la pratique chez les hommes. . . . Mes actes ont été de l'ancienne cité, mes pensées de la nouvelle; les premiers de mon devoir, les dernières de ma nature" (MOT I, 662). He finds in himself, when forced, a political energy in the service of the royalists, and yet in him reigns "l'ennui, le dégoût de tout, le doute perpétuel. . . . J'allai à Rome chercher parmi les ruines mon autre moi-même, car il y a dans ma personne deux êtres distincts, et qui n'ont aucune communication l'un avec l'autre" (MOT II, 149).[21] The meaning of this last sentence in its place at the end of a paragraph about his departure for Rome is by no means clear, but it seems to refer in part at least to the author's conflicting desires for peace and meditation, on the one hand, and political activity on the other. Such a mixture is a perpetually surprising aspect of his last eighteen years—one thinks of his "embassies" to Prague and his trip to London in 1843; literarily such confrontations are at the origin of everything from "Cynthie" in the *Mémoires d'Outre-Tombe* to that astounding passage in *Rancé* terminating with "Rancé va quitter Chambord, il faut donc que je quitte aussi cet asile où je crains de m'être trop oublié" (ORV I, 1032). Literarily conflicts in character and experience, which in life are expressed in mobility, find expression in the themes of passage and metamorphosis that we have seen on all sides. As for all the

---

[21] Cf. passages quoted *supra*, pp. 43-44 and MOT I, 435: ". . . c'était un autre *moi*, un *moi* de mes premiers jours finis, qui jadis habita ces lieux."

temporal discontinuities everywhere apparent in his works, we saw earlier how Chateaubriand spoke of them in the context of the Revolutionary days of July, 1830; he relates them there specifically to his desire for emotional salvation:

> Pardon de tous ces souvenirs; mais peut-être la tyrannie de ma mémoire, en faisant entrer le passé dans le présent, ôte à celui-ci une partie de ce qu'il a de misérable. (MOT II, 452)

Rejoining, assembling, combining, reminding: such are the duties of "composition" imposed by the consciousness of all these divisions. They are processes susceptible of falling happily within the domain of writing. "Mon imagination allumée, se propageant sur tous les objets, ne trouvait nulle part assez de nourriture et aurait dévoré la terre et le ciel. C'est cet état moral qu'il faut maintenant décrire. Replongé dans ma jeunesse, je vais essayer de me saisir dans le passé, de me montrer tel que j'étais, tel peut-être que je regrette de n'être plus. . ." (MOT I, 85). The very fluidity of this passage, which passes curiously from the description of his childhood dreams in the medieval tower where his father made him sleep alone, to his writing of the past in the present, by means of a triple movement originating in "imagination" (which is the source first of fears and terrors, then daydreams and desires, and finally evocation, "décrire" becoming through an imaginative act "me saisir dans le passé")—one of his more daring and subtle transitions—shows us how directly for Chateaubriand the vivid, imaginative perception of the diverse moments of his life leads to a consciousness of the duty to write. And to write in such a way that the unity of the self writing does not overpower or conceal the diversity and discontinuousness of the past. The recent interpreters of Chateaubriand's literary landscape have given much attention to this simultaneous presence of unity and juxtaposed diversity: "un brusque retour en arrière, procédé caractéristique traduisant les affres d'une conscience qui se cherche dans le temps";[22] "cette fusion d'époques et de lieux à partir d'une indication infime . . . la volonté expresse de léguer à la postérité la signification secrète des incidents minimes qui se sont associés à sa vie."[23] The figure of "Le vent . . . est complice de notre tohu-bohu intérieur, de ce désordre dont les meilleurs critiques de Chateaubriand . . . ont pu noter qu'il était consubstantiel à son génie."[24]

As Chateaubriand's style and artistic independence evolve, then, the perception and inner conviction of discontinuity becomes the basis of a method of discontinuity, visible on many levels. The simplest, the one that

[22] Grevlund, *Paysage intérieur et paysage extérieur dans les Mémoires d'Outre-Tombe*, p. 175.
[23] *Ibid.*, p. 176.
[24] Richard, *Paysage de Chateaubriand*, p. 26.

will be so much a part of Hugolian Romanticism, is the love of contrast and antithesis: this, characteristically Chateaubriand's trait in satirical or comic passages, is notable in various forms throughout his work; indeed, as Mourot has remarked, "on pourrait même dire que l'opposition est la catégorie selon laquelle Chateaubriand figure ses rapports avec les autres."[25] A more exclusively stylistic kind of discontinuity than antithesis, that again is everywhere apparent, is the generous use of quotations, variously assimilated.[26] More peculiarly Chateaubriand's, more stunningly surprising, more demanding on the reader is the gamut of discontinuities that has occupied our attention throughout this study: the juxtapositions that have gone under the various names of echoes, *rapprochements*, metaphors; that Chateaubriand himself is conscious of how outrageous they can be is apparent often, as in one of the more particularly daring (or carefree) notes of the *Essai sur les révolutions*: "Il faut convenir que c'est accrocher subtilement une note à un mot."[27] There is no absolute distinction,[28] other than purely mechanical, that can be made among these forms if one considers them from the point of view of the demands that their use places on the imagination of the reader. An apt remark of Miss Lehtonen, noting already in the "Tableaux de la nature" the predominance of metaphors over similes, suggests a general feature of the author's method: ". . . la prédominance de la métaphore dépendrait-elle d'un choix conscient? L'imagination de Chateaubriand procédait, sans doute, par des associations rapides et directes: en concevant l'image, il 'identifiait', le plus souvent, les deux termes, au lieu de chercher une ressemblance logique entre ceux-ci."[29] Such identifications, with the responsibility that they place on the reader to work out the concealed analogy, characterize even more the writings of the author's old age: in the *Mémoires d'Outre-Tombe*, writes Miss Grevlund, "un paysage n'est plus un paysage, il est l'espace privilégié d'où l'imagination s'envole vers des ailleurs, la pierre mémoriale derrière laquelle se révèlent le pays et le temps perdus."[30]

[25] Laulan, "La Part de l'humour dans les *Mémoires d'Outre-Tombe*," BSC, I (1957), 80; Mourot, "Chateaubriand satirique; quelques aspects de son style," CAIEF, XXI (May 1969), 176.

[26] Note Chateaubriand's declaration to Marcellus quoted in chap. 3, n. 16, *supra*, p. 59.

[27] Chateaubriand, *Essai sur les révolutions*, in *Oeuvres*, ed. Ladvocat, II, 233, n. (a); cf. Lebègue, "Réalités et résultats du voyage de Chateaubriand en Amérique," RHLF, LXVIII, 6 (Nov.-Dec. 1968), 924.

[28] See Richard's admirable analysis of *rapprochement* and *métaphore* in *Paysage de Chateaubriand*, pp. 122-23 ff.

[29]Lehtonen, *L'Expression imagée dans l'œuvre de Chateaubriand*, p. 66.

[30] Grevlund, *Paysage intérieur et paysage extérieur dans les Mémoires d'Outre-Tombe*, p. 185; cf. Riffaterre's analysis of the "monument," "lieu de rencontre de personnages et d'époques que la réalité sépare," in "Chateaubriand et le monument imaginaire," *Chateaubriand, Actes du Congrès de Wisconsin*, p. 66.

The concealed analogies caught in Chateaubriand's metaphors and *rapprochements* are an aspect of another constant in the method of discontinuity: Chateaubriand's phenomenal concision, "ce resserrement foudroyant, cette science de l'effet," as Madame Durry[31] puts it. It is such evocative and metaphorically ambiguous concentration, joined to the art of balancing parts and especially weaving his themes together[32] that finally, most powerfully, makes Chateaubriand's discontinuities poetic and makes a generation of readers sensitized by the prose poems of a Rimbaud turn to Chateaubriand's most mature works with a pleasure sometimes not shared by the readers of Chateaubriand's own day.

Chateaubriand must surely be considered one of the originators of the prose poem in France. Strictly a "classic" himself, and not "un de ces barbares qui confondent la prose et les vers," (Préface d'*Atala*, ORV I, 18, n.) he is not beyond referring to some of his prose, from beginning to end, as poetry: *Atala*, "une sorte de poème, moitié descriptif, moitié dramatique" (*Ibid.*); "Tel livre de mes *Mémoires* est un voyage, tel autre s'élève à la poésie."[33] His critics and panegyrists of the twentieth century have frequently found in him impressive foreshadowings of Baudelaire, Mallarmé, Claudel, and most insistently Rimbaud.[34] Georges-Emmanuel Clancier finds in him an imposing array of themes and sentiments— feelings of solitude and perpetual exile, impossible or forbidden love, preference for everything in nature that has reached its autumn, carefully cultivated melancholy, nostalgia for the past coupled with a feeling for modernity—that remind him of Baudelaire and his ennui. Julien Gracq's analysis, poetic in itself, of the language of *La Vie de Rancé*, that "enfonce vers l'avenir une pointe . . . mystérieuse: ses messages en morse, saccadés, déphasés, qui coupent la narration tout à trac comme s'ils étaient captés d'une autre planète, bégayent déjà des nouvelles de la contrée où va s'éveiller Rimbaud," finds in Chateaubriand even more a stylistic foreshadowing of the post-Romantic poets. Themes or techniques, the most daring of Chateaubriand's innovations or the developments that most closely correspond to a future vision or malaise, have with regularity been considered by the most sensitive critics in the context of the later poets.

[31] Durry, *La Vieillesse de Chateaubriand*, I, 254-55. Cf. Lehtonen, *L'Expression imagée*, pp. 527-28: "le langage imagé de Chateaubriand a évolué vers une concision toujours plus grande."

[32] Durry, *op. cit.*, I, 531.

[33] Letter, 24 April 1834, to Edouard Mennechet, quoted by Biré in *Les Dernières Années de Chateaubriand*, p. 211.

[34] Clancier, *De Chénier à Baudelaire*, p. 48; Busset, "Actualité de Chateaubriand," *Table Ronde*, CCXLI (Feb. 1968), 8; Gracq, *Préférences*, p. 168; Grevlund, *Paysage intérieur et paysage extérieur*, pp. 120, 132, 145.

Some of the poetical elements in Chateaubriand's prose are of a traditional sort, the kind that tends to "date" important portions of his work. In one of the very rare playful moments to be found anywhere in his work, in a letter dated from Lyon, 29 May 1803, to Chênedollé and Joubert,[35] he writes: "Un petit bout du croissant de la lune était dans le ciel, tout justement pour m'empêcher de mentir, car je sens que, si la lune n'avait pas été là réellement, je l'aurais toujours mise dans ma lettre." Thematic maneuverings of such a kind, when they appear in his narratives, give a "poetic" flavor of the "Rousseau through Romanticism" style, but they are no less objectionable to many a would-be modern reader than is "cette complaisance à gémir, cette *littérature* des *chants désespérés*" that Clancier despairs of.[36]

But in Chateaubriand there are genuine poetical innovations. Julien Gracq points out that the *Mémoires d'Outre-Tombe* open "les temps modernes de la littérature" "[par] l'irruption neuve de l'histoire comme dimension souffrante, inguérissable, de la sensibilité."[37] The composition of many a page of the *Mémoires*, like in their general form *Atala* and *René*, presents a tightly organized unit, lyrical, meticulously composed, full of concrete images, even of abstractions, turning back on themselves, like a prose poem.[38] But most particularly, and this is what the present study has sought to illustrate, there is to be found a formidably suggestive and original poetry of juxtaposition and inexplicitness that is simply ahead of Chateaubriand's time.

"Chateaubriand, quand il écrit, est à la fois présent et absent. Présent par la vigueur et la couleur, absent à cause d'une certaine indifférence souveraine, d'une certaine façon de suggérer: 'Et après tout, si je me trompe, tant pis!' D'où ces ruptures, ces syncopes dans ces pages dont le léché n'est qu'un vernis qui cache mal de profondes fissures."[39] This curious analysis goes straight to the heart of the matter. Chateaubriand in the most developed of his literary works charms the reader both by what is there on the page—new images, strong colors, daring combinations of words—and by what is not there. There is an unusual abundance of things left unsaid, and that cannot be allowed to remain unsaid, in Chateaubriand. The sequences of images, abstract or pictorial, flow together at a

---

[35] *Correspondance générale*, I, 92.

[36] Clancier, *De Chénier à Baudelaire*, pp. 47-48.

[37] Gracq, *Préférences*, p. 159. Cf. the remark of Barbéris quoted in chap. 5, n. 27, and his remark, in *Chateaubriand, une réaction au monde moderne*, p. 130, about "l'expérience moderne de l'obscur, de l'absurde et de l'incomplet. Tout cela va être dit par une littérature nouvelle qui manifestera un étrange pouvoir. . . ."

[38] Clancier, *De Chénier à Baudelaire*, p. 46; Lehtonen, *L'Expression imagée dans l'œuvre de Chateaubriand*, pp. 75, 80.

[39] Busset, "Actualité de Chateaubriand," *Table Ronde*, CCXLI (Feb. 1968), 8.

dream-like speed, with a dream's incoherence.[40] In between the sentences, the paragraphs, the chapters, the reader has to interpret. It is an aspect of Chateaubriand's art that brings strangely to mind at last—by the force of the color and the clear delineation of detail as much as the mystery of the sequence—the Surrealists, whom one does not usually think of in connection with Chateaubriand. The following description concerning André Breton seems to me an apt characterization of Chateaubriand's poetry of discontinuity. "A l'inverse de la phrase de roman, la phrase poétique, si objective qu'elle paraisse au premier abord, doit toujours traduire une relation Choses-Poète, ou Choses-Lecteur. Le poème nous fournit une information fragmentée, éparpillée en multiples segments. Il faut le lire phrase isolée par phrase isolée et se laisser envahir par le kaléïdoscope des sensations. Chaque phrase vaut par la qualité de ses images et par l'insolite des sensations qu'elle nous procure. . . . Tout cela se résume en une formule qui, si elle n'explique pas tout, peut expliquer beaucoup: l'Art Poétique de Breton est un Art du Discontinu."[41]

If the satisfaction of the reader does indeed demand that the abundance of things left unsaid not remain absent, the reader himself is obliged to intervene. The pictures transmitted by Chateaubriand's imagination into the analytic decomposition of writing call out to the reader's imagination for recomposition. It is finally in this appeal to the reader's imagination that the poetry in Chateaubriand is felt the most as poetry.

"Chaque homme porte en lui un monde composé de tout ce qu'il a vu et aimé, et où il rentre sans cesse, alors même qu'il parcourt et semble habiter un monde étranger" (ORV II, 1443). So wrote Chateaubriand in his *Voyage en Italie*, describing how on a stormy night in Tivoli, in 1803, suddenly appeared to him, through the mist of the waterfall, the "souvenirs du toit paternel," "dans les bruyères de mon Armorique." The leaps and jumps he imposes on his reader by suppressing transitions, boldly daring juxtapositions, piling together matters of uncertain compatibility, are finally a stimulus to the reader's imagination to bring forth from his own depths, as he passes through the foreign world of Chateaubriand's imagination, that "monde composé de tout ce qu'il a vu et aimé," just as Chateaubriand's came forth under the stimuli of his own disconnected and contradictory and incoherent experience of life. And that reader's effort is, for me, the source of "Chateaubriand's Poetry": "The grandest efforts of poetry are where the imagination is called forth, not to produce a distinct

---

[40] Cf. Richard, *Paysage de Chateaubriand*, p. 140.
[41] Chesneau, "La marquise sortit à cinq heures," PMLA, LXXXIV, 6 (Oct. 1969), 1648.

form, but a strong working of the mind . . . namely, the substitution of a sublime feeling of the unimaginable for a mere image."[42]

---

[42] Coleridge, "The Grandest Efforts of Poetry": see epigraph to this chapter. Cf. Cohen, *Structure du langage poétique*, p. 222, defining the "fonction poétique" of "le langage": "forcer l'âme à *sentir* ce qu'elle se contente d'ordinaire de *penser*."

List of Books and Articles Referred to

WORKS OF CHATEAUBRIAND

Atala. Ed. Armand Weil. Paris: José Corti, 1950.

Atala, René, Les Aventures du Dernier Abencérage. Ed. Fernand Letessier. Classiques Garnier. Paris: Garnier frères, 1962.

Congrès de Vérone. Guerre d'Espagne. Négociations. Colonies espagnoles. In *Oeuvres complètes*, X. Paris: Furne, 1862.

Correspondance générale. Ed. Louis Thomas. 5 vols. Paris: Champion, 1912-24.

Essai historique, politique et moral, sur les Révolutions Anciennes et modernes, considérées dans leurs rapports avec La Révolution Françoise. London: J. Deboffe [etc.], 1797.

Itinéraire de Paris à Jérusalem. Ed. Emile Malakis. 2 vols. Baltimore: The Johns Hopkins Press, 1946.

Lectures des Mémoires de M. de Chateaubriand. Paris: Lefèvre, 1834.

Lettres à Madame Récamier. Ed. Maurice Levaillant and E. Beau de Loménie. Paris: Flammarion, 1951.

Mémoires de ma vie. Première version des Mémoires d'Outre-Tombe (Livres I, II et III). Ed. Maurice Levaillant. Paris: Jacques et René Wittmann, 1948.

[MOT] *Mémoires d'Outre-Tombe*. Ed. Maurice Levaillant and Georges Moulinier. Bibliothèque de la Pléiade. 3rd ed. 2 vols. Paris: Gallimard, 1957.

Mémoires d'Outre-Tombe. Ed. Maurice Levaillant. Edition du Centenaire. 2nd ed. 4 vols. in 2. Paris: Flammarion, 1964.

Oeuvres complètes. 28 vols. in 31. Paris: Ladvocat, 1826-31.

Oeuvres complètes. 36 vols. Paris: Pourrat frères, 1836-39.

[ORV] *Oeuvres romanesques et voyages*. Ed. Maurice Regard. Bibliothèque de la Pléiade. 2 vols. Paris: Gallimard, 1969.

René. Ed. Armand Weil. Nouvelle éd. Genève: Droz, 1947.

René. Ed. J.-M. Gautier. Genève: Droz, 1970.

Vie de Rancé. Ed. Fernand Letessier. Paris: Marcel Didier, 1955.

141

OTHER WORKS

Ages, Arnold. "Chateaubriand and the Philosophes." *Chateaubriand. Actes du Congrès de Wisconsin.* Ed. Richard Switzer. Genève: Droz, 1970. Pp. 229-41.

Barbéris, Pierre. *Chateaubriand, une réaction au monde moderne.* Paris: Larousse, 1976.

Barbéris, Pierre. *"René" de Chateaubriand, un nouveau roman.* Paris: Larousse, 1973.

Bédé, Jean-Albert. "De Chateaubriand à André Malraux." *Cahiers de l'Association internationale des études françaises,* XXI (May 1969), 209-24.

Biré, Edmond. *Les Dernières Années de Chateaubriand (1830-1848).* Paris: Garnier frères, 1902.

Boorsch, Jean. "Chateaubriand and Napoleon." *Yale French Studies,* XXVI (Fall-Winter 1960-61), 55-62.

Boorsch, Jean. "Motion and Rest in *René.*" *Yale French Studies,* XIII (Spring-Summer 1954), 76-82.

Bourrienne, Louis Antoine Fauvelet de. *Mémoires de M. de Bourrienne . . . sur Napoléon . . .* 10 vols. Paris: Ladvocat, 1829.

Boutet, Gilbert. "Un 'Art Poétique' de Chateaubriand: *Cynthie.*" *Les Lettres romanes,* XXI, 4 (1 Nov. 1967), 311-38 and XXII, 1 (1 Feb. 1968), 20-39.

Busset, Jacques de Bourbon. "Actualité de Chateaubriand." *Table Ronde,* CCXLI (Feb. 1968), 7-10.

Butor, Michel. *Répertoire II.* Paris: Editions de minuit, 1964.

Charlton, D.G. "The Ambiguity of Chateaubriand's *René.*" *French Studies,* XXIII, 3 (July 1969), 229-43.

Chesneau, Albert. "'La marquise sortit à cinq heures.'" *PMLA,* LXXXIV, 6 (Oct. 1969), 1644-48.

Clancier, Georges-Emmanuel. *De Chénier à Baudelaire. Panorama critique.* Paris: Seghers, 1963.

Clarac, Pierre. *A la recherche de Chateaubriand.* Paris: Nizet, 1975.

Clarac, Pierre. "L'Exemplaire Pourrat de Chateaubriand." *Société Chateaubriand Bulletin,* nouvelle série, XIII (1970), 13-22.

Clarac, Pierre. "Mémoires d'Outre-Tombe: le manuscrit de Genève (suite)." *Société Chateaubriand Bulletin,* nouvelle série, X (1967), 73-82.

Clarac, Pierre. "Quelques remarques sur les relations de Chateaubriand et de Victor Hugo." *Revue d'Histoire littéraire de la France,* LXVIII, 6 (Nov.-Dec. 1968), 1005-17.

Clarac, Pierre. "Une version inédite de l'Avant-propos des 'Mémoires.'" *Société Chateaubriand Bulletin,* nouvelle série, IX (1965-66), 62-72.

Cohen, Jean. *Structure du langage poétique.* Paris: Flammarion, 1966.

Dollinger, Albert. *Les Etudes historiques de Chateaubriand.* Paris: Les Belles Lettres, 1932.

Durry, Marie-Jeanne. *En marge des Mémoires d'Outre-Tombe.* Paris: Le Divan, 1933.

Durry, Marie-Jeanne. "Un Manuscrit retrouvé des Mémoires d'Outre-Tombe." *Revue des Deux Mondes,* CI, 6 (1 Dec. 1931), 664-74.

Durry, Marie-Jeanne. *La Vieillesse de Chateaubriand 1830-1848.* 2 vols. Paris: Le Divan, 1933.

Etudes françaises. "Chateaubriand et ses précurseurs français d'Amérique." IV, 3 (Aug. 1968).

Gagnebin, Bernard. "'J'ai fait la connaissance de M. Rigaud': cinq lettres inédites de Chateaubriand." *Revue d'Histoire littéraire de la France*, LXVIII, 6 (Nov.-Dec. 1968), 1038-47.

Gautier, Jean-Maurice. *Le Style des Mémoires d'outre-tombe de Chateaubriand*. Genève: Droz, 1959.

Gracq, Julien. "Le grand Paon." [Dated 1960, in] *Préférences*. Paris: José Corti, 1961. Pp. 151-68.

Grevlund, Merete. *Paysage intérieur et paysage extérieur dans les Mémoires d'Outre-Tombe*. Paris: A.-G. Nizet, 1968.

Laulan, Robert. "La Part de l'humour dans les Mémoires d'Outre-Tombe." *Société Chateaubriand Bulletin*, nouvelle série, I (1957), 79-80.

Lebègue, Raymond. "Essai sur Chateaubriand lecteur de Montaigne." *Société Chateaubriand Bulletin*, nouvelle série, XVI (1973), 54-63.

Lebègue, Raymond. "Réalités et résultats du voyage de Chateaubriand en Amérique." *Revue d'Histoire littéraire de la France*, LXVIII, 6 (Nov.-Dec. 1968), 905-33.

Lebègue, Raymond. "Le succès d'une image mennaisienne: la Bretonne noyée." *Société Chateaubriand Bulletin*, nouvelle série, IV (1960), 32-35.

Lebègue, Raymond. "Le Thème de la 'Bretonne noyée' chez Lamennais et Chateaubriand." *Mercure de France*, CCCXXII, 1093 (1 Sept. 1954), 176-81.

Lebègue, Raymond. "Le Thème du 'Miserere' de la Sixtine." *Revue d'Histoire littéraire de la France*, LXXII, 2 (Mar.-Apr. 1972), 247-63.

Lebègue, Raymond. "Versions inédites des Livres IX et X des 'Martyrs.'" *Société Chateaubriand Bulletin*, nouvelle série, X (1967), 12-51.

Leguat, François. *Voyage et Avantures de François Leguat. . .* 2 vols. Londres: David Mortier, 1708.

Lehtonen, Maija. "Chateaubriand et le thème de la mer." *Cahiers de l'Association internationale des études françaises*, XXI (May 1969), 193-208.

Lehtonen, Maija. "L'Evolution du langage imagé de Chateaubriand." *Société Chateaubriand Bulletin*, nouvelle série, IX (1965-66), 20-24.

Lehtonen, Maija. *L'Expression imagée dans l'œuvre de Chateaubriand*. Mémoires de la Société Néophilologique de Helsinki, XXVI. Helsinki: Société Néophilologique, 1964.

Lemaître, Jules. *Chateaubriand*. Paris: Calmann-Lévy, 1912.

Le Nain, Dom Pierre. *La Vie du R.P. dom Armand-Jean Le Boutillier de Rancé*. Paris: Louis d'Hotelfort, 1719.

Levaillant, Maurice. *Deux livres des Mémoires d'Outre-Tombe*. 2 vols. Paris: Delagrave, 1936.

Levitine, George. "Some Unexplored Aspects of the Illustrations of *Atala*: the *Surenchères Visuelles* of Girodet and Hersent." *Chateaubriand. Actes du Congrès de Wisconsin*. Ed. Richard Switzer. Genève: Droz, 1970. Pp. 139-45.

Lowrie, Joyce O. "Motifs of Kingdom and Exile in *Atala*." *French Review*, XLIII, 5 (April 1970), 755-64.

Lynes, Carlos Jr. *Chateaubriand as a Critic of French Literature*. Baltimore: The Johns Hopkins Press, 1946.

Marcellus, le Comte de. *Chateaubriand et son temps*. Paris: Michel Lévy frères, 1859.

Milton, John. *Paradise Lost*. Ed. Merritt Y. Hughes. New York: Odyssey Press, 1962.

Monod-Cassidy, Hélène. "Amours sauvages, Amours chrétiennes: Quelques pré-décesseurs peu connus d'*Atala*." *Chateaubriand. Actes du Congrès de Wisconsin*. Ed. Richard Switzer. Genève: Droz, 1970. Pp. 243-51.

Montesquieu, Charles-Louis de Secondat, baron de La Brède et de. *Oeuvres complètes*. Ed. Daniel Oster. Collection l'Intégrale. Paris: Aux éditions du Seuil, 1964.

Mourot, Jean. *Chateaubriand. Rythme et sonorité dans les Mémoires d'Outre-Tombe*. Edition revue. Paris: Armand Colin, 1969.

Mourot, Jean. "Chateaubriand satirique; quelques aspects de son style." *Cahiers de l'Association internationale des études françaises*, XXI (May 1969), 167-91.

Mourot, Jean. *Etudes sur les premières œuvres de Chateaubriand. Tableaux de la Nature–Essai sur les Révolutions*. Paris: A.-G. Nizet, 1962.

Mourot, Jean. "Réflexions sur quelques variantes de 'L'Itinéraire de Paris à Jérusalem.'" *Revue d'Histoire littéraire de la France*, LXVIII, 6 (Nov.-Dec. 1968), 953-80.

O'Flaherty, Kathleen. "Adolescence in the Work of Chateaubriand." *Chateaubriand. Actes du Congrès de Wisconsin*. Ed. Richard Switzer. Genève: Droz, 1970. Pp. 273-81.

Poulet, Georges. *Etudes sur le temps humain*. Edinburgh: University Press, 1949.

Proust, Marcel. *A la recherche du temps perdu*. Ed. Pierre Clarac and André Ferré. Bibliothèque de la Pléiade. 3 vols. Paris: Gallimard, 1954.

Revue d'Histoire littéraire de la France. "Chateaubriand." LXVIII, 6 (Nov.-Dec. 1968).

Revue des Sciences Humaines. "Chateaubriand. L'œuvre et la Pensée. Chateaubriand et son temps." Fasc. 132 (Oct.-Dec. 1968).

Riberette, Pierre. "La lettre de Chateaubriand à Lucien Bonaparte: documents inédits." *Société Chateaubriand Bulletin*, nouvelle série, XIV (1971), 63-68.

Richard, Jean-Pierre. *Paysage de Chateaubriand*. Paris: Editions du Seuil, 1967.

Riffaterre, Michael. "Chateaubriand et le monument imaginaire." *Chateaubriand. Actes du Congrès de Wisconsin*. Ed. Richard Switzer. Genève: Droz, 1970. Pp. 63-81.

Rousseau, Jean-Jacques. *Oeuvres complètes*. Ed. Bernard Gagnebin and Marcel Raymond. Bibliothèque de la Pléiade. 4 vols. Paris: Gallimard, 1959-69.

Sainte-Beuve, Charles-Augustin. *Chateaubriand et son groupe littéraire sous l'empire*. Ed. Maurice Allem. Classiques Garnier. 2 vols. Paris: Garnier, 1948.

Sainte-Beuve, Charles-Augustin. *Vie, Poésie et Pensées de Joseph Delorme*. Ed. Gérald Antoine. Paris: Nouvelles éditions latines, 1956.

Sand, George. *Oeuvres autobiographiques*. Ed. Georges Lubin. Bibliothèque de la Pléiade. 2 vols. Paris: Gallimard, 1970-71.

Shackleton, Robert. "Chateaubriand and the Eighteenth Century." *Chateaubriand. Actes du Congrès de Wisconsin*. Ed. Richard Switzer. Genève: Droz, 1970. Pp. 15-28.

Starobinski, Jean. *Jean-Jacques Rousseau: La transparence et l'obstacle*. 2nd ed. Paris: Gallimard, 1971.

Stein, Gertrude. "How Writing Is Written." In W. Somerset Maugham's *Introduction to Modern English and American Literature*. 1943; rpt. Garden City: Garden City Books, 1952. Pp. 356-65.

Stendhal. *Oeuvres intimes*. Ed. Henri Martineau. Bibliothèque de la Pléiade. Paris: Gallimard, 1955.

Storzer, Gerald H. "Chateaubriand and the 'Fictional Confession.'" *Chateaubriand. Actes du Congrès de Wisconsin*. Ed. Richard Switzer. Genève: Droz, 1970. Pp. 123-31.

La Table Ronde. "Actualité de Chateaubriand." CCXLI (Feb. 1968).

Thoraval, Jean. "Chateaubriand Paysagiste d'après ses variantes." *Société Chateaubriand Bulletin*, nouvelle série, I (1957), 30-35.